EDUCATION, DISABILITY AND SOCIAL POLICY

Second edition

Edited by
Steve Haines and David Ruebain

First published in Great Britain in 2025 by

Policy Press, an imprint of
Bristol University Press
University of Bristol
1–9 Old Park Hill
Bristol
BS2 8BB
UK
t: +44 (0)117 374 6645
e: bup-info@bristol.ac.uk

Details of international sales and distribution partners are available at policy.bristoluniversitypress.co.uk

© Bristol University Press 2025

British Library Cataloguing in Publication Data
A catalogue record for this book is available from the British Library

ISBN 978-1-4473-6984-4 hardcover
ISBN 978-1-4473-6985-1 paperback
ISBN 978-1-4473-6986-8 ePub
ISBN 978-1-4473-6987-5 ePdf

The right of Steve Haines and David Ruebain to be identified as editors of this work has been asserted by them in accordance with the Copyright, Designs and Patents Act 1988.

All rights reserved: no part of this publication may be reproduced, stored in a retrieval system, or transmitted in any form or by any means, electronic, mechanical, photocopying, recording, or otherwise without the prior permission of Bristol University Press.

Every reasonable effort has been made to obtain permission to reproduce copyrighted material. If, however, anyone knows of an oversight, please contact the publisher.

The statements and opinions contained within this publication are solely those of the editors and contributors and not of the University of Bristol or Bristol University Press. The University of Bristol and Bristol University Press disclaim responsibility for any injury to persons or property resulting from any material published in this publication.

Bristol University Press and Policy Press work to counter discrimination on grounds of gender, race, disability, age and sexuality.

Cover design: Lyn Davies Design
Front cover image: iStock/Rafa Irusta

Contents

List of figures and tables	iv
Notes on contributors	v
Foreword by Sam Freedman	ix
Foreword by Dame Christine Lenehan	xi
Foreword by Professor Tom Shakespeare	xiii

Introduction   1
David Ruebain and Steve Haines

1   Disability and education in historical perspective   6
    Anne Borsay

2   Continuity and tensions between the SEND framework and disability rights legislation in recent legislative reforms   20
    Brian Lamb

3   Multi-agency working and children and young people with disabilities: from 'what works' to 'active becoming'   51
    Liz Todd and Jo Rose

4   Disabled students in higher education: what progress has been made over the last 30 years?   74
    Sheila Riddell and Elisabet Weedon

5   Meeting the standard but failing the test: the case of children and young people with sensory impairments and access to assessments and qualifications   94
    Caireen Sutherland and Martin McLean

6   Exploring the intersection of race and disability in English schools   107
    Valentina Migliarini and Chelsea Stinson

7   The hidden world of within-school exclusion   119
    Rob Webster

8   Social, emotional and mental health needs in educational settings: putting wellbeing into socio-relational context   142
    Robin Banerjee

Conclusion   154
David Ruebain and Steve Haines

Index   157

List of figures and tables

Figures

4.1	Proportion of disabled students in the UK undergraduate student population	76
4.2	Proportion of disabled students in receipt of DSA by jurisdiction, 2015–21	77
4.3	UK domiciled undergraduate enrolments by type of impairment 2016–17 and 2021–22	78
4.4	UK domiciled undergraduate enrolments by type of impairment, no disability and sex, 2021–22	79
4.5	Disabled students by type of impairment and socio-economic background compared to non-disabled students, percentages	81
4.6	Employment rates of disabled and non-disabled people and gaps by highest qualification level, 2019	82

Tables

4.1	Outcomes of disabled and non-disabled graduates (by qualification level), percentages	83
4.2	Graduate outcomes by disability type for first degree graduates	84
5.1	Proportion of English 16-year-olds achieving five GCSE passes or equivalent qualifications in 2008 and 2019 and the attainment gap between SI students and all students	102

Notes on contributors

Robin Banerjee is Pro-Vice-Chancellor for Global and Civic Engagement, and Professor of Developmental Psychology at the University of Sussex. Formerly Head of the School of Psychology, his research focuses on the social and emotional development of young people, and he works closely with practitioners and policymakers in the areas of education and mental health. He founded the Sussex Centre for Research on Kindness, an interdisciplinary research centre focused on illuminating the nature of kindness and its impacts on people and communities. Professor Banerjee recently led the world's largest ever public science project on kindness, The Kindness Test, in partnership with the BBC. In his role as Pro-Vice-Chancellor, he leads the university's strategic work on local and global engagement activities.

Anne Borsay was Professor of Healthcare and Medical Studies at the University of Wales, Swansea. Her principal research interests were in the social and cultural history of disability, and she was committed to teasing out the implications of perspectives from history, literature and the visual arts for contemporary policy and practice. Her single-authored publications include *Disabled People in the Community: A Study of Housing, Health and Welfare Services* (1986), *Medicine and Charity in Georgian Bath: A Social History of the General Infirmary, c.1739–1830* (1999) and *Disability and Social Policy in Britain since 1750: A History of Exclusion* (2005). Anne sat on the editorial board of Disability and Society and was a member of the Wellcome Trust's Medical History and Humanities Funding Committee.

Steve Haines was formerly the Executive Director of Policy and Campaigns at the National Deaf Children's Society and a Member of the Ministerial Advisory Group for the SEND System Leadership Board. He was Head of Policy and Policy Manager for Education at the Disability Rights Commission.

Brian Lamb was the Chair of the Lamb Inquiry into Parental Confidence in SEND which helped form the basis of the current legislation and SEN Code of Practice in England. He was a member of the Disability Rights Task Force 1997–99. He was also chair of the Special Education Consortium from 2000 to 2010 and is the policy adviser for the National Sensory Impairment Partnership. He is a Visiting Professor of Special Educational Needs and Disability at Derby University and has published widely on special needs education.

Martin McLean, who was born profoundly deaf, has had his perspectives on education and disability shaped in part by his firsthand experience within the education system. Holding a Master's Degree in Policy, he is also a qualified teacher with a PGCE in post-16 education and training, with experience of working in the FE and HE sectors. In his role as a policy adviser for the National Deaf Children's Society, where he progressed to lead its policy and campaigns team, Martin strove to positively influence education and employment policy for deaf young people. Martin has been an active member of advisory groups for the Department for Education, Ofqual, Student Loans Company and the Office of the Independent Adjudicator. Moreover, he has spearheaded the creation of professional resources co-developed with the National Sensory Impairment Partnership and Education and Training Foundation, including quality standards for deaf students in FE.

Valentina Migliarini is Assistant Professor in Education Studies in the School of Education in the Department of Education and Social Justice at the University of Birmingham. Her work, both in research and teaching, focuses on increasing access to equitable education for students from multiply marginalised communities, specifically disabled students from migrant and forced migrant backgrounds, in secondary education. She is at the forefront of researchers using the Disability Critical Race Theory in Education (DisCrit) framework as an intersectional lens to examine inclusive policies and practices in education systems in Europe and in the United States. Through her research agenda, she addresses mainstream conceptualisations of inclusion, highlighting how these reproduce micro-exclusions for students living at the intersections of multiple forms of oppression.

Sheila Riddell is a member of the Centre for Research in Education Inclusion and Diversity at the Moray House School of Education and Sport, University of Edinburgh. She previously worked as Director of the Strathclyde Centre for Disability Research, University of Glasgow. Her research interests are in the broad field of education, equality and inclusion, including school and higher education.

Jo Rose is Associate Professor of Social Psychology of Education at the University of Bristol. Her background is in social psychology, and she has been working in educational research since 2001. Her research interests lie specifically in relational dynamics, considering how people from different backgrounds work together. She has explored this in the areas of educational partnerships (including parental engagement in education) and collaborative working, and young people's trajectories through the educational system. Jo's work uses a wide diversity of methods: both quantitative and qualitative, both large- and small-scale, and both fixed and emergent designs. Many of her projects incorporate mixed methods, and she often works across disciplinary boundaries. This presents interesting methodological challenges and questions, and has helped to develop her range of methodological expertise. Jo is co-Editor in Chief of the *International Journal of Research and Method in Education*, and co-edits the book series Emerald Studies in Out-of-School Learning.

David Ruebain is Pro-Vice-Chancellor for Culture, Equality and Inclusion and Professor of Culture, Diversity and Inclusion in the School of Law, Politics and Sociology at the University of Sussex. He is a consultant to Chair of the Premier League's EDI Standard (PLEDIS) on equalities issues, and previously held the post of Chief Executive of the Conservatoire for Dance and Drama and Chief Executive of Advance HE's Equality Challenge Unit. He began his career as a solicitor and practised for 21 years; latterly as Director of Legal Policy at the Equality and Human Rights Commission of Great Britain following a career in private practice as a Partner at and founder of the department of Education, Equality and Disability Law at Levenes Solicitors.

Chelsea Stinson is Assistant Professor of Inclusive Education in the Foundations and Social Advocacy Department at the State University of New York at Cortland. Her research focuses on the experiences of emergent bilingual youth labelled as disabled and their families across migration and education contexts, as well as the knowledge, emotions, and policy contexts of teachers who support multiply marginalised students at the intersections of language, race, disability and migration.

Caireen Sutherland is a qualified teacher with the mandatory qualifications for vision and multi-sensory impairment (MSI) and has been working in the field of special educational needs and disabilities (SEND) for over 20 years. She currently works as Programme Lead and Senior Lecturer for the Mandatory Qualification (MQ) in MSI at Seashell. Previously as head of education at the RNIB she was instrumental in the work of the Curriculum Framework for Children with Vision Impairment and she continues this work as project sponsor, as well as being co-chair at the National Sensory Impairment Partnership and a committee member of VIEW. During her career, Caireen has worked in specialist settings, Local Authority Sensory Support services, in the third sector and as a freelance consultant. Her particular passions include: ensuring equal access to assessments for those with sensory impairment, improving use of technology to support students to achieve their potential, developing tactile learning skills and optimising independence for children and young people with sensory impairments.

Liz Todd is Professor of Educational Inclusion at Newcastle University. Liz engages in research with a strong social justice agenda, being known for her work on the interaction between communities and schools, the engagement of young people in societal agendas and in research, and respectful democratic approaches to change (personal and organisational). Liz is Director of Newcastle University's Institute for Social Science which is committed to celebrating engaged critical social science, fostering an inclusive research culture and developing interdisciplinary research. Liz was awarded an OBE for services to education and to young people in 2025.

Rob Webster researches and writes on SEND, inclusion and the role of teaching assistants. He co-directed the UK's largest longitudinal cohort study of the everyday educational experiences of pupils with SEND, and was a researcher on the ground-breaking Deployment and Impact of Support Staff project. Rob is a Senior Research Fellow at the University of Greenwich, and a joint coordinator of the SEN Policy Research Network. He is the author of *The Inclusion Illusion: How Children with Special Educational Needs Experience Mainstream Schools* (2022).

Elisabet Weedon is now retired. For many years she worked as a Senior Research Fellow in the Centre for Research in Education Inclusion and Diversity at the Moray House School of Education, University of Edinburgh. Her main research areas are lifelong learning and additional support for learning with a focus on issues around equality and social justice. She has been involved in large-scale European projects on lifelong learning, religious education and workplace learning. Economic and Social Research Council (ESRC) funded projects have focused on disability and additional support for learning as well as Scottish Government-funded research in areas such as restorative practices in education. Her most recent work was in higher education with a focus on widening access in the UK and Europe.

Foreword

Sam Freedman

One of the few things that everyone in the education world agrees on is that the special educational needs and disabilities system is broken. Parents are deeply frustrated at having to fight for their children to have access to necessary resources.

Mainstream schools feel unable to provide the support they know pupils need, due to a lack of funding. Special schools are in an even tougher financial position. Many local authorities have been plunged into debt they have no route to paying off, which risks the financial health of the whole council.

Central government knows this situation is unsustainable. Gillian Keegan, the last Conservative education secretary, called it a 'lose, lose, lose' system. Her new Labour replacement, Bridget Phillipson, has firmly agreed with this assessment. But solutions are not obvious, or at least not affordable ones, given the straightened times.

It feels like a lot of important questions – many of which are highlighted in this valuable guide – have been ignored for a long time. Not least, why have we seen such a substantial rise in the number of young people with certain conditions, that has driven huge year-on-year cost increases. This applies to conditions like autism and ADHD but also broader behavioural challenges, and mental illnesses like anxiety and depression.

There has been a remarkable lack of curiosity about these trends among policymakers, perhaps because there are no easy or obvious answers. But without halting, and ideally reversing these trends, or at least applying different approaches to managing them, it is hard to see how any government can get a grip. They tie into a wider array of problems affecting the most vulnerable young people, including rising poverty and an increase in instances of abusive or neglectful parenting.

Dealing with these challenges goes well beyond the school system. Recent analyses of labour markets have shown marked changes to the more youthful end, with a significant rise in those not working and/or in receipt of disability benefits; something that has been driven almost entirely by greater incidence of mental illness. When you also take into account the costs this imposes on a creaking NHS, it is not an exaggeration to say that, even in a crowded field, this is one of the biggest public policy problems around. As ever, one of the big challenges in

Whitehall is communications and cooperation between all the different departments involved.

As new ministers (hopefully) prioritise these issues and start to work through them, one hopes they will consult the learned essays in this book, to help them understand the history of previous efforts, and how aspects of the education system could be rethought in more radical ways.

Foreword

Dame Christine Lenehan

When the Children and Families Act was published in 2014 it was described as the biggest reform to child welfare legislation in 30 years. It set a strong vision for a system which put children and families at the centre and was built on joined up services which focused on delivering the best outcomes. There is no doubt that was its intent. So how did we lose this?

Partly those joined up services changed, the reorganisation of health services and schools had a fundamental impact on structure and accountability, local authorities also entered a period of austerity and then there was a pandemic.

One of the unintended impacts of the changing education system was the creation of a hostile environment for children and young people with SEND. The previous government's focus on narrow attainment measures reinforced by an attendance and behaviour approach which did not recognise an increasing number of children and young people struggling to find a confident and secure environment at school, led to a system where children who could not conform where increasingly excluded.

The SEND system also acquired its own identity and bureaucracy, leading to an 'othering' of children with SEND, a view that there were children, and then a separate category of SEND children, where the same understanding of valuing childhood and achievement did not apply. If we add to this the fundamental impact of the pandemic on young people and the broader understanding of the impact of autism on girls and young women, and the rising prevalence of mental health needs, a system which needed greater flexibility became increasingly inflexible.

The last 10 years has also seen a rise in parental dissatisfaction. All parents want the very best for their children; why we should think this would be any different for parents of children with SEN is a mystery. Wanting the education and support that children deserve in an increasingly fraught, complex system which is financially challenged and where accountability can seem opaque can lead to anger and distrust on the part of parents, and frustration and despair for professionals. It is why the system needs a reset, a fundamental relook at the tangled web we have created and a clarity about the state offer for children, young people and their families.

The publication of this book of essays provides an important contribution to the debate and an opportunity to reflect on how we fulfil the 2014 vision. The new government has indicated that they want to create a positive, inclusive culture for all young people; it is the least they deserve and essential to deliver the best outcomes for all children, young people and their families.

Foreword

Professor Tom Shakespeare

I start from thinking that every school should be barrier-free for all, and every child is special and should get their needs met. That way, disabled kids would be the same as everyone else, and there would be no 'special needs' stigma talk. But I recognise that this utopian answer is some way off.

In the meantime, we need to concentrate resources on some schools, and develop expertise to work with disabled children, so that we can enable them to develop and grow, as we expect with all our children. I do not think that it is about young people with disabilities having the same outcomes as everyone else, because that will not be possible for all. But everyone develops and grows, so the gap I am interested in is between where they are now, and where they will be in five years' time, with all the educational input they will have received.

Let me say something about disability. I think that disability is complex: people are disabled by social barriers and oppression, and also by bodies and minds which work in different ways, or not as well as the average. I think embodiment is a challenge for everyone, although this is usually only evident by mid-life, when everyone realises that they have special needs for some sort of repair or other. I want us to see our commonalities. As a group of young disabled people said to me more than 30 years ago: they are just like young people without disabilities.

I want everyone, particularly children and young people, to feel okay about having bodies or minds that work differently. I want them to be told all about what people have achieved, with different bodies or minds, because this learning that it is okay to be disabled or neurodivergent cannot begin early enough. After all, we tell girls what women have achieved, and we tell kids from different ethnic backgrounds what people like them have achieved, and I hope the same about gay people, so I definitely think we should tell disabled and non-disabled children that disability is not the opposite to success. In fact, we have built some of the world that they now live in.

I have worked in higher education for nearly 40 years, in which time I have met blind students, and deaf students, and students with bipolar condition, and students with dyslexia, and students with autism, and students with all kinds of physical impairments. I have met students who have been blown up, and students who lived in countries where measles made people blind, and students who were crippled by polio, again because they lived in poor parts of the world.

In all this time, I have never met a disabled student who was not working hard to achieve their potential. In many cases, I know they went on to great things. From my personal experience, I know that disability is not the opposite to success, and that disabled children and young people can achieve great things, if we are able to help them grow and succeed.

I have come to the conclusion that if you are disabled, you are even more committed to your studies. I never forget the gentleman I met in Zambia: his mother had said to him, 'You, of all my children, must go to school'. In Kenya, I met the extraordinary Deaf woman; from Tahiti, I remember the inspirational blind man. As the late great Stella Young said, we are not here to be your inspiration, but I hope she would forgive me for finding so much that we do impressive. And I say that, knowing that I could not achieve a fraction of what others have.

In conclusion, this book explores the detail, but we should not lose sight of the prize: disabled children and young people deserve no less and no more than what all children and young people deserve, which is an education that lasts a lifetime. The rest is up to them.

Introduction

David Ruebain and Steve Haines

Over a decade ago, and after nearly 30 years of policy changes and legislative reform, we sought to take stock of progress in the provision of effective education for disabled children and young people and for those otherwise defined as having special educational needs (SEN). We brought together leading thinkers from a range of perspectives in the field and asked them to consider ongoing challenges and opportunities in a series of chapters for our book, *Education, Disability and Social Policy*.

This revised and updated second edition considers progress and revisits those challenges and opportunities, as well as new ones that have arisen since then. We have returned to some of the original authors to consider developments on the topics they covered in their chapters, and have also included several new voices to consider other themes that were not as visible to us, or which have surfaced since the first edition; such as school exclusion, the intersection of SEN with race and racism, and the increasing prevalence and understanding of the social, emotional and mental health needs of young people, which has driven much of the increase in demand for support.

While we were writing the introduction to the first edition in 2010, a general election resulted in a change in government. After 13 years in power, Labour were defeated and replaced with a Conservative/Liberal Democrat Coalition. In turn, this resulted in a new approach to SEN policy which sought to combine disconnected twin manifesto commitments of meeting the needs of every child and ending the supposed 'bias towards inclusion'. In 2015 the Conservative Manifesto stated 'we have made improving support for children and young people with special educational needs and disabilities a priority' and in 2019 new funding and a commitment to create more school places for children with complex SEN were included in the manifesto, alongside raising standards and improving behaviour for all young people. After 14 years of first the Coalition and, later, three successive terms of a Conservative government, our authors have reflected on the distance travelled in implementing these commitments and the experiences of children with SEN.

The historical arc of provision for children with SEN and the social history of disabled people continue to inform these challenges and we have included again Anne Borsay's essay on the history of SEN which situated these in this context. Anne sadly died in 2014, but her analysis remains deeply relevant, and Brian Lamb's following chapter picks up the historical narrative.

Our approach has always been rooted in the social model of disability, which in summary foregrounds disabling barriers and attitudes in society which prevent disabled people from full participation and inclusion. In August 2014, the social model was endorsed by the Government Equalities Office who recommended its use by all government departments. In education, arguably both the social model and its forerunner medical model, frame the duties now contained in the Equality Act 2010, to proactively remove barriers to inclusion, alongside the assessment of needs and provision of support from the SEN framework. Cherie Booth, Marc Bush and Ruth Scott's chapter in the first edition argued that, in reality, this would leave parents of children with SEN and those responsible for meeting their needs in an invidious position. In many ways, this situation has worsened over the past decade, with under resourced local authorities forced to suppress demand for support, in some cases by making the system more arduous for parents. They posited that this 'jigsaw of provision', which tried to knit together the approach set out in the Warnock Report in 1978 and the Equality Act, required a rethink.

The Children and Families Act 2014 aimed to address this challenge by clarifying the frameworks for support. It updated and extended statements of SEN, introducing in their place Education Health and Care (EHC) plans and clarifying the previous system of in-school support. But by 2020, the Westminster Parliament's Public Accounts Committee had concluded that:

> Education, Health and Care plans have become a 'golden ticket' that parents fight for to secure access to adequate support for their children. Children with SEND [special educational needs and disabilities] but who do not have EHC plans risk missing out on the support they need, especially in mainstream schools that are under significant financial pressure. Parents still feel left out of decisions that affect their children, and they do not have full confidence in the system. We remain to be convinced that the Department has sufficient grip on what needs to be done to tackle the growing pressures on the SEND system.

In response, the previous government took steps to develop a new Special Educational Needs and Disability and Alternative Provision Improvement Plan which promises to support children with SEN to fulfil their potential, restore parents' trust and provide financial stability.

In his chapter, Brian Lamb reflects on the strengths and weaknesses of these reforms and concludes that, to some extent due to the wider pressures on schools in a decade of austerity, the core challenges these reforms sought to resolve were not adequately addressed. He argues that the opportunity should now be taken to go further and reframe the legislation with a capability approach, which would move from a deficit model of meeting needs to identifying the support children and young people need to flourish. This builds on the suggestion of Neil Crowther in his chapter in our previous edition. Since then academic literature on this framing has been building and warrants serious consideration by policymakers looking to form a more ambitious approach to reform.

In the first edition, we asked Liz Todd to reflect on the role of professionals. Charting the rise of 'multi-agency working', she outlined the need to become 'privilege cognisant', reflecting on power and relationships with and between young people and professionals. The 2014 reforms sought to strengthen co-production with families, but again underfunding has made the culture change difficult to deliver in practice with parents driven into taking adversarial positions to professionals. In this context, Liz Todd and Jo Rose suggest evolving the role of professionals from providing expertise to that of a guide working dynamically with parents and disabled young people as partners.

Sheila Riddell and Elisabet Weedon's chapter, which reviews the participation of disabled students in higher education, stood out in the first edition as a success story. The authors' updated chapter continues to chart this success, with increasing numbers and proportions of disabled students participating in higher education. However, the authors raise concerns about new challenges caused by the long-term impact of the COVID-19 pandemic which puts at risk this progress. They also reflect on our greater understanding of the barriers to participation in higher education and call for more funding and, in particular, a stronger appreciation of the intersection of class and disability.

Cobb, Miller and Simpson's chapter on assessment and qualifications through the lens of young people with sensory impairments in our first edition pointed out the fundamental flaw in thinking that defends a system which claims that all learners are placed on an equal footing and measured fairly against assessment objectives that are 'in some sense pure and universal' and 'access arrangements' which are 'subsequently "bolted on" to take account of minorities, such as disabled candidates'. Revisiting this chapter, Martin McLean and Caireen Sutherland find many of the same challenges today in a high-stakes examination system that does not always recognise individual strengths and does not always allow for students learning with different styles or working at a different pace. But they also find there are reasons to feel optimistic with the advent of the GCSE in British Sign Language and an, albeit overdue, move to a more inclusive design approach to the development of qualifications and assessments, rather than relying solely on post-hoc access arrangements. As the new government takes forward its review of curriculum and assessment there is a significant opportunity to take forward this inclusive design approach, finally dispensing with the flawed thinking that has defined the system to date.

With hindsight, we recognised that our first edition gave insufficient attention to the intersection of race and SEN and we have sought to address this with a new chapter on the topic. Referencing Bernard Coard's 1971 pamphlet 'How the West Indian child is made educationally subnormal in the British school system', Valentina Migliarini and Chelsea Stinson consider the legacy of institutional racism which resulted in children of the Windrush generation being disproportionally labelled as having SEN. By adopting Disability Critical Race Theory (DisCrit) the authors examine current education policy and practice and show how the intersection of perceptions of Black and marginalised students and reactions to disability and behaviour have contributed to inequitable educational opportunities for these students. The authors make a powerful call to all those involved in education policy, practice and research to name and address these wrongs and cultivate radical hope to challenge this embedded narrative.

Over a decade ago, the chapter from Anne Lewis in our first edition, on including the voice of disabled young people and their families, seemed radical. Today, including the views of disabled young people is commonplace, reflecting a wider change towards participatory approaches to policymaking. In a recent report for the Cabinet Office to inform the Disability Action Plan, the Office of the Children's Commissioner worked with disabled young people to share their experiences. The report sent a clear message from disabled young people: they want the right support, provided early enough to support their education, and support for transition to a good job and thriving future. The report also paints the reality of the opposite picture: a failure to provide support early enough, a frequent lack of confidence that the education system will deliver, and fractured transition.

Similarly, Nigel Utton's chapter in our first edition, which charted one headteacher's journey towards leading an inclusive school, felt like a trailblazer. Notwithstanding the 2010 manifesto commitment to 'remove the bias towards inclusion', our view as editors was that school leaders have largely adopted a mindset of pursuing an inclusive school environment. However, this is not to say that we have made sufficient progress or that the path is untroubled. To understand this, we sought a contribution that investigated some of the hidden narratives and disincentives in the school system. Rob Webster's chapter shows that, despite the good intentions of school leaders, organisational arrangements in schools still disproportionately exclude children with SEN, either due to conflicting incentives or inherited practice. He calls for a more aligned and intentional policy framework and investment in building an inclusive school culture in practice as well as in principle, through greater training to increase teacher confidence and competence in inclusive approaches.

Last, we asked Robin Banerjee to explore the rise in reported social emotional and behavioural difficulties and underlying mental health needs as a proportion of the numbers of young people classified as having SEN. Echoing many other chapters in this second edition, he argues for abandoning the deficit model of 'needs to be corrected' and instead understanding these needs as relational, arguing for a strengths-based approach to supporting human flourishing. The promising findings of his work show that prevention and intervention through emotional skills that promote wellbeing and flourishing for all, not just reducing distress for individuals labelled as having 'difficulties', can benefit the whole school community.

Following our first edition there was recognition by Stephen Ball (2013) in *The Education Debate* that disability needs to be a much greater part of education debate and policymaking. The revised chapters and new contributions in this second edition demonstrate that the dated approach of considering SEN as a separate concern to be retrofitted after the policy has been made not only fails huge numbers of young people, but undermines the very principles of those policies, be they focused on qualifications, behaviour, ethos or any other aspect of education.

We publish this collection, as we did a decade ago, hopeful that proposed reforms will be successful. But we urge decision makers to be more ambitious in creating an education system that supports young people's flourishing, with families and professionals working together to promote agency for disabled children and young people and for those otherwise defined as having SEN.

References

House of Commons (2020) Committee of Public Accounts Support for children with special educational needs and disabilities First Report of Session 2019–21.

Ball, S. (2013) *The Education Debate* (2nd edn), Bristol: Policy Press.

1

Disability and education in historical perspective

Anne Borsay

Introduction

The human rights agenda, broadly defined, promotes health and wellbeing by upholding 'opportunity and choice, freedom of speech, respect for individuality and an acceptance of difference in all spheres of life' (Armstrong and Barton, 1999: 211). For disabled people, the realisation of these aspirations is an inclusive society, where the economic, political, ideological, social and cultural barriers that underpin inequality and discrimination are dismantled. The purpose of this chapter is to assess the historical development of education for disabled children against the human rights yardstick, focusing on Britain between the late 18th century and the early 1980s. Three main themes will be pursued: the inability of legal entitlements to replace segregated with inclusive schooling; the contribution of the professions to this failure; and the threat to human rights posed by schooling that compromised participation in family, community and employment. The chapter will conclude by locating education within a broader framework of social exclusion that encompasses cultural representation as well as public policy.

From segregation to inclusion?

Charitable origins

Segregated education for disabled children dates back to the early modern period when dedicated institutions emerged from private tuition. Sensory impairments – judged to be particularly pernicious because they denied full access to the word of God – were the initial category of disability to attract attention. Thus, the first 'special' school – opened in Edinburgh in 1764 – was for deaf pupils. Although this was a commercial venture, the institutions for deaf and blind pupils that multiplied from the 1790s were charitable foundations, resting upon voluntary donations and subscriptions (Phillips, 2004; Borsay, 2007). From the 1840s, the same formula was applied to institutions for intellectually impaired children, inspired by the belief that 'idiocy' was no longer beyond education (Wright, 2001). The result was a network of segregated schooling. By the end of the 19th century, there were in Britain over 50 institutions for blind children; 26 for deaf children; and a National Asylum for Idiots at Earlswood in Surrey, on which four regional asylums had also been modelled (Haswell, 1876; Woodford, 2000; Wright, 2001).

The charitable ethos of these foundations was incompatible with the concept of education as a human right. First, pupils – typically aged between six and 12 – had no entitlement to a place. On the contrary, they were elected by benefactors on the basis of biographical notes that were circulated prior to electoral meetings. Second, the compassion that was used to generate funds disempowered disabled children by construing them as helpless objects of pity rather than future citizens with a right to education (Borsay, 2007). This denial of rights was compounded by the discourse of degeneration, which gathered momentum after the publication of Charles Darwin's *On the Origin of Species* in 1859 (Darwin, 1996) and was consolidated by the formation of the Eugenics Education Society in 1907. Far from promoting education, however, the Society advocated sterilisation, marital regulation, birth control and segregation to prevent the spread of 'mental deficiency' (King, 1999).

Although all disabled people were tainted by this eugenic message, children with intellectual impairments were most directly affected. This was because a new emphasis on their untreatable condition led to the establishment of permanent institutions, committed to lifelong residence rather than the completion of a fixed-term programme of education and training. Some such foundations – like Sandlebridge Boarding School and Colony in Cheshire, which opened in 1902 – were charitable (Jackson, 2000). Far more numerically significant, however, were the local authority 'mental deficiency' institutions, which stemmed from legislation in 1913. By 1939 they were accommodating over 40,000 people (Walmsley et al, 1999), including among their inmates those incapable of being educated at school (Jones, 1972).

Statutory origins

The earlier arrival of mainstream state schooling had done little to improve the human rights of disabled children. Central government had topped up charitable general-purpose schools since the 1830s, but it was only the 1870 Education Act that authorised statutory provision to fill the gaps left by voluntary endeavour. When, a decade later, school attendance became compulsory for five to ten year olds, all children acquired the right to at least an elementary education (Harris, 2004). However, like the charitable societies whose activities it complemented, the 1870 Act was not concerned with disabled children (Tomlinson, 1982). Consequently, they were detected by default as those who had stayed at home or remained undifferentiated at school (McCoy, 1998).

Children with physical as well as sensory and intellectual impairments were caught up in this process, triggering the launch of over 40 agencies for the newly identified young 'cripples' by 1914. The charitable orthopaedic hospitals into which some of these initiatives grew during the interwar period provided a new educational destination for disabled children: the hospital school, set up to teach patients institutionalised for long periods as a result of orthopaedic surgery or the appliance of plaster casts, splints and frames (Cooter, 1993). However, the most significant outcomes of the childhood disability revealed by compulsory education arose from the Royal Commission, which reported in 1889.

Among the recommendations of the Royal Commission was schooling for blind, deaf and 'dumb' children. What drove this recommendation was the financial burden that disability imposed. Therefore, education was promoted not as a right that disabled children enjoyed by virtue of being human, but as a means of reducing pauperism (Tomlinson, 1982). In 1893, responsibility for the education of blind and deaf children was thus transferred from the poor law authorities to local education authorities (LEAs), who were given a duty to develop their own segregated schools or to grant-aid charitable schools. Six years later, LEAs received enabling but not mandatory powers to provide special schools for intellectually impaired children. Not until 1918, however, was schooling for mentally and physically 'defective' children made compulsory (Hurt, 1988).

By the 1920s, Britain had over 500 institutions for children with sensory or physical impairments (Humphries and Gordon, 1992). The extension of the franchise, which had begun in earnest in the late 19th century, was beginning to affect the outlook of these specialist institutions whose publicity spoke in terms of preparing responsible citizens (Thomson, 1998). This 'civic' consciousness, however, was undermined by the continuing eugenic mindset, which attributed 'mental deficiency' and 'much physical deficiency' to 'poor mental endowment' (Jones, 1982: 723). Therefore, the duty of local authorities to provide special schools for disabled children was 'inscribed within the rhetorical and ideological framework of eugenics' rather than of citizenship and human rights (Koven, 1994: 1173).

The welfare state

This eugenic mindset was challenged by the education policy of the postwar welfare state. Reaching the statute book towards the end of the Second World War, the 1944 Education Act embraced the optimistic ethos of social reconstruction that the conflict had engendered, by establishing the right of all children to a schooling suited to their 'age, aptitude and ability' (Lowe,

1993). In line with this agenda, all those 'able to benefit' from education were brought under the local authority umbrella, leaving only 'ineducable' children within the National Health Service (NHS) (Henderson, 1974). In addition, however, it was conceded that where possible disabled children were best taught in mainstream schools. Additional facilities were accordingly made available under the Handicapped Pupils and Medical Services Regulations of 1945. Therefore, as well as special attention from the teacher, disabled children in ordinary schools were to be allowed 'a favourable position in the classroom', special furniture, aids and equipment, and tuition in lip-reading if they were partially deaf (Clarke, 1951: 127–128).

The promise of integration implicit in these arrangements was fundamentally flawed. Special education was defined as a 'treatment' in which 'methods appropriate for persons suffering from disability of mind and/or body' were expertly applied (see the 1944 Education Act, available at: www.opsi.gov.uk/acts/acts1944/pdf/ukpga_19440031_en.pdf [accessed 1 September 2009]). This encouraged an essentially medical system of classification in which children were placed in one of 11 categories ranging from blind and deaf to physically handicapped and educationally subnormal. Parental choice only came into play if it was 'compatible with efficient instruction and training and the avoidance of unreasonable public expenditure'. Educational authorities – anxious to avoid any disruption to the new 'co-ordinated system of compulsory mass primary and secondary education' – were, therefore, free 'to exclude as many children as possible who might obstruct or inconvenience the smooth running of normal schools' (Tomlinson, 1982: 50). The combined effect of these limitations was an expansion of segregated schools (Oliver, 1998; French, 2006). Consequently, despite the alleged policy of integration, the number of pupils in special schooling climbed from 38,499 in 1945 to 106,367 in 1972 (Topliss, 1975).

From the 1960s, the case for segregation was increasingly undermined by the growth of all-inclusive comprehensive education, which abandoned selection by ability at the age of 11. At the same time, the debate about integrating disabled children was advancing. An early sign was the transfer of junior training centres for children deemed 'ineducable' from the NHS to LEAs in 1970 (Fulcher, 1989). However, the most significant development was the 1981 Education Act. Drawing on the 1978 Warnock Report, the Act dropped medical classification and the concept of educational treatment and replaced them with 'special educational needs', which was defined as 'having a learning difficulty which calls for special educational provision'. There were two constructions of learning difficulty: having 'a significantly greater difficulty in learning than the majority of children of his [sic] age'; or having a 'disability which either prevents or hinders ... making use of educational facilities of a kind generally provided in schools' (see the 1981 Education

Act, available at: www.opsi.gov.uk/acts/acts1981/pdf/ukpga_19810060_en.pdf [accessed 1 September 2009]).

Although these two definitions were intended to replace the categorisation of disabled children with 'a continuum of need', they merely produced a change of terminology as medical classification gave way to three bands of learning difficulty: moderate, severe and profound and multiple (Swain et al, 2003: 126). Moreover, neither definition acknowledged Warnock's contention that special educational needs were relative, or dependent upon the physical and social environment of the school; as the report elaborated: 'Schools differ, often widely, in outlook, expertise, resources, accommodation, organization and physical and social surroundings', and so it is 'impossible to establish precise criteria for defining what constitutes handicap' (Warnock, 1978: 37). The monies to adapt these varying environments were not guaranteed because the obligation to accommodate disabled children in mainstream schools was again conditional upon 'the efficient education' of other children and the efficient use of resources. Therefore, although the 1981 Act aspired to reduce the number of disabled children in segregated schooling, it did not facilitate the inclusive education essential to human rights in which mainstream classrooms became accessible.

Medicine, psychology and teaching

Medicine, psychology and teaching – the occupational groups who competed for professional kudos within the sphere of special schooling – were implicated in its failure to deliver inclusive education. The first institutions for blind and deaf children specifically ruled out medical intervention and insisted that pupils were admitted for educational purposes only (Borsay, 2005). The teachers offering this instruction were initially of low status with poor wages, long hours and spartan residential facilities (Beaver, 1992). In the second half of the 19th century, however, they began to organise to protect their interests. Command of the communication skills used to educate children with sensory impairments was critical to this process. Therefore, after 1880, ambitious teachers seized on the conclusion of the infamous Milan Congress that 'only oral instruction could fully restore deaf people to society' (Lane, 1993: 113–114). Its imposition contributed to the professionalisation of deaf education by identifying teachers with the dominant linguistic culture and denigrating or excluding those who practised sign language. At a time, though, when three quarters of British schools supported this manual method rather than the oral method or a combination of the two (Branson and Miller, 2000), the effect was to deny deaf pupils the right to talk in the language of their choice.

Although the early blind and deaf institutions resisted medicine, doctors were later to play a central role in the management of special education.

Learning difficulty came under medical control from the mid-19th century with doctors dominating the new 'idiot' asylums. John Langdon Down was medical superintendent at Earlswood between 1858 and 1868. While there, he not only 'classified a new type of mental disability' – named Down's syndrome in his honour – but also 'pioneered the medical treatment of "idiocy"' (Wright, 2001). Drugs were part of this treatment, but Langdon Down also applied a moral method of instruction, based on rewards and punishments. This embryonic form of behaviour modification was employed within an existing programme of physical activity, designed to improve the mind by disciplining the unruly movements of the body (Wright, 2001: 199). Similar programmes, comprising drill and gymnastics, were adopted in blind and deaf institutions with games, dancing and swimming added to the repertoire to discipline the effects of sensory impairment (Borsay, 2005).

Medical intervention in special education went beyond the endorsement of physical exercise to include intrusive treatments. One of the more recent manifestations is the controversial cochlear implant (Hogan, 1998), but medical technologies were also a problem in the past. Children with partial sight, for instance, found that the contact lenses developed in the 1950s were awkward and painful to use, despite the enthusiasm surrounding their arrival (French, 2006). Furthermore, orthopaedic institutions like the Heritage Craft Schools and Hospital at Chailey in Sussex had ambitious plans to remould the disabled child, medical treatment featuring as one element within a package that also included education, vocational training and leisure (Koven, 1994). Yet many of the cumbersome aids fitted to thalidomide children resident in the 1960s impeded rather than enhanced their functioning (Medus, 2009). In closed environments, however, it was difficult for children or parents either to complain about the institutional regime, or to demand non-interference, against the power of the medical establishment.

With the advent of state education from the 1890s, doctors became increasingly involved in the assessment as well as the management and treatment of disabled children. Their vehicle was the local authority School Medical Service, founded in 1907 with a statutory duty to inspect children's health (Harris, 2004). The Board of Education regarded the Service as pivotal to the expansion of special schooling (Thomson, 1998). Doctors were soon joined by psychologists following the introduction of the IQ test as an assessment tool. Gillian Sutherland has argued that this test had benign potential because it identified a continuum of ability that stretched from the normal to the abnormal and hence discredited segregation (Sutherland, 1984). By the 1920s, however, 'Psychologists, through mental testing procedures, were acquiring the power to legitimate the removal of large numbers of children from normal education' (Tomlinson, 1982: 48).

Despite the reliance on the IQ test, doctors continued to lead the 'ascertainment' of physically and mentally impaired children after the 1944

Act. Thirty years later, psychologists had achieved parity, as evidenced by the additional report that they were now required to provide for the assessment process (Russell, 1978; Tomlinson, 1982). This new-found power was not rooted in more reliable testing, and, although the measurement of IQ continued to discriminate against all children by failing to recognise the effects of social background (Lowe, 1993), disabled children were further disadvantaged. Rather than blurring the normal–abnormal boundary, testing firmed up the deviance of those with intellectual impairments. Moreover, as the Board of Education had recognised as long ago as 1936, to 'apply the ordinary tests of intelligence to a child who is defective in sight or in hearing is to do him [*sic*] serious injustice' (Hurt, 1988: 164). On both grounds, therefore, psychology justified the special school by supplying spurious scientific criteria for demarcation. In consequence, with this institution ensconced, segregation became an all too easy means for not only regulating any 'disruptive' behaviour, but also reducing tolerance of difference (Tomlinson, 1982). School exclusions subsequently took on this role, as new categories of disturbing behaviour (like Attention Deficit Disorder) were increasingly medicalised and responsibility was increasingly located with children or their 'inadequate' families rather than the educational system (Armstrong and Barton, 1999).

The 1981 Act's concept of special educational needs, which sought to capture this diversity, strengthened the professional standing of teachers by ceasing to construe education as a treatment in the domain of medicine or psychology. However, the model of professionalisation advanced was a bureaucratic and not substantive one. Scant attention was thus paid to how the curriculum might aggravate the difficulties of disabled children; and the skills to teach them remained the preserve of in-service training, a post-qualification add-on rather than an intrinsic part of the syllabus. Conversely, the bureaucratic process of 'statementing' was championed as teachers became heavily involved in the multi-professional assessments that released special provision (Fulcher, 1989). However, only a minority of disabled children – those with more serious special educational needs – were actually 'statemented'. Integration rather than inclusion was the goal (French, 2006). Furthermore, while consultation was compulsory, LEAs were not obliged to obtain parental approval and parents had only limited rights of appeal to a local committee, which was authorised to ask for reconsideration but not to overrule a decision (Fulcher, 1989). Even the Special Education Needs and Disability Tribunal (now Panel), set up later under the 1993 Education Act and independent of local authorities, had on its own admission 'quite limited' powers, which were restricted to demanding an assessment or a statement where one was refused or insisting on alterations to the statement's content. If disability discrimination was proved, reasonable action to remedy it could be ordered, though not financial compensation. The Tribunal/Panel did produce a guide for children and young people. However, the dominance of the professions undermined both them and their families in the determination of provision and, in any event, their own requirements were not guaranteed by parental involvement. Consequently, the dominance of the professions disempowered families in the determination of needs (Oliver, 1996) and the requirements of disabled children were not guaranteed by parental involvement where there was a conflict of interest (Oliver, 1998) – for example, a preference for social training (Glendinning, 1983). Therefore, the victory of the teaching profession over medicine and psychology did not ensure that human rights in education were protected.

Family, community and employment

Despite the human rights deficiencies, by no means all educational experiences were negative. Alice – educated after 1981 – who became deaf as a baby due to meningitis, had a positive experience of mainstream education at both primary and secondary level. Though the school was not designed for deaf pupils and had no visual alarms or electronic displays, she was supported through a deaf unit where teachers 'made sure I got on well with the work and mixed with hearing people' but also taught her sign language and introduced her to the Deaf community. Consequently, she remained comfortable about going 'into both worlds' (Jasvinder et al, 2008: 123–124). Disabled children were also happily absorbed into mainstream education before the 1980 Act took effect, including migrants from special schools; and not all those who were segregated expressed dissatisfaction (Madge and Fassam, 1982). Moreover, even where institutional regimes were harsh and punishments were brutal, friendships were sustaining (Humphries and Gordon, 1992; French with Swain, 2000; Cook et al, 2001).

Yet whatever the quality of their internal relationships, schools that forced pupils to board denied them the sense of inclusion that Alice enjoyed and restricted their right to participate in family life, the local community and employment. The late Victorian commentator D.O. Haswell lambasted this exile. Writing with particular reference to blind institutions, he complained that they intensified the visual incarceration already inflicted on blind people and subjected them to a regime that not only failed to develop their abilities, but also weakened their physical and mental health (Haswell, 1876). Conversely, many early 20th-century reformers – under the influence of eugenic thinking – welcomed the removal of disabled children whose parents were poor, blaming the impoverished home environment for endangering morality as well as causing impairment. By the early 1950s, however, the Chief Medical Officer was declaring that: 'A child should never be removed from home unless it is quite certain that there is no practicable alternative' because the family was 'the fundamental basis for the child's emotional development and security' (French, 2006: 124).

Disabled children's experiences of segregation testify to the force of this argument. The pain of initial desertion was acute; and if returning after the school holidays was hard, so was going home. Indeed, it was 'more traumatic ... because, although in your head you knew about mothers, grandmothers and whoever, these people were basically strangers to you' (French, 2006: 182–183). Long distances aggravated this alienation. Some children were able to see their parents only once a year, but even where families were nearby, face-to-face contact was discouraged and visits allowed just once a month. Access to community participation was also limited. Not only were special schools often isolated from local neighbourhoods, but the children who attended them were also acutely conscious of their difference and hence had difficulty in forging friendships during holidays or weekends at home. Though their loneliness may have eased when day schools became more common in the 1970s, there was still the stigma of the special school bus (Oswin, 1978; Campbell and Oliver, 1996; French, 2006). Consequently, it was disabled children educated with their non-disabled peers who mixed most frequently with school friends out of school (Madge and Fassam, 1982).

In addition to eroding rights to family and community engagement, segregated schooling put at risk disabled children's employment opportunities in adult life. The reason was low expectations. From the first days of the blind and deaf institutions, the formal curriculum was combined with vocational training, which reinforced the divisions of class and gender: boys were engaged in workshops learning how to make baskets, mats, clothing and boots; girls were engaged in institutional housework, learning how to wash, clean and sew (Borsay, 2005). The preoccupation with manual skills, which extended to all disabled children and endured into the post-war period, discouraged schools from entering pupils for public examinations (Barnes et al, 1999). Therefore, in the early 1970s, a national survey revealed that 60 per cent of impaired men and women had no formal qualifications or skills – compared with 47 per cent of the population as a whole (Buckle, 1971).

This shortage of educational credentials curtailed employment opportunities in adulthood. True, the post-war period saw a severing of the link between the special school and workshop, which had so invidiously portrayed manual labour as the natural destination for disabled children. At the same time, a raft of policy measures was introduced, including the notorious quota scheme that was so inept in compelling larger employers to recruit 3 per cent of their workforce from the disabled population (Jordan, 1979). However, careers advice was poor and job opportunities remained typecast, as being a typist, telephonist or piano tuner replaced the traditional craft occupations.

Some individuals escaped: for example, David, who became a basket maker in the late 1950s, was subsequently employed as a home teacher of blind people, a computer programmer and a social welfare officer (French, 2006). Overall, however, disabled people were concentrated at the bottom of the labour market and exposed to high unemployment. Therefore, in a study of children born during one week in 1958, 22 per cent of those ascertained as disabled under the 1944 Education Act had taken a first job that was unskilled, compared with 9 per cent of all 15 to 24 year olds. Two thirds of this 'handicapped' group had experienced unemployment: twice as many as the 'non-handicapped' group (Walker, 1982).

Of course, segregated schools were not alone in denying the right to well-paid, secure employment. In a society where discrimination against disabled people was rampant, they were just one conduit for transmitting deep-seated prejudices rooted in bodily perfection and full economic productivity. Therefore, for Jock Young – a pupil at the Glasgow Deaf and Dumb Institution in the 1930s – the employer was the obstacle: 'they wouldn't take me because of my deafness and I was sent to cobblers' workshops employing deaf people. Deaf people could get jobs as joiners, painters, and cobblers, but I wanted to be an electrical engineer' (Hutchinson, 2007: 273). Nevertheless, by removing disabled children from everyday social interaction, special schools compounded the negative attitudes that frustrated the achievement of an inclusive society with the full spectrum of human rights.

Conclusion

This chapter has evaluated the development of education policies for disability; explored the contributions of doctors, psychologists and teachers to their shortcomings; and examined access to family, community and work. The segregated system that evolved from the late 18th century prevented disabled children from obtaining the full rights of citizenship. This exclusion was multifaceted. As the American political theorist, Iris Young, has argued, social oppression may involve violence, powerlessness, marginalisation, exploitation and cultural imperialism. Historically, disabled education was guilty on all five counts. First, disabled children were subjected to physical and psychological violence at school. Second, both they and their families were powerless to influence the school environment. Third, this school environment marginalised pupils in and excluded them from mainstream education, their families and local communities, and the labour market. Fourth, it left them prone to economic exploitation in an economy that rewarded educational qualifications. Finally, the special school fed cultural imperialism: 'the paradox of experiencing oneself as invisible at the same time that one is marked out as different' (Young, 1990: 60). By separating disabled children, segregation ensured that the experience of disability remained remote from non-disabled people. Consequently, what it was like to be disabled found little expression in the dominant culture because literature and the visual arts reproduced stereotyped images that sustained isolation.

The task of the historian is to analyse the past because the changing context in which human experiences occur make predicting the future impossible. Nevertheless, the broad-ranging social oppression perpetrated by education policies in previous centuries does not bode well for social inclusion today. In the 1995 Disability Discrimination Act (DDA), education was exempt. Six years later, the 2001 Special Educational Needs and Disability Act did make it unlawful for schools to discriminate against disabled children and this requirement was strengthened by the extension of the DDA to education in 2005. However, neither piece of legislation was sufficiently ambitious to allow children to bring a case in their own right, and the implementation of both Acts continues to be frustrated by budgetary constraints, professional shortcomings and prejudicial attitudes towards disability. History suggests that such barriers to the educational rights of disabled children will be slow to break down.

References

Armstrong, F. and Barton, L. (1999) '"Is there anyone there concerned with human rights?" Cross-cultural connections, disability and the struggle for change in England', in F. Armstrong and L. Barton (eds) *Disability, Human Rights and Education: Cross-Cultural Perspectives*, Buckingham: Open University Press, pp 210–229.

Barnes, C., Mercer, G. and Shakespeare, T. (1999) *Exploring Disability: A Sociological Introduction*, Cambridge: Polity.

Beaver, P. (1992) *A Tower of Strength: Two Hundred Years of the Royal School for Deaf Children, Margate*, Lewes: The Book Guild.

Borsay, A. (2005) *Disability and Social Policy in Britain since 1750: A History of Exclusion*, Basingstoke: Palgrave Macmillan.

Borsay, A. (2007) 'Deaf children and charitable education in Britain, 1790–1944', in A. Borsay and P. Shapely (eds) *Medicine, Charity and Mutual Aid: The Consumption of Health and Welfare in Britain, c.1550–1950*, Aldershot: Ashgate, pp 71–90.

Branson, J. and Miller, D. (2000) 'From myth to history: Maginn, Gallaudet and the destruction of the BSL-based manualism in deaf education in Britain', *Deaf History Journal*, 4(1): 7–17.

Buckle, J.R. (1971) *Work and Housing of Impaired Persons in Great Britain*, London: HMSO.

Campbell, J. and Oliver, M. (1996) *Disability Politics: Understanding Our Past, Changing Our Future*, London: Routledge.

Clarke, J.S. (1951) *Disabled Citizens*, London: Allen and Unwin.

Cook, T., Swain J. and French, S. (2001) 'Voices from segregated schooling: towards an inclusive education system', *Disability and Society*, 16(2): 293–310.

Cooter, R. (1993) *Surgery and Society in Peace and War: Orthopaedics and the Organization of Modern Medicine, 1880–1948*, Basingstoke: Macmillan.

Darwin, C. (1996) *On the Origin of Species*, 1st pub. 1859, edited by G. Beer, Oxford: Oxford University Press.

French, S. (2006) *An Oral History of the Education of Visually Impaired People*, Lewiston, Queenston and Lampeter: Edwin Mellen Press.

French, S. with Swain, J. (2000) 'Institutional abuse: memories of a "special" school for visually impaired girls – a personal account', in J. Bornat, R. Perks, P. Thompson and J. Walmsley (eds) *Oral History, Health and Welfare*, London: Routledge, pp 159–179.

Fulcher, G. (1989) *Disabling Policies? A Comparative Approach to Education Policy and Disability*, London, New York and Philadelphia: Falmer Press.

Glendinning, C. (1983) *Unshared Care: Parents and Their Disabled Children*, London: Routledge and Kegan Paul.

Harris, B. (2004) *The Origins of the British Welfare State: Social Welfare in England and Wales, 1800–1945*, Basingstoke: Palgrave Macmillan.

Haswell, D.O. (1876) *The Social Condition of the Blind*, published by the author.

Henderson, P. (1974) *Disability in Childhood and Youth*, Oxford: Oxford University Press.

Hogan, A. (1998) 'Carving out a space to act: acquired impairment and contested identity', *Health*, 2(1): 75–90.

Humphries, S. and Gordon, P. (1992) *Out of Sight: The Experience of Disability 1900–1950*, Plymouth: Northcote House.

Hurt, J.S. (1988) *Outside the Mainstream: A History of Special Education*, London: Batsford.

Hutchinson, I. (2007) *A History of Disability in Nineteenth-Century Scotland*, Lewiston, Queenston and Lampeter: Edwin Mellen Press.

Jackson, M. (2000) *The Borderland of Imbecility: Medicine, Society and the Fabrication of the Feeble Mind in Late Victorian and Edwardian England*, Manchester: Manchester University Press.

Jasvinder, A., Geoff and Alice (2008) 'Disabled people's testimonies', in J. Swain and S. French (eds) *Disability on Equal Terms*, London: Sage Publications, pp 115–126.

Jones, G. (1982) 'Eugenics and social policy between the wars', *Historical Journal*, 25(3): 717–728.

Jones, K. (1972) *A History of the Mental Health Services*, London: Routledge and Kegan Paul.

Jordan, D. (1979) *A New Employment Programme Wanted for Disabled People*, London: Disability Alliance.

King, D. (1999) *In the Name of Liberalism: Illiberal Social Policy in the United States and Britain*, Oxford: Oxford University Press.

Koven, S. (1994) 'Remembering and dismemberment: crippled children, wounded soldiers, and the Great War in Great Britain', *American Historical Review*, 99(4): 1167–1202.

Lane, H. (1993) *The Mask of Benevolence: Disabling the Deaf Community*, New York: Vintage.

Lowe, R. (1993) *The Welfare State in Britain since 1945*, Basingstoke: Macmillan.

Madge, N. and Fassam, M. (1982) *Ask the Children: Experiences of Physical Disability in the School Years*, London: Batsford.

McCoy, L. (1998) 'Education for labour: social problems of nationhood', in G. Lewis (ed) *Forming Nation, Framing Welfare*, London: Routledge, pp 93–138.

Medus, L. (2009) *No Hand to Hold and No Legs to Dance on: Laughing and Loving – a Thalidomide Survivor's Story*, Bedlinog, Mid-Glamorgan: Accent Press.

Oliver, M. (1996) *Understanding Disability: From Theory to Practice*, Basingstoke: Macmillan.

Oliver, M. (1998) 'The social and political context of education policy: the case of special needs', in L. Barton (ed) *The Politics of Special Educational Needs*, London, New York and Philadelphia: Falmer Press, pp 13–31.

Oswin, M. (1978) *Holes in the Welfare Net*, London: Bedford Square Press.

Phillips, G. (2004) *The Blind in British Society: Charity, State and Community, c.1780–1930*, Aldershot: Ashgate.

Russell, P. (1978) *The Wheelchair Child*, London: Souvenir Press.

Sutherland, G. (1984) *Ability, Merit and Measurement: Mental Testing and English Education, 1880–1940*, Oxford: Clarendon Press.

Swain, J., French, S. and Cameron, C. (2003) *Controversial Issues in a Disabling Society*, Buckingham: Open University Press.

Thomson, M. (1998) *The Problem of Mental Deficiency: Eugenics, Democracy, and Social Policy in Britain, c.1870–1959*, Oxford: Clarendon Press.

Tomlinson, S. (1982) *A Sociology of Special Education*, London: Routledge and Kegan Paul.

Topliss, E. (1975) *Provision for the Disabled*, Oxford and London: Basil Blackwell and Martin Robertson.

Walker, A. (1982) *Unqualified and Underemployed: Handicapped Young People and the Labour Market*, Basingstoke: Macmillan.

Walmsley, J., Atkinson, D. and Rolph, S. (1999) 'Community care and mental deficiency, 1913 to 1945', in P. Bartlett and D. Wright (eds) *Outside the Walls of the Asylum: A History of Care in the Community, 1750–2000*, London: Athlone, pp 181–203.

Warnock, M. (1978) Special educational needs: Report of the Committee of Enquiry into the Education of Handicapped Children and Young People, Cmnd 7212, London: HMSO.

Woodford, D.E. (2000) *Touch, Touch and Touch Again*, Feltham, Middlesex: British Deaf History Society.

Wright, D. (2001) *Mental Disability in Victorian England: The Earlswood Asylum 1847–1901*, Oxford: Clarendon Press.

Young, I.M. (1990) *Justice and the Politics of Difference*, Princeton, NJ: Princeton University Press.

2

Continuity and tensions between the SEND framework and disability rights legislation in recent legislative reforms

Brian Lamb

Introduction

The needs based special education framework established after the Warnock Report has endured for over 40 years, despite its progenitor more than once calling for its abolition (Warnock, 1978, 1993: xi, 2005; Education Act, 1981). A limited extension of a disability rights-based approach to special education was introduced through the Special Educational Needs and Disability Act (2001), followed by an extension of its measures in the revised Disability Discrimination Act (2005) and the Equality Act (2010) which unified discrimination legislation and extended protections to individual disabled children.

Following the reforms in the Children and Families Act 2014, the Code of Practice 2015 (DfE/DoH, 2015) attempted to integrate the rights provisions within the overall special educational needs (SEN) framework, but in practice the rights framework has played an ancillary role to the dominant Warnock framework. Essentially both legal frameworks seek to remove barriers to learning (DfE/DoH 2015: 1.33) but operate on entirely different principles and apply to overlapping but not coterminous groups of children and young people. The Warnock framework seeks to identify SEN needs and the Equality Act framework to prevent discrimination. The failure to address the discontinuities between the two legislative strands within the Special Educational Needs and Disabilities (SEND) framework undermines the aims of the reforms and is a barrier to equitable provision.

The Warnock framework and the 2014 reforms

Who are we talking about?

The number of children identified with SEND, compared to the overall school population, has gradually increased reaching a peak of around

21 per cent in 2010. The SEND incidence rate then declined and reached its lowest level in 2016 and 2017 (around 14 per cent), before increasing again to 18.4 per cent as of January 2024 (HoC, 2023; DfE, 2024a, 2024b). These figures obscure the fact that at some point in their school journey four in ten children may be identified as having SEND (Hutchinson, 2017). Identification will be influenced by how the school and SEND professionals interpret the definition of SEN, the quality of teaching and the resources available to the school (Hutchinson, 2021). The SEND figures cover a wide range of disabilities which may impact on learning, such as autism, ADHD, dyslexia, sensory impairment, mental health and learning disabilities. At least three quarters of children with a disability will also meet the SEN definition (Porter et al, 2008). In 2022–23, 11 per cent of children in the UK had a disability and the number has been increasing since 2011–12 when it was 6 per cent. The most reported disabilities are social and behavioural (50 per cent), learning impairment (32 per cent) and mental health (30 per cent) (DWP, 2023). There has also been a substantive growth in the number of children with more complex needs (Pinney, 2017). This growth would suggest that the number of children with disability will encompass an increasing proportion of children who would be covered by the Equality Act 2010 definition. The interface between the SEN and disability definitions complicates estimates of how many children are covered by the legislation.

The number of children and young people covered by the statutory assessment framework has fluctuated significantly. The number grew between 1989 and 2001, then decreased because of specific policy initiatives from 2002 onwards (DfES, 2004) until 2010. Statutory assessments have then increased every year since 2010 (Marsh, 2014, 2021, 2023; DfE, 2024a). This increasing reliance on the statutory framework has been framed as a key problem by successive governments and statutory bodies almost from the framework's inception and reforms have been aimed at reducing reliance on statutory provision and supporting early intervention at the pre-statutory stage to reduce costs and ensure more appropriate services (DfEE, 1997; Pinney, 2002; Audit Commission, 2002; DfES, 2004; DfE, 2011, 2012, 2022a).

Changes in the Warnock framework: the more things change the more they stay the same?

Despite the Children and Families Act (CFA) (2014) being presented as a radical reform of the Warnock framework, most of the key concepts in the first circular, equivalent to the code of practice, issued in 1983 (DES, 1983), are retained in current legislation (Lamb, 2019), even if the language has changed (Norwich and Eaton, 2015). These include educational need remaining the trigger for a statutory assessment, the importance of working with parents, the core definition of SEN and cooperation between statutory bodies.

Statutory provision

Replacing statements of special educational need with Education, Health and Care Plans (EHCPs) was one of the main changes of the CFA (2014). The aim of EHCPs was to provide a comprehensive assessment and support for children and young people with SEND from 0–25 years, extending the coverage to health, and social care services to provide personalised assessment and support. Legally the joint plan is only triggered by an education need which confers rights to education services, while health and social care are not covered by the same legal obligations (Norwich and Eaton, 2015). An attempt has been made to extend legal coverage in that First Tier Tribunal cases can now make recommendations that are intended to be binding on health and social care services through a 'voluntary' agreement (DfE, 2021).

Strengthening joint commissioning was also seen as a means of ensuring that joined-up assessments were delivered and that the costly discontinuity of assessments and services between different agencies and professionals would be reduced. The assumption was that coordinated planning would reduce pressure on the statutory system as services would be more personalised and consistently delivered across different agencies (DfE/DoH, 2015). The Act also introduced a new mediation and disagreement resolution process to help resolve disputes between parents, young people and local authorities (LAs) regarding EHCP assessments and plans. Mediation and dispute resolution provides an alternative to going to court and aims to encourage collaborative problem solving and reduce conflict. In addition, those with an EHCP could ask for a personal budget to facilitate personalisation through direct payments (CFA, 2014; DfE/DoH, 2015).

Non-statutory provision

The reforms abolished the old distinction between School Action and School Action Plus replacing this with a new 'SEN support' category to denote non-statutory provision which is 'ordinarily available' in schools, aiming to simplify the approach and reduce the conflation between SEN and pupils who had simply 'fallen behind' (Lamb, 2009; Ofsted, 2010; DFE, 2011). Needs are identified through a graduated approach of assess, plan, do and review once a child or young person meets the definition of SEND (DfE/DoH, 2015: Chapter 6). Schools and settings are expected to meet SEN through the school budget up to a 'notional' additional amount of £6,000 per pupil, not updated for inflation in the last ten years, before triggering discussions about additional support through the statutory route. The monetary limit is not formally intended as a trigger point and LAs have some discretion to top up schools' funding before recourse to statutory assessment. Schools must report on their provision through the Schools Information Report which is available for parents on the school's website, which built on previous information requirements (DfE/DoH, 2015).

The most significant legal innovation was the legal requirement to consult with parents, children and young people (CFA, 2014: Clause 19) which applied to both individual provision and the strategic delivery of the overall service, changing the conceptualisation of parental engagement from partnership to co-production (Lamb, 2013; Smith, 2022). The Local Offer was established as a means of effecting strategic co-production through a requirement to be consulted concerning the provision of local services and information on their provision (Lamb, 2013). The aim was to enhance parental rights to engagement over provision locally, as well as the ability to make more informed decisions about provision which would also help make services more appropriate and save money.

Have the reforms worked?

Statutory provision

> Generally, it is desirable that funds are spent on special education itself (in an inclusive setting), instead of on bureaucratic procedures such as diagnosis, categorisation, appeals and litigation.
> (Meijer, 1999: 168)

The aims of improving outcomes, greater personalisation and improved parental engagement gained wide support across professionals and parents' groups. Early evaluations of EHCPs with parents and young people were positive (Adams et al, 2017, 2018), especially in respect of the focus on personalisation and clarifying the outcomes to be achieved. As the system bedded down, the quality of EHCPs has suffered (Ofsted, 2021a, 2021b, 2022a; Ahad et al, 2022), reflected through increasing criticism by a series of parliamentary reports (HCESSC, 2019; NAO, 2019; HCCPA, 2020), Ofsted Reviews (Ofsted, 2021a, 2021b) and user groups (Disabled Children's Partnership, 2023). The reports identified poor implementation of the new assessment systems, with lack of staff expertise and capacity (HCESSC, 2019; NAO, 2019; Ahad et al, 2022). A systematic review of the implementation of EHCPs found that professionals required more training, especially in procedural aspects of the process, while parents required greater support and access to knowledge to enable informed engagement (Ahad et al, 2022). The system is still struggling to join services together as the DfE concluded 'The system relies on families engaging with multiple services and assessments, making it difficult to navigate, especially for the families of children and young people with the most complex needs' (DfE, 2022a: 10).

The number of EHCPs has increased against a background of growing need for statutory support and tighter school budgets which impacted on the 'ordinarily available' offer (Parish et al, 2018; ISOS, 2024). This has led to a greater reliance on the statutory framework, with the number of children and young people with EHCPs rising from 240,183 in 2014/15 (which includes EHCPs and statements) to 575,963 in 2023/24. This is an increase of 140 per cent (ISOS, 2024) over the period since their introduction and an average yearly increase of approximately 10 per cent since 2014 (DfE, 2024a). This is also an increase compared to the total proportion of pupils, up from 2.8 per cent in 2015 to 4.8 per cent (DfE, 2024a). On current trends, the number will reach 10 per cent by 2042 (Marsh, 2023). Pupils with an EHCP made up one quarter (26.0 per cent) of all pupils with SEN in January 2024 compared to 19.3 per cent in 2016 (DfE, 2024b). For children and young people there were 84,428 new plans issued in 2023, an increase on the previous year of 26.6 per cent. In 2023, the number of initial requests for an EHCP was 138,242, an increase from the previous year of 20.8 per cent (DfE, 2024a, DfE, 2024b). The system has become ever more reliant on statutory assessment to meet need as parental confidence in non-statutory provision has dropped (Lamb, 2019; DfE, 2022a). The additional growth threatens to overwhelm LA capacity without additional funding, though there are very different rates of statutory provision in different LAs even where they have similar characteristics (Marsh, 2014, 2022; DfE, 2022a; Marsh et al, 2024; ISOS, 2024).

While the initial growth was from the extension of the EHCPs to young people up to 25 years of age, growth is now driven across the age range. For children of compulsory school age, the number of EHCPs rose by 11.6 per cent. Children aged under five accounted for 4.6 per cent of EHCPs in 2024. The number of plans for children in this age group increased to 26,500 in 2024, a 25.8 per cent increase from 2023 (DfE, 2024a).

While the number of pupils with an EHCP in special schools increased between 2023 and 2024, the percentage of pupils with an EHCP attending state-funded special schools has dropped from 37.9 per cent to 35.8 per cent. At the same time, the percentage of pupils with an EHCP attending independent schools has increased significantly in recent years, rising from 5.3 per cent of all pupils with statements attending independent schools in January 2015, to 7.7 per cent of all pupils with an EHCP in January 2024 (DfE, 2024c). Overall, the trend has been for an increasing use of special school provision from 2014 to 2022 (Marsh et al, 2024) with a rise of 60 per cent in state funded special schools and 132 per cent in the number placed in non-maintained special schools (ISOS, 2024). As a percentage of the school population, the number of pupils placed in special schools rose from 1.4 per cent in 2015/16 to 2.1 per cent in 2023/24 (ISOS, 2024), illustrating that resources are being concentrated in specialist provision without developing a more sustainable integration between specialist and mainstream support.

LAs have managed the growth in EHCPs through longer waiting times. In 2022, the number of new EHCPs finalised within the statutory 20-week timescale fell to its lowest national level of only 49.2 per cent. This recovered slightly to 50.3 per cent being issued within 20 weeks in 2023. At the same time, refusal to assess showed an increase of initial EHC needs assessment requests turned down from 22.1 per cent in 2022 to 24 per cent (33,141) in 2023 (DfE, 2024a). Early diagnosis and assessment of need is crucial to access appropriate services (Sapiets et al, 2023) and delays risk increasing costs and complexity of interventions while restricting life chances.

A recent analysis also shows that the growth in the numbers of EHCPs is 'irrespective of affluence, geography or size' (ISOS, 2024: 27), though another study also suggests that the chance of a primary school child with SEND having an EHCP is higher if they live in an affluent local area than if they live in a deprived area, and that this holds true within LAs, not just between LAs (Campbell, 2023). Overall, there is a strong association between social disadvantage and being in receipt of an EHCP, with 42.2 per cent of pupils with a plan in 2023 being eligible for free school meals, the main indicator of children in low-income families (DfE, 2024b). This matches with the previous statementing system where an analysis concluded that 'Children with a statement of need experience more socio-economic disadvantage than children with SEN. … the most disadvantaged children, and those who are persistently disadvantaged, are more likely to have a Statement at age 7' (Parsons and Platt, 2017). The evidence undermines the perception that it is mainly middle-class parents who monopolise statutory provision (Lamb, 2023) even if they do make more use of the Tribunal (Marsh, 2022).

The response from DfE to the increasing financial pressure brought about by the growth in EHCPs has been to plug the overall funding gap with additional resources to the LAs' high needs budget, planned to grow to £10.54 billion in 2024–25 – an increase of over 60 per cent in just five years (DfE, 2022a, 2023a). The current system is financially unstable while not fully meeting needs despite the additional investment. There is also a distortion in how funding is calculated, as the National Funding Formula for High Needs applies a 32 per cent weight to historical spend, with those authorities spending more historically on specialist provision having larger spends than authorities who have invested in early intervention (Marsh, 2002, Marsh et al, 2024). This also leads to dramatic variation between authorities that is not obviously based only on current local needs or delivering in the most cost-effective way (NAO, 2019; Marsh et al, 2024).

There has also been a reduction in the overall value of an EHCP as the average spend per plan decreased from £26,700 to £23,800 between 2014 and 2018 (Bryant and Swords, 2018). Another study suggests a 20 per cent fall in value from 2014/15 to just over £19,000 (Hunter, 2019), while a more recent calculation suggests a lessening of value to £14,536 in 2017 recovering somewhat to £17,446 in 2022 (ISOS, 2024). Whichever figures are taken, the variation in provision, declining overall value of statutory provision from previous levels and limited access to specialist support suggests the Warnock system is failing in its primary purpose of identifying and meeting need in an equitable way, despite very significant extra resource being invested in recent years (DfE, 2022a).

It remains to be seen how far the combination of changes to the way the High Needs Budget is funded, together with the proposed national banding system (DfE, 2022a, 2023a) will be able to address the issue of variable funding and produce more consistency of provision. The Delivering Better Value in SEND programme (DfE, 2022b) and the 'Safety Valve' programme, which supports LAs to focus their assessment systems to bring a downward pressure on EHCPs in return for additional funding, are also intended to address financial pressure in the system by improving early intervention. This has been controversial with parent's groups (Kerr, 2024) and crucially, in terms of its stated aims, there is no significant evidence from the latest DfE figures that the number of EHCPs being completed is significantly lower in Safety Valve areas (DfE, 2024a). The new government has announced that the scheme will not be continued (Hansard, Dec 2024).

Overall, when Ofsted/Care Quality Commission (CQC) finished their inspections of all LAs under the old inspection regime in 2022, 82 out of 149 had received requests for written statements of action to remedy poor implementation (Ofsted, 2022a). There has also not been evidence of the expected dividend in joined-up working between education, health and social care. Ofsted/CQC reported 60 per cent of inspected areas have significant weaknesses and the lack of joined-up services was often cited along with poor practice in assessments and a lack of parental engagement (Ofsted, 2022b). Other reviews found the assessments to be fragmented, of low quality and failing to account for children's and families' own voices (Palikara et al, 2018; Castro-Kemp et al, 2019). The aspirations to involve children and young people also encountered multiple barriers. Participation in statutory assessment was poor, with only 44 per cent of children asked if they wanted to participate in the preparation of their EHCP and only 19 per cent offered a choice in how they might participate (Adams et al, 2017). A number of barriers were identified to their participation including little change in service culture and children and young people still having to listen to adults (Castro-Kemp et al, 2019; Sharma, 2021). The continued power of professionals over the process and decision-making about resources has brought into question how far the aspirations for co-production of individual provision have been met: requests from a professional for an EHCP are 1.4 times more likely to be issued than requests from families (Boddison and Soan, 2021).

The increase in the numbers of cases and growth in successful cases being taken by parents to the First Tier Tribunal illustrates the growing failure of confidence in the non-statutory system to meet needs, and in the fairness of the process. The overall number of appeals about statutory assessment increased 250 per cent between 2015 and 2022 (Marsh, 2023). While the overall number of Tribunal appeals, as a proportion of the total potential appealable decisions for EHCPs, is relatively low, there were 15,615 appeals registered in 2023 (calendar year), which is equivalent to an estimated 2.5 per cent of appealable decisions or approximately 1 tribunal appeal for every 38 children with an EHCP. This is an increase of 22 per cent compared to the previous year when there were 12,796 appeals registered, equivalent to an estimated 2.3 per cent of appealable decisions (MoJ, 2024; ISOS, 2024). Of these, 98 per cent have been found wholly or partly in the appellant's favour (MoJ, 2024). Rates of appeal to the Tribunal are lower in areas with lower socio-economic status and are significantly higher in the least deprived areas (Marsh, 2023). However, these figures do not support the narrative of system being driven by appeals to Tribunal rather than being a symptom of the failure of the system to meet its statutory obligations and LAs being able to resolve differences without parents having recourse to legal remedies.

The SEND tribunals dealt with 160 Disability Discrimination claims in 2022/23, 20 per cent up from 135 in the previous year. Of those decided at hearing, 64 per cent were dismissed and 36 per cent upheld – compared to 71 per cent dismissed and 29 per cent upheld in 2021/22 (MoJ, 2023). It is not clear if the lower level of claims related to discrimination cases is due to it being harder to prove discrimination or greater reluctance from parents to allege discrimination against schools (Porter et al, 2012).

Discontent with how the system is working is also reflected in the reports from the Local Government and Social Care Ombudsman (LGSCO) where they found fault in 92 per cent of cases in education and a substantial proportion of these were on issues relating to EHCPs (LGSCO, 2024). This led the Ombudsman to conclude that 'Special educational needs provision is an existential threat for the local authorities' (LGSCO, 2024: 6). These trends are indicative of a rising lack of confidence in the system and poor practice and illegality by LAs in assessment and following up with provision (AJC 2023; LGSCO, 2024).

Non-statutory provision

The growth in statutory provision and requests for provision reflect legitimate requests for support but begs the question whether this is the only way to meet the needs of disabled children and parents. At 'SEN support' there was a change from a graded identification system of 'school action' and 'school action plus' to a single 'SEN support' category with a graduated approach to identify and address learning needs. The more iterative approach was helpful in not having such rigid categories but also removed a level of clarity for parents about what support is being made without recourse to statutory provision. Schools have struggled to deliver confidence in the non-statutory offer, with concerns about access to specialist provision (HCESSC, 2019; NAO, 2019) and the capacity of schools to meet children's needs (Ofsted, 2021a, Ofsted, 2021b). A lack of understanding of the implications and obligations of the legislation within schools (Dunleavy and Sorte, 2022) has also driven the growth in EHCPs (DfE, 2023a).

Crucially, children with SEND continue to have poor outcomes even after contextual factors are taken into account (Parsons and Platt, 2017). One analysis argues that children and young people with SEND have performed worse overall since the reforms than before, and their Progress 8 attainment figures have remained broadly the same over the period 2018/19 to 2022/23 (ISOS, 2024). School accountability systems such as Attainment and Progress 8 scores have also been shown to impact negatively on how disabled children are assessed and also on schools' competence in supporting them, creating disincentives for schools to take children with SEND (Leckie and Goldstein, 2019). Children and young people with SEND fall behind their peers at every stage of education, regardless of their prior attainment (DfE, 2022a) and the gap is widening in most SEND categories (Daniel, 2024). While parental engagement is a focus in guidance and inspection, the monitoring of this within schools has been patchy (Ofsted, 2021a). Despite the requirements for parental engagement at school there is still not a focus on systematic parental engagement to ensure good home school working, which has the most evidence of improving outcomes (Lamb, 2022, 2023; Jones and Palikara, 2023).

Schools continue to manage challenging SEND pupils through suspensions and exclusion.

> The rate of suspensions among those pupils who have an EHCP is 21.60 compared to 24.42 for children at SEN support. This compares to 6.38 for pupils with no SEN. The rate of permanent exclusions among those pupils who have an EHC plan is 0.20, which is lower than for those with SEN without an EHC plan (SEN support) at 0.37. This compares to 0.07 for pupils with no SEN. (DfE, 2024d)

Historically, permanent exclusion rates for those with EHCPs are approximately half the rate of those on SEN support (Lamb, 2019; Black, 2022), which may be explained by the fact schools are required to strive to avoid exclusions for pupils on EHCPs and another reason why securing a statutory plan is attractive to parents.

From the beginning of the Warnock framework there has been a paradox where securing individual statutory provision drains the capacity of the system to meet the needs of all children with SEND, leading to more parents seeking statutory provision (Lamb, 2019). As the previous government's analysis argued, this creates

> a vicious cycle of late intervention, low confidence from parents, carers and providers, and inefficient allocation of support which is driving the spiralling costs in the system. This cycle begins in early years and mainstream schools ... settings are frequently ill-equipped to identify and effectively support children and young people's needs. (DfE, 2022a: 12)

The Green Paper and improvement plan

The Green Paper (DfE, 2022a) accepted and amplified the analysis of the failings identified by recent reviews. The SEND review programme originally intended to pursue legislative changes but, without the planned Education Bill envisaged by the previous administration, has become an administrative improvement plan within the current framework. The plan outlined a vision 'to create a more inclusive society ... to offer every child and young person the support that they need to participate fully, thrive and fulfil their potential' (DfE, 2023a: 7). To address the problems identified it proposed enhancing and tightening the accountability framework, with the introduction of a number of new bodies, standards and processes which adds to the complexity of an already Byzantine system.

The key changes proposed are:

- a national SEND and alternative provision implementation board to oversee the improvement plan and provide challenge and support to the system;
- establishment of local SEND and alternative provision partnerships that bring together partners to plan and commission support for children and young people with SEND and in alternative provision;
- a standard template for EHCPs, and to support the plans' transition to digital formats;
- integrating alternative provision, which now mainly provides for children with SEND, more directly into SEND provision in mainstream with additional funding;
- restricting parental rights to choice of school and potentially to Tribunals;
- development of National Special Educational Needs and Alternative Provision Standards;
- a new national and local inclusion dashboard;
- refocused inspections of local SEND provision by Ofsted and the CQC.

Mandating better joint working through National SEND boards and giving Integrated Care Board members a SEND brief (DfE, 2023a) are attempts to address the problems produced by the lack of legislative and organisational integration. The proposals face significant challenges of implementation without legislative powers or the cultural change that might follow within services (Disabled Children's Partnership, 2023). The improvement plan may just ensure more compliance with process measures developed by oversight boards and partnerships that mirror many of the current requirements without substantially altering the culture or focus of provision, thereby encouraging a performative adherence to targets generated by the current system without a focus on the outcomes achieved for children, which is part of the current problems (Hellawell, 2018; Lamb, 2023).

The improvement plan is vague about the legal status and content of the standards and targets, with the danger that they could simply be a restatement of existing legal duties or undermine them by lowering what is required, confusing parents and settings. Co-producing the standards with parents and stakeholders is, in principle, helpful, but this depends how much parents and young people can really frame and structure the scope of the policies rather than be co-opted to respond to a pre-given agenda (Lamb, 2022). Pragmatically, measures might be arrived at for indicators of inclusion, improved provision of support and processes but questions then remain about what happens if these are not met.

Simplifying and standardising the EHCP process and providing more guidance to assessment staff is a welcome point of consensus across most stakeholders as inconsistency was a major criticism (HCESSC, 2019; Ahad et al, 2022). Ensuring that assessment meets legal requirements by a more simplified and consistent application of the assessment process and understanding of its legal requirements could improve experience of the system. Any changes need to ensure that assessment retains the core principle of personalisation which was a popular part of the reforms (Adams et al, 2017).

The proposal to make mediation mandatory before parents are allowed to appeal to the First Tier Tribunal about an EHCP plan has been paused due to the negative reaction during the consultation, with the DfE now examining options to strengthen the mediation process (DfE, 2023a). Mediation works precisely because it is voluntary and engenders trust between the parties. Making mediation compulsory would risk destroying that trust and undermine the effectiveness of the current mediation process. The DfE (2023a: 76) has committed to examining if the LGSCO should have an expanded remit given it has been taking an increasingly important role in dealing with administrative complaints against LAs (LGSCO, 2019). The Ombudsman process is simpler and more direct than appeals to the First Tier Tribunal and it can use financial remedies.

While the plan supports co-production at the strategic level and has helpfully committed to developing a clearer definition of what co-production might require, it then seeks to restrict rights of access to redress and choice at the individual level, where the government perceives it leads to additional costs. The implementation plan proposes setting limits on parental choice of schools through a tailored list of educational settings provided through the Local Offer as a way to promote local provision and reduce 'the need for costly independent provision' (DfE, 2023a), though special schools providers have also argued that appropriate special school provision can ensure significant savings (Clifford et al, 2023). In principle, it is good to ensure more specialist provision locally, as part of a more inclusive system, but encouraging this by imposing restrictions on parental choice is dubious. The strategy should be first to ensure that provision locally meets need so that parents are not driven to make difficult choices about specialist provision.

There is recognition in the improvement plan of specific problems with the implementation of the current equality framework and the plan commits to seeking to 'prevent discrimination from arising in the first place by supporting schools to comply with their duties under the Equality Act 2010' (DfE, 2023a: 78) but has only proposed producing a good practice guide for schools following from this. The plan also commits to considering how policy on disability discrimination claims against schools are dealt with, following calls for the Tribunal to have the power to award financial compensation as part of making redress more successful (DfE, 2023a: 78).

By not addressing the discontinuities in legislative obligations between the two frameworks, the reforms risk introducing more layers of accountability and process without addressing the underlying contradictions in the Warnock framework. The new government will now be faced with a decision to either continue with these ameliorative 'improvements' which are already partially underway or opt for a more root and branch reform, especially given the potential financial challenges the system needs to address. The danger is that a reform programme working within the constraints of the current framework will get bogged down in trying to fix the financial challenges but not address the underlying framework that continues to drive a lack of parental confidence in the system. Currently the government will find it difficult to make the necessary investment in mainstream provision while maintaining funding for EHCPs (Sibieta and Snape, 2024). What is needed is a reframing of the reforms in terms of the rights and positive duties to children with SEND, which could transcend the contradictions of the Warnock framework (Sayers, 2018; Lamb, 2019).

Relationship with rights legislation

From the introduction of rights legislation to the SEND framework in 2001 with the Disability Rights Act, the system has struggled with what Warnock called the 'forced marriage' of the two approaches (Warnock and Norwich, 2010: 133). Following the work of the Disability Rights Task Force, proposals to extend the rights framework to education were included in the 1999 Task

Force Report (Disability Rights Task Force, 1999). These proposals were enacted incrementally with the Special Educational Needs and Disability Act 2001 and, following further pressure from stakeholders, the Disability Discrimination Act 2005. These measures were then incorporated into the Equality Act 2010. The extension of the legislation to include individual rights to reasonable adjustments was only implemented in 2012. The SEND CoP (DfE/DoH, 2015) then attempted to integrate the Equality Act 2010 requirements with the Warnock framework.

The key elements of the Rights framework are the non-discrimination requirements, including addressing direct and indirect discrimination and making reasonable adjustments to procedures, criteria and practices to ensure that disabled children are not at a substantial disadvantage compared to their peers, which is an anticipatory duty (Equality Act, 2010: Sections 13, 19, 20). These measures require the provision of auxiliary aids and adaptations. The Act has general duties for schools to publish accessibility plans setting out how they plan to increase access for disabled pupils to the curriculum, the physical environment and to information (Equality Act, 2010: Sched. 10). Schools also must publish information demonstrating how they have complied with the public sector equality duty, and update this a year after the last information was published; prepare and publish equality objectives, within four years after the last equality objectives were published. Compliance with the duties is proactive and failure to meet the requirements can be appealed at a First Tier Tribunal irrespective of whether a child has an EHCP, giving much broader legal entitlement and protection to provision than the Warnock framework (Sayers, 2018; Lamb, 2019).

The DfE did not commission the Equality and Human Rights Commission (EHRC) to issue statutory guidance, so the commission was limited to issuing non-statutory technical guidance (EHRC, 2014). The Equality Act (2010) has therefore tended to work as an ancillary layer of obligations, underutilised and poorly monitored (Beckett et al, 2009; Bukowski et al, 2011) and guidance has emphasised its role as a safety net (DfE/DoH, 2015; EHRC, 2015). This has been reflected in the absence of the rights obligations within Local Offers which are the key planning and accountability mechanism for LAs. Only 8 per cent of the Local Offer websites referred to the Equality Act (2010) in the preparation, development and/or review of the Local Offer, including specific and measurable objectives (Matthews et al, 2024). Despite the lack of promotion, schools which have followed a rights-based approach identified a number of positive outcomes from increasing access, improved pupil progress and achievements, better relationships with parents or specific changes within the school that increased participation (Beckett et al, 2009; Bukowski et al, 2011; Porter et al, 2012). The failure to fully integrate the frameworks has meant that the 'system is divided against itself' (Peacey, 2015).

How could a disability rights approach address the structural failings of the Warnock framework?

A different approach to the improvement plan would be to extend and develop the rights-based approach by building on the Equality Act (2010) requirements and potentially extending the legislation to address the current problems. Combined with other confidence-building measures such as greater investment in the schools ordinarily available offer, joint budgets for specialist services and improved parental and young people's engagement, it would be possible to consider reviewing the reliance on the Warnock framework in favour of a more comprehensive rights approach in a phased way.

1. Reframe the basis of SEND provision to align with a rights approach

Producing a particular type of statutory protection (EHCPs) is not the only way of producing a legally binding right to the services needed (Florian, 2002). A fundamental legal change took place in 2012 with the implementation of the right to reasonable adjustments for auxiliary aids and adjustments for individual disabled pupils (Equality Act, 2010; EHRC, 2015). This established individual rights to support, and adjustments aimed at removing barriers to learning which would include the services and support normally associated with the SEN provision, thus providing comprehensive support to remove educational barriers. Failure to make adjustments would result in discrimination, in which case there would be the right to appeal to the First Tribunal. Reasonable adjustments also retain a resource allocation mechanism through the concept of reasonableness and is not therefore an open-ended funding commitment for LAs or schools (EHRC, 2015). The 2012 change addressed criticisms that rights approaches focus only on common or generic barriers but do not address specific individual needs where this requires additional support (Norwich in Warnock and Norwich, 2010).

Reasonable adjustments could be seen as analogous to the provision that should be 'ordinarily available' within a school which is properly funded to meet needs. To support this, specific guidance on what should be 'ordinarily available' in terms of the anticipatory duty in the Equality Act 2010 could be provided to cover assessment, curriculum and pedagogy and provision of auxiliary aids (Peacey, 2015). There is a continuing debate about the allocation of schools funding and the role of current notional budget of £6,000 which, in theory, is allocated to schools and could be increased and schools held accountable for its deployment as part of any reforms. Increasing school funding to meet these general needs could be a more effective and inclusive means of funding provision (Lamb, 2019) and has been shown to be effective in supporting quality education for learners with disabilities (Ebersold and Meijer, 2016).

In principle, extending reasonable adjustments to individual disabled children should have rendered the SEN framework subordinate to the disability rights framework for disabled children (Crowther, 2011). However, guidance continued to position the reasonable adjustment measures as a safety valve for the Warnock framework if SEN provision has not been secured (DfE/DoH, 2015). A different approach to how reasonable adjustments is conceived and promoted could still effect a significant change in practice.

Funding reform, with schools receiving more delegated funding, is crucial for this approach to work. More legal security (reasonable adjustments are a statutory right) and comprehensive provision at the pre-statutory level could build confidence in the non-statutory offer, with changes being actively embraced from below rather than imposed from above and any reduction in statutory plans being a by-product of the process (Lamb, 2009).

Wales has moved to an integrated legislative approach, removing the gatekeeper role for statutory assessment by allowing anyone who receives an individual development plan, which is a wider category than an EHCP, as a result of being identified with an Additional Learning Need (ALN), to have recourse to the Tribunal (Welsh Government, 2021). While Scotland has moved to a focus on provision before the statutory stage and restricted statutory provision, through a Coordinated Support Plan, to a much smaller group of children (Scottish Government, 2017; Riddell and Gillooly, 2019; Harris and Riddell, 2022; Marsh, 2023). Both approaches were introduced as part of a wider rights-based approach with a focus on improving overall access to services and support.

Changing the focus of the legal basis of provision could also enable a different concept of children's development based on fulfilling a child's capability (Terzi, 2005; Norwich, 2014b; Broderick, 2018), replacing concepts of need and the deficit model. A focus on capability could also help reframe how inclusion is conceptualised so that it moves the debate beyond some of the polarising dichotomies of the traditional debate (Terzi, 2014; Broderick, 2018). A capability approach would also help in contextualising what supports children with disability need to achieve better outcomes, looking at wider determinates and the support needed and how we measure these (Mihut et al, 2021). This could be applied to current academic accountability models. Progress 8 measures currently disadvantage disabled children by expecting them to perform to a particular standard without value added measures and disadvantage disincentives for schools to focus on disabled children. For example, a capabilities approach to Progress 8 would weight more heavily the progress of those pupils who have not yet achieved sufficient capabilities to lead a dignified and autonomous life and identify what additional adjustments and support they needed to do so (Roberts, 2020).

2. Align the accountability and the rights framework

The government cannot easily extend the unique educational rights to health and social care just for children with SEND and this creates a significant anomaly for service providers and families. DfE addressed this problem by giving powers to the First Tier Tribunal to make non-binding judgements and recommendations in respect of health and social care which providers agree voluntarily to honour but which have no formal legal force (DfE, 2021). While these 'extended appeals' are an ingenious practical solution they do not provide a long-term sustainable basis to ensure integration across these provisions. Mandating better joint working through National SEND boards and giving Integrated Care Board members a SEND brief (DfE, 2023a) are also attempts to address the problems produced by the lack of legislative and organisational integration but face significant challenges of implementation without legislative powers to enforce decisions or the cultural change that might follow within the services from such changes (Disabled Children's Partnership, 2023).

There are a number of measures which could be taken to improve accountability:

a. *Merge accountability and budgets for EHCPs.* A recent systematic review of research into the issues with EHCPs found that '[t]he structural reform needs to be one which subsumes health care, social and educational services for children and young people under a single accountability system' (Ahad et al, 2022). It would also help if legislative entitlements, accountability and provision were covered within one budget bringing both budgetary clarity and legal consistency (Audit Commission, 2002; Pinney, 2002; Russell, 2011). Education, health and social care are already covered by the public duties under the Equality Act (Russell, 2011) so unifying these areas grounded in a rights-based framework would also bring more coherence.

b. *Improve the remedies available to Tribunals and enhanced role for the Ombudsman.* Criticisms that the Tribunal should be able to use financial remedies has led DfE to committing to examining the issue further for Disability Discrimination appeals (DfE, 2023a: 77–78). While there has been little research on this area, limited evidence suggests that parents do not apply on grounds of disability as they are reluctant to claim discrimination by their child's school and that there is no financial remedy for redress (Porter et al, 2012). It may well be helpful both as a potential deterrent and as quicker remedy in some circumstances for this to form part of the Tribunal's potential powers. This could be combined with the often-recommended extension of the powers of the LGSCO as a route to quicker resolution of administrative issues (Lamb, 2009; HCESSC, 2019; DfE, 2023a).

c. *Ensure better access for young people.* The extension of rights to lodge an appeal to the Tribunal in their own right to young people over 16 years of age in the CFA 2014 has been welcomed by disabled young people despite some complexities in its exercise (Cullen and Cullen, 2021). A power was also included in the CFA 2014 to pilot an independent appeal right for children under 16 and to introduce such a right on a permanent basis provided the right has first been piloted following a recommendation in the Lamb Inquiry (2009). There has been no full trial in England as, following a small pilot, it was decided not to go ahead. The Scottish Government, in contrast, has gone much further than England in giving those aged 12–15 years, judged to have competence, the same rights as parents and young people – apart from requesting mediation and making a request or appeal regarding placement (Harris and Riddell, 2022). As the principle of consultation is becoming more embedded in English legislation the age limit for competence in these areas should be reviewed with a view to reducing the age limit.

d. *Require more comprehensive accountability for the planning of services.* The anticipatory and planning duties provide a powerful framework for ensuring that Education, Health and Care provide access under the Equality Act 2010 requirements. The Equality Act 2010 duty to produce an accessibility plan and report on progress should create the framework to secure a more inclusive school environment and ethos (Stobbs, 2022). However, a review of access plans found that adherence is often lacking, with parents often unaware of its existence, access measures non-existent or poorly implemented, and that the framework is poorly enforced (Soorenian, 2019). Ofsted's schools inspection framework does require measuring compliance with the Equality Act 2010 but it is not clear how far the specific SEND elements of this are routinely taken into account and enforced as the Ofsted Annual Report has not covered this (Ofsted, 2022b). Development and adherence to Equality Plans could be made the core of the DfE's proposed national standards (DfE, 2023a) and more centrally woven into the Ofsted/CQC area inspection framework. It would need a level of willingness to both inspect and enforce those entitlements in a way that has been absent from the system to date and involve Ofsted/CQC in a more active inspection and compliance role in respect of the revised SEND area inspection framework.

e. *Improve reporting by schools.* LAs have powers through their cooperation duties with schools (CFA, 2014) to hold schools to account through the Schools Information Report which could be developed into a more robust accountability framework, ensuring schools detail what is 'ordinarily available' in their provision. This should also include what steps schools are taking to provide reasonable adjustments to meet their equality duties.

f. *Integrate the wider children's rights framework into SEND legislation.* It is important to recognise the fundamental right of all children to be heard and consulted on their educational provision on an equal basis. These requirements are enshrined in international law and provide a wider framework that encompasses specific SEND-related measures (Sayers, 2018). The UN Convention on the Rights of the Child 1989 (UNCRC), the UN Convention on the Rights of Persons with Disabilities 2006 (UNCRPD), and the European Convention on Human Rights Article 14s (ECHR) are an important context for the domestic legislative framework (Sayers, 2018; Mangiaracina et al, 2021). Both the English framework on SEND and the Scottish ASN framework make reference to the UNCRC which provides an overall framework for children's rights (Sayers, 2018; Riddell and Gillooly, 2019; Harris and Riddell, 2022). Scotland has also recently integrated the UNCRC into Scottish legislation (Scottish Government, 2023, 2024; Harris and Riddell, 2022). The revised Welsh SEND legislation explicitly used the principles of the UNCRC in how it has framed the overall approach in its new framework and especially the rights of parents and young people to be consulted (Welsh Government, 2021). The more these frameworks are integrated into the principles informing the delivery of SEND provision the more the culture of provision will be aligned with a rights-based rather than needs-led Warnock model.

3. Review the current definition of SEND

Warnock criticised the introduction of the rights framework into SEN legislation without at the same time addressing the different definitions of SEND contained within the legislation (Warnock and Norwich, 2010). The CoP tried to align the definitions of SEN with disability: 'Where a disabled child or young person requires special educational provision, they will also be covered by the SEN definition' (DfE/DoH, 2015: 16). However, this attempt has left the framework with an uneasy tension between different definitions and approaches (Norwich, 2014a).

The SEN definition has been consistently challenged on the basis that it is a relative definition and therefore often leads to mistaking poor progression due to poor teaching with SEN (Lamb, 2009; Ofsted, 2010, 2021a), it relies on labelling to deliver resources (Lauchlan and Boyle, 2020), identification fluctuates significantly based on social class, school policies and location (Hutchinson, 2021) and it promotes a deficit model of disability (Runswick-Cole and Hodge, 2009).

Scotland moved to using a broader concept of Additional Support Needs as the trigger to access support (Scottish Government, 2017; Harris and

Riddell, 2022). Wales has also introduced a new descriptor of Additional Learning Needs, but the underlying definitions of SEN and disability remain the same and therefore the measures are in danger of simply reproducing the same issues under a different heading while also ignoring specific SEN needs (Welsh Government, 2021). A consequence of the new definition has been a 20 per cent reduction in the number of children identified with SEN leading to questions about its effectiveness (Dauncey, 2022).

The Equality Act 2010 measures include disabled children and young people whether or not they have SEN. The disability definition focuses on the definition of who has a disability, not learning difficulty, but relies on a within-child definition of impairment that is in danger of reinforcing the central legacy of the Warnock approach with its focus on individual entitlement and provision (Norwich and Eaton, 2015). Nevertheless, the disability definition has the potential to be widened or altered, combining an individual approach with a broader social ecological approach (Rees, 2017) using a more holistic assessment approach such as the International Classification of Functioning Disability and Health for Children and Youth where aspects of this approach have been successfully trialled (Norwich, 2014a, 2016; Castro-Kemp and Palikara, 2016; Palikara et al, 2018, 2019).

There are also proposals for how the definition could be expanded. Evans (2007) suggested that the definition of SEND could be amended to ensure learning difficulty is included as a disability, bringing SEN within the orbit of the equality legislation and having one consistent legal framework and approach based on those values. Peacey (2015: 9) also argues for a focus on the fact 'that someone has been assessed as having the right to additional or different provision and encourage "SEN" to wither away'. While needing further analysis these approaches suggest that the disability definition could be expanded in ways which address its current limitations and provide a sounder basis for a new approach to identification and assessment.

Any change of definition is unlikely to move totally away from identification and assessments which will use specific labels relating to disability, given the need to define who might be covered by legal protections is a central prerequisite of any system of entitlements to specific interventions or protections (Lamb, 2009; Lauchlan and Boyle, 2020). As Sayers argues, 'Removing labels removes the obligation to provide support' (2018: 626). Additional support is triggered by identification or diagnosis (Sapiets et al, 2023) and failure to identify specific impairments which can also lead to discrimination by not addressing individuals' specific issues (Macdonald, 2010). The focus should be on how appropriate identification (labels) for specific disabilities can be refined to make a positive difference to a child or young person's development (Lauchlan and Boyle, 2020) within an overall rights framework that guarantees the removal of barriers through appropriate support and access arrangements.

4. Change the culture of provision and support the workforce to achieve more equity

The Carter Review of Initial Teacher Training (Carter, 2015) identified significant gaps in training for SEND which needed to be addressed if the 2014 reforms were to be successful. The Teacher Development Agency responded by producing a five-year plan with the aim of improving initial teacher training (ITT). Yet a recent survey found that only 46 per cent of Early Career Teachers (ECTs) felt well prepared for teaching pupils with SEND, with 23 per cent saying they were badly prepared (DfE, 2023b). A large-scale survey of teacher views also found that eight in 10 (83 per cent) teachers believed that students with SEND and/or additional needs in primary school are not being effectively supported in their aspirations and achievements by the current education system (Pearson, 2024).

Other studies have questioned the training and capacity of the workforce to support children with disability and competing notions of inclusion within a school framework which emphasises normative achievement but this is not yet routinely part of ITT training. The models for teacher training for inclusion need to be reviewed if they are to be successful in meeting the practice and values identified as crucial for success (Robinson, 2024). Staff training in SEND pupil engagement and disability inclusion training were identified as key to addressing pupil dissatisfaction in their relations with teachers and peers (Dimitrellou and Male, 2020). Young people also identified better staff understanding of their needs as important to support inclusion (National Census, 2022). While research found that teachers should receive education training to provide them with the values and competencies to accommodate inclusive environments (Goodall and Mackenzie, 2018). Staff training specifically in disability rights is fundamental to altering the culture of provision and in supporting staff to become more aware of the implications of equality legislation (Dunleavy and Sorte, 2022; Stobbs, 2022). At the LA level there also needs to be change, as a survey of professionals' attitudes found they 'felt more comfortable operating within discourses of needs, whereby professionals reserved the right to make key decisions on educational provision, rather than adopting a discourse of rights' (Riddell and Gillooly, 2019: 24; Harris and Davidge, 2018).

The government should commission the EHRC to produce separate statutory guidance on the equality measures as they apply to SEND given the acknowledgement of schools' weakness in this area (DfE, 2023a). Ideally this would be part of an extended approach that resets the role of rights legislation and is accompanied with new materials and practical guidance for teachers and support staff. Ofsted and the EHRC could also be asked to report on the impact of schools' accountability measures and Progress 8 on disabled students as a specific human rights issue.

Conclusion

The attraction of the Warnock framework can be seen in the legal protection and support it provides for a growing number of children and families. A focus on better implementation, more coordinated provision and national standards may bring improvements to the current framework. But, as with previous attempts at reform, the measures proposed have not fully addressed the fault lines in the current framework which creates ever more pressure for statutory protection and renders the framework unsustainable. Governments then respond by resorting to restricting services and support without addressing the underlying problems that led to growth in the use of the statutory framework in the first place. For over 20 years, a complementary system of rights and protections has been available but underpromoted and underused. The strength of a rights-based approach is not only in the wider legislative protections it affords but also that it encapsulates an inclusive set of values upon which to reset the culture of provision for disabled children, moving from a needs-led model to one based on rights and capability.

A rights-based approach could provide a more solid foundation on which to improve disabled children's and young people's outcomes especially if harnessed to full engagement of parents and young people. But legislation on its own is not enough unless underpinned by values that support changed practice (Lamb, 2022; Harris and Riddell, 2022). Unless there is a better integration, if not full replacement, of the Warnock framework with a rights-based approach the alternative seems to be the never-ending cycle of ameliorative reforms, sustaining a framework that continues to labour under its central contradiction of only securing legal protections for some children based on a flawed concept of needs rather than rights.

References

Adams, L., Tindale, A., Basran, S., Dobie, S., Thomson, D., Robinson, D., et al (2017) Experiences of Education, Health and Care Plans: A survey of parents and young people. DfE Research Report.

Adams, L., Tindale, A., Basran, S., Dobie, S., Thomson, D., Robinson, D., et al (2018) Education, Health and Care Plans: A qualitative investigation into service user experiences of the planning process. DfE Research Report.

Ahad, A., Thompson, A.M. and Hall, K.E. (2022) 'Identifying service users' experience of the education, health and care plan process: a systematic literature review', *Review of Education*, 10: e3333. doi: 10.1002/rev3.3333

AJC (Administrative Justice Council) (2023) Special educational needs and disability: Improving local authority decision making. Report of the AJC's Working Group on Special Educational Needs and Disability. https://www.judiciary.uk/wp-content/uploads/2024/08/SEND-Improving-Local-Authority-Decision-Making.pdf

Audit Commission (2002) Special educational needs: A mainstream issue. ISBN: 1862404097, 9781862404090.

Beckett, A., Ellison, N., Barrett, S., Shah, S., Buckner, L. and Byrne, D. (2009) Disability equality in English primary schools: Exploring teaching about disability equality and non-disabled children's perceptions of disability: Full research report. ESRC End of Award Report RES-062-23-0461. Swindon: ESRC.

Black, A. (2022) '"But what do the statistics say?" An overview of permanent school exclusions in England', *Emotional and Behavioural Difficulties*, 27(3): 199–219.

Boddison, A. and Soan, S. (2021) 'The coproduction illusion: considering the relative success rates and efficiency rates of securing an Education, Health and Care plan when requested by families or education professionals', *Journal of Research in Special Educational Needs*, 22(2): 89–205.

Broderick, A. (2018) 'Equality of what? The capability approach and the right to education for persons with disabilities', 6(1): 29–39.

Bryant, B. and Swords, B. (2018) Developing and sustaining an effective local SEND system: A practical guide for councils and partners. ISOS Partnership. https://www.local.gov.uk/developing-and-sustaining-effective-local-send-system-practical-guide-councils-and-partners

Bukowski, G., Roberts, H., Fraser, J., Johnson, F. and Ipsos MORI (2011) The equality duties and schools. Equality and Human Rights Commission Research Report 70. www.equalityhumanrights.com/sites/default/files/research-report-70-equality-duties-and-schools_0.pdf

Campbell, T. (2023) Inequalities in provision for primary children with special educational needs and/or disabilities by local area deprivation, LSE. https://sticerd.lse.ac.uk/CASE/_NEW/PUBLICATIONS/abstract/?index=10538

Carter, A. (2015) Carter Review of Initial Teacher Training. www.gov.uk/government/publications/carter-review-of-initial-teacher-training

Castro-Kemp, S. and Palikara, O. (2016) 'Mind the gap: the new special educational needs and disability legislation in England', *Frontiers in Education*, 1: 4. doi: 10.3389/feduc.2016.00004

Castro-Kemp, S., Palikara, O. and Grande, C. (2019) 'Status quo and inequalities of the statutory provision for young children in England, 40 years on from Warnock', *Frontiers in Education*, 4: 76. doi: 10.3389/feduc.2019.00076

Children and Families Act (2014) Children and Families Act. Legislation UK. London: HMSO.

Clifford, J., Hutchison, E., Kemp, J. and Cooke, C. (2023) Reaching My Potential: The value of SEND provision demonstrated through learners' stories. A report for the National Association of Independent Schools and Non-Maintained Special Schools (NASS), London: Sonnet Impact.

Crowther, N. (2011) 'From SEN to Sen: could the capabilities approach transform educational opportunities for disabled children?', in S. Haines and D. Ruebain (eds) *Education, Disability and Social Policy*, Bristol: Policy Press, pp 47–64.

Cullen, M.A. and Cullen, S. (2021) 'Young people's right to appeal to the English First-tier Tribunal (Special Educational Needs and Disability): learning from the first two years', *Journal of Social Welfare and Family Law*, 43(77): 1–21. doi: 10.1080/09649069.2021.1876308

Dauncey, M. (2022) Identifying Additional Learning Needs: Has the bar been raised or was it previously too low? SENEDD. https://research.senedd.wales/research-articles/identifying-additional-learning-needs-has-the-bar-been-raised-or-was-it-previously-too-low/

Daniel, J. (2024) The academic achievement gap between students with and without special educational needs and disabilities. European Journal of Special Needs Education. 1–18. https://doi.org/10.1080/08856257.2024.2400771

DES (Department of Education and Science) (1983) Assessments and statements of special educational need. Circular 1/83. London. www.educationengland.org.uk/documents/des/circular1-83.html

DfE (2011) Support and aspiration: A consultation. https://assets.publishing.service.gov.uk/media/5a751423e5274a3cb28697c7/Support_and_Aspiration_Green-Paper-SEN.pdf

DfE (2012) Support and aspiration: A new approach to Special Educational Needs and Disability: progress and next steps.

DfE (2014) The Equality Act 2010 and Schools Departmental Advice for School Leaders, School Staff, Governing Bodies and Local Authorities.

DfE (2021) SEND Tribunal: Extended appeals guidance for local authorities, health commissioners, parents and young people. https://assets.publishing.service.gov.uk/media/612f43fe8fa8f5033264a132/DBOT_2122_single_route_of_redress_guidance_-_1_September_2021.pdf

DfE (2022a) SEND Review: Right support, right place, right time. Government consultation on the SEND and alternative provision system in England. https://www.gov.uk/government/consultations/send-review-right-support-right-place-right-time

DfE (2022b) Guidance on our intervention work with local authorities. https://assets.publishing.service.gov.uk/government/uploads/system/uploads/attachment_data/file/1110657/Sustainable_high_needs_systems_guide_-_SV_and_DBV_updates_-_Oct22.pdf

DfE (2023a) Special Educational Needs and Disabilities (SEND) and Alternative Provision (AP) Improvement Plan. service.gov.uk/media/63ff39d28fa8f527fb67cb06/SEND_and_alternative_provision_improvement_plan.pdf

DfE (2023b) Working lives of teachers and leaders – Wave 1. www.gov.uk/government/publications/working-lives-of-teachers-and-leaders-wave-1

DfE (2024a) Education, health and care plans, 2024. https://explore-education-statistics.service.gov.uk/find-statistics/education-health-and-care-plans

DfE (2024b) Special educational needs in England, academic year 2023/24. https://explore-education-statistics.service.gov.uk/find-statistics/special-educational-needs-in-england

DfE (2024c) Special educational needs and disability: an analysis and summary of data sources, August 2024.

DfE (2024d) Permanent exclusions and suspensions in England: 2022 to 2023.

DfE/DoH (2015) Special educational needs and disability: Code of practice. https://www.gov.uk/government/publications/send-code-of-practice-0-to-25

DfEE (1997) Excellence for all children: Meeting special educational needs. https://www.education-uk.org/documents/pdfs/1997-green-paper.pdf

DfES (Department for Education and Skills) (2004) Reducing reliance on statements: An investigation into local authority practice and outcomes. Research Report RR508. https://publications.parliament.uk/pa/cm200506/cmselect/cmeduski/478/478i.pdf

Dimitrellou, E. and Male, D. (2020) 'Understanding what makes a positive school experience for pupils with SEND: can their voices inform inclusive practice?' *Journal of Research in Special Educational Needs*, 20(2): 87–96.

Disabled Children's Partnership (2023) Failed and forgotten: Research by the Learning Hub at the Disabled Children's Partnership. https://disabledchildrenspartnership.org.uk/wp-content/uploads/2023/03/Failed-and-Forgotten-DCP-report-2023.pdf

Disability Discrimination Act (2005) Legislation UK, HMSO. https://www.legislation.gov.uk/ukpga/2005/13/contents

Disability Rights Task Force (1999) From exclusion to inclusion: A report of the Disability Rights Task Force on Civil Rights for Disabled People, London: DfEE. https://dera.ioe.ac.uk/id/eprint/4553/1/drtf.pdf

Dunleavy, A. and Sorte, R. (2022) 'A thematic analysis of the family experience of British mainstream school SEND inclusion: can their voices inform best practice?' *Journal of Research in Special Educational Needs*, 22(4): 332–342.

DWP (2023) Family Resources Survey. https://www.gov.uk/government/statistics/family-resources-survey-financial-year-2022-to-2023

Ebersold, S. and Meijer, C. (2016) 'Financing inclusive education: policy challenges, issues and trends', in A. Watkins and C. Meijer (eds) *Implementing Inclusive Education: Issues in Bridging the Policy-Practice Gap (International Perspectives on Inclusive Education, Vol. 8)*, Bingley: Emerald Group Publishing Limited, pp 37–62.

Education Act (1981) London: HMSO. https://www.legislation.gov.uk/ukpga/1981/60/enacted

Equality Act (2010) Legislation UK. HMSO. https://www.legislation.gov.uk/ukpga/2010/15/contents

EHRC (Equality and Human Rights Commission) (2014) Technical Guidance for Schools in England. https://www.equalityhumanrights.com/sites/default/files/technical_guidance_for_schools_england.pdf

Evans, W. (2007) 'Reforming special educational needs law: vocabulary and distributive justice', in R. Cigman (ed) *Included or Excluded? The Challenge of the Mainstream for Some Children with SEN*. London: Routledge, pp 85–94.

Florian, L. (2002) 'The more things change the more they stay the same?' *British Journal of Special Education*, 29(4).

Goodall, C. and Mackenzie, A. (2018) 'What about my voice? Autistic young girls' experiences of mainstream school', *European Journal of Special Needs Education*, 34(4): 499–513.

Hansard (2024) SEND Capital Funding Volume 758: Wednesday 4 December 2024.

Harris, N. and Davidge, G. (2018) Analysis of key informant interviews: England (Autonomy, Rights and Children with SEN/ASN: Working Paper 6). Edinburgh: CREID, University of Edinburgh. https://www.research.ed.ac.uk/en/publications/working-paper-6-literature-review-autonomy-rights-and-children-wi/publications/

Harris, N. and Riddell, S. (2022) 'Ensuring rights matter: England's and Scotland's frameworks for implementing the rights of children and young people with special educational needs and disabilities', *The International Journal of Human Rights*, 26(9): 1671–1690.

HCCPA (House of Commons Committee of Public Accounts) (2020) Support for children with special educational needs and disabilities. https://committees.parliament.uk/work/35/support-for-children-with-special-educational-needs-and-disabilities/publications/reports-responses/

HCESSC (House of Commons Education and Skills Select Committee) (2019) Special educational needs and disabilities: Government response to the Committee's first report of Session 2019. First special report of Session 2019–21, House of Commons. https://publications.parliament.uk/pa/cm201919/cmselect/cmeduc/20/20.pdf

Hellawell, B. (2018) '"There is still a long way to go to be solidly marvellous": professional identities, performativity and responsibilisation arising from the SEND Code of Practice 2015', *British Journal of Educational Studies*, 66(2): 165–181.

House of Commons Library Briefing Paper (2023) Special Educational Needs: support in England. Number 07020.

Hunter, J. (2019) Plans that work: Employment outcomes for people with learning disabilities. IPPR North.

Hutchinson, J. (2017) 'How many children have SEND?' Education Policy Institute. https://epi.org.uk/wp-content/uploads/2021/03/SEND-Indentification_2021-EPI.pdf

Hutchinson, J. (2021) 'Identifying pupils with special educational needs and disabilities', Education Policy Institute and Nuffield Foundation. https://epi.org.uk/wp-content/uploads/2021/03/SEND-Indentification_2021-EPI.pdf

ISOS Partnership (2024) Towards an effective and financially sustainable approach to SEND in England. https://www.local.gov.uk/publications/towards-effective-and-financially-sustainable-approach-send-england

Jones, C. and Palikara, O. (2023) 'How do parents and school staff conceptualize parental engagement? A primary school case study', *Frontiers in Education*, 8: 990204. doi: 10.3389/feduc.2023.990204

Kerr, M. (2024) 'Does the SEND Safety Valve scheme have a future under the Labour Government? And if so, who's next?' Special Needs Jungle, 31 July. www.specialneedsjungle.com/send-safety-valve-scheme-future-labour-government-whos-next/

Lamb, B. (2009) Lamb Inquiry, Special Educational Needs and Parental Confidence. DCSF.

Lamb, B. (2013) 'Accountability, the local offer and SEND reform: a cultural revolution?' *Journal of Research in Special Educational Needs*, 15: 70–75.

Lamb, B. (2019) 'Statutory assessment for special educational needs and the Warnock Report; the first 40 years', *Frontiers in Education*, 4: 51.

Lamb, B. (2022) Parental engagement in schools and beyond: What works and the implications for SEND? SEN Policy Forum Paper. https://www.researchgate.net/publication/367656415_Parental_engagement_in_the_early_years_schools_and_beyond_what_works_and_the_implications_for_SEND

Lamb, B. (2023) 'SEND legislation, parental engagement and coproduction', in Green, H. and Edwards, B., *True Partnerships in SEND*, Abingdon: Routledge, pp 3–14.

Lauchlan, F. and Boyle, C. (2020) 'Labelling and inclusive education', in U. Sharma (ed) *Oxford Research Encyclopaedia of Education*, New York: Oxford University Press. https://www.researchgate.net/publication/341189693_Labelling_and_Inclusive_Education

Leckie, G. and Goldstein, H. (2019) 'The importance of adjusting for pupil background in school value-added models: a study of Progress 8 and school accountability in England', *British Educational Research Journal*, 45(3): 518–537.

LGSCO (Local Government and Social Care Ombudsman) (2019) Not going to plan? Education, health and social care plans two years on. London. https://www.lgo.org.uk/assets/attach/5693/EHCP-2019-vfC.pdf

LGSCO (Local Government and Social Care Ombudsman) (2024) Annual review of local government complaints. London. https://www.lgo.org.uk/information-centre/news/2019/oct/a-system-in-crisis-ombudsman-complaints-about-special-educational-needs-at-alarming-level

Macdonald, S. (2010) *Crime and Dyslexia: A Social Model Approach.* VDM Verlag.

Mangiaracina, A., Kefallinou, A., Kyriazopoulou, M. and Watkins, A. (2021) 'Learners' voices in inclusive education policy debates', *Education Sciences,* 11(10): 599. doi: 10.3390/educsci11100599

Marsh, A.J. (2014) 'Statements of special educational needs and tribunal appeals in England and Wales 2003–2013 – in numbers', *Educational Psychology in Practice,* 30: 393–408.

Marsh, A.J. (2021) 'Special educational needs and disability tribunals in England 1994–2019', *Research Papers in Education,* 37(6): 797821.

Marsh, A.J. (2022) 'Special educational needs and disability tribunals in England 1994–2019', *Research Papers in Education,* 37(6): 797–821.

Marsh, A.J. (2023) 'Education health and care plans (EHCPs) and statements in England: a 20 year sustainability review', *Educational Psychology in Practice,* 39(4): 457–474.

Marsh, A.J., Gray, P. and Norwich, B. (2024) 'Fair funding for pupils with special educational needs and disability in England?' *British Educational Research Journal,* 50: 1064–1083.

Matthews, J., Black-Hawkins, K., Basu, A., Necula, A.I., Downs, J., Ford, T. et al (2024) 'To what extent do England's local offer websites adhere to the statutory guidance as set out in the Special Educational Needs and Disabilities Code of Practice?' *British Educational Research Journal,* 50(4): 1724–1740.

Meijer, C. (1999) Financing special education: A seventeen-country study of the relationship between financing of special needs education and inclusion. European Agency for Development in Special Needs Education. https://www.european-agency.org/sites/default/files/financing-of-special-needs-education_Financing-EN.pdf

Mihut, G., McCoy, S. and Maître, B. (2021) 'A capability approach to understanding academic and socio-emotional outcomes of students with special educational needs in Ireland', *Oxford Review of Education,* 48. doi: 10.1080/03054985.2021.1973982

MoJ (Ministry of Justice) (2023) Tribunal Statistics Quarterly: July to September 2023.

MoJ (Ministry of Justice) (2024) Tribunal Statistics Quarterly: January to March 2024.

NAO (National Audit Office) (2019) Support for pupils with special educational needs and disabilities in England, London: NAO.

National Census (2022) Educational experiences of young people with special educational needs and disabilities in England: February to May 2022. https://www.nasschools.org.uk/wp-content/uploads/2023/10/Full-Report-Reaching-my-potential-The-value-of-SEND-provision-demonstrated-through-learners-stories.pdf

Norwich, B. (2014a) 'Changing policy and legislation and its effects on inclusive and special education: a perspective from England', *British Journal of Special Education*, 41: 403–425.

Norwich, B. (2014b) 'How does the capability approach address current issues in special educational needs, disability and inclusive education field?' *Journal of Research in Special Educational Needs*, 14: 16–21.

Norwich, B. (2016) 'Conceptualizing special educational needs using a biopsychosocial model in England: the prospects and challenges of using the international classification of functioning framework', *Frontiers in Education*, 1: 5. doi: 10.3389/feduc.2016.00005

Norwich, B. and Eaton, A. (2015) 'The new special educational needs (SEN) legislation in England and implications for services for children and young people with social, emotional and behavioural difficulties', *Emotional and Behavioural Difficulties*, 20(2): 117–132.

Ofsted (2010) The Special Educational Needs and Disability Review. A statement is not enough. https://www.gov.uk/government/publications/special-educational-needs-and-disability-review

Ofsted (2021a) SEND: old issues, new issues, next steps. June 2021. https://www.gov.uk/government/publications/send-old-issues-new-issues-next-steps

Ofsted (2021b) Supporting SEND. https://www.gov.uk/government/publications/supporting-send/supporting-send

Ofsted (2022a) Main findings: Area SEND inspections and outcomes in England as at 31 August 2022. Published 17 November 2022. https://www.gov.uk/government/statistics/area-send-inspections-and-outcomes-in-england-as-at-31-august-2022

Ofsted (2022b) The Annual Report of His Majesty's Chief Inspector of Education, Children's Services and Skills 2021/ 22. https://www.gov.uk/government/publications/ofsted-annual-report-202122-education-childrens-services-and-skills/the-annual-report-of-his-majestys-chief-inspector-of-education-childrens-services-and-skills-202122

Palikara, O., Castro-Kemp, S., Gaona, C. and Eirinaki, V. (2018) 'Capturing the voices of children in the Education Health and Care Plans: are we there yet?' *Frontiers in Education*, 3: 24. doi: 10.3389/feduc.2018.00024

Palikara, O., Castro-Kemp, S., Gaona, G. and Eirinaki, V. (2019) 'Professionals' views on the new policy for special educational needs in England: ideology versus implementation', *European Journal of Special Needs Education*, 34: 83–97.

Parish, N., Bryant, B. and Swords, B. (2018) Have we reached a 'tipping point'? Trends in spending for children and young people with SEND in England. ISOS Partnership. https://www.local.gov.uk/have-we-reached-tipping-point-trends-spending-children-and-young-people-send-england

Parsons, S. and Platt, L. (2017) 'The early academic progress of children with special educational needs', *British Educational Research Journal*, 43(3): 466–485.

Peacey, N. (2015) A transformation or an opportunity lost? The education of children and young people with special educational needs and disability within the framework of the Children and Families Act 2014. Research and Information on State Education. https://dera.ioe.ac.uk/id/eprint/38597/1/A%20transformation%20or%20an%20opportunity%20lost.pdf

Pearson (2024) School Report. https://www.pearson.com/en-gb/schools/insights-and-events/topics/school-report/2024.html

Pinney, A. (2002) 'In need of review? The Audit Commission's report on statutory assessment and statements of special educational need', *British Journal of Special Education*, 29: 3. doi: 10.1111/1467-8527.00253

Pinney, A. (2017) Understanding the needs of children with complex needs or life-limiting conditions. Council for Disabled Children/True Colours Trust. https://councilfordisabledchildren.org.uk/sites/default/files/uploads/attachments/Data%20Report.pdf

Porter, J., Daniels, H., Georgeson, J., Hacker, J., Gallop, V., Feiler, A. et al (2008) Disability data collection for children's services research report. Department for Children, Schools and Families: RR062.

Porter, J., Georgeson, J., Daniels, H., Martin, S. and Feiler, A. (2012) 'Reasonable adjustments for disabled pupils: what support do parents want for their child?', *European Journal of Special Needs Education*, 28(1): 1–18. https://doi.org/10.1080/08856257.2012.742747

Rees, K. (2017) 'Models of disability and the categorisation of children with severe and profound learning difficulties: informing educational approaches based on an understanding of individual needs', *Educational and Child Psychology*, 34(4): 30–39.

Riddell, S. and Gillooly, A. (2019) Autonomy, rights and children with special needs: A new paradigm? The Rights of Children with Special and Additional Support Needs in England and Scotland Report June 2019. ESRC. https://www.docs.hss.ed.ac.uk/education/creid/Projects/39_vi_ESRC_SENChildren_FinalRpt.pdf

Roberts, J. (2020) 'Thinking about accountability, education and SEND', in Accountability, performance management and inspection: how to enable positive responses to diversity? SEN Policy Research Forum, *Journal of Research in Special Educational Needs*, 20(2): 146–171.

Robinson, D. (2024) *Effective Teacher Education for Inclusion: Critical Perspectives on the Role of Higher Education* (1st edn), Abingdon: Routledge.

Runswick-Cole, K. and Hodge, N. (2009) 'Needs or rights? A challenge to the discourse of special education', *British Journal of Special Education*, 36(4): 198–203.

Russell, P. (2011) 'Building brighter futures for all our children: education, disability, social policy and family', in S. Haines and D. Ruebain (eds) *Education, Disability and Social Policy*, Bristol: Policy Press, pp 105–130.

Sapiets, S.J., Hastings, R.P. and Totsika, V. (2023) 'Predictors of access to early support in families of children with suspected or diagnosed developmental disabilities in the United Kingdom', *Journal of Autism and Developmental Disorders*, 54(4): 1628–1641.

Sayers, D. (2018) 'Rights not needs: changing the legal model for Special Educational Needs (SEN)', in K. Runswick-Cole, T. Curran and K. Liddiard (eds) *The Palgrave Handbook of Disabled Children's Childhood Studies*, London: Palgrave Macmillan, pp 617–642.

Scottish Government (2017) Additional support for learning: statutory guidance 2017. https://www.gov.scot/publications/supporting-childrens-learning-statutory-guidance-education-additional-support-learning-scotland/

Scottish Government (2023) www.gov.scot/policies/human-rights/childrens-rights/

Scottish Government (2024) Statutory guidance on Part 2 of the UNCRC (Incorporation) (Scotland) Act 2024. https://www.gov.scot/publications/statutory-guidance-part-2-uncrc-incorporation-scotland-act-2024-2/pages/1/

SENEDD (2022) Identifying Additional Learning Needs: Has the bar been raised or was it previously too low? https://research.senedd.wales/research-articles/identifying-additional-learning-needs-has-the-bar-been-raised-or-was-it-previously-too-low/#:~:text=The%20Welsh%20Government%20has%20revealed%2C%20under%20scrutiny%20by,were%20incorrectly%20identified%20and%20over-reported%20in%20the%20past.

Sharma, P. (2021) 'Barriers faced when eliciting the voice of children and young people with special educational needs and disabilities for their Education, Health and Care Plans and Annual Reviews', *British Journal of Special Education*, October. doi: 10.1111/1467-8578.12386

Sibieta, L. and Snape, D. (2024) Spending on special educational needs in England: Something has to change. IFS Report R341. https://ifs.org.uk/sites/default/files/2024-12/Spending-on-special-educational-needs-in-England.pdf

Smith, S. (2022) Overview of parental partnership: assumptions, changes over time and consequences. SEND Policy Forum Paper 47. https://senpolicyresearchforum.co.uk/wp-content/uploads/Parent-policy-seminar-paper-June-22.pdf

Soorenian, A. (2019) Accessibility plans as effective tools for inclusion in schools: Are they working? Alliance for Inclusive Education. https://www.allfie.org.uk/wp-content/uploads/2020/02/AccessibityPlans-Report.pdf

Special Educational Needs and Disability Act (2001) London: HMSO. https://www.legislation.gov.uk/ukpga/2001/10/contents

Stobbs, P. (2022) Disabled Children and the Equality Act 2010: What teachers need to know and what schools need to do. Council for Disabled Children. https://www.ncb.org.uk/sites/default/files/uploads/attachments/Equality%20Act%20Guide%20for%20schools%20-%20FINAL.pdf

Terzi, L. (2005) 'Beyond the dilemma of difference: the capability approach to disability and special educational needs', *Journal of Philosophy of Education*, 39: 443–459.

Terzi, L. (2014) 'Reframing inclusive education: educational equality as capability equality', *Cambridge Journal of Education*, 44(4). doi: 10.1080/0305764X.2014.960911

UNCRC (1989) United Nations Convention on the Rights of the Child, London: UNICEF. https://www.unicef.org.uk/wp-content/uploads/2016/08/unicef-convention-rights-child-uncrc.pdf

UNCRPD (2006) United Nations Convention on the Rights of Persons with Disabilities. https://www.un.org/disabilities/documents/convention/convoptprot-e.pdf

Warnock, M. (1978) Special Educational Needs: Report of the Committee of Enquiry Into the Education of Handicapped Children and Young People, London: HMSO; DES.

Warnock, M. (1993) 'Introduction', in J. Visser and G. Upton (eds) *Special Education in Britain After Warnock*, London: Routledge, pp vii–xi.

Warnock, M. (2005) *Special Educational Needs: A New Look*, London: Philosophy of Education Society of Great Britain.

Warnock, M. and Norwich, B. (2010) *Special Educational Needs: A New Look*, edited by L. Terzi, London: Continuum.

Welsh Government (2021) The Additional Learning Needs Code for Wales 2021. https://www.gov.wales/sites/default/files/publications/2024-04/220622-the-additional-learning-needs-code-for-wales-2021%20%282%29.pdf

3

Multi-agency working and children and young people with disabilities: from 'what works' to 'active becoming'

Liz Todd and Jo Rose

Introduction

This chapter considers the assumptions and implications of policy developments in multi-agency working over at least the last 40 years for the support of children and young people with disabilities. We look at four policy strands: that of post-Warnock statutory SEN assessment, inclusive education, the Every Child Matters (ECM) agenda and the era of Education, Health and Care plans. Our focus is on education, and although the actual policies referred to would vary in other contexts, the overall argument will, we claim, apply to all. For most of the last four decades there has been a constantly renewed call to improve multi-agency working and, more recently, far-reaching structural changes to integrate services. However, it is questionable whether this has been for the benefit of children and young people with disabilities. Additionally, in the last decade, as multi-agency working has become more of a taken for granted, the trend of considering how to improve processes has diminished. We make the case that problems in multi-agency working have been repeatedly conceptualised in ways that do not tell the whole story and therefore do not make it easy for improvements to happen.

Multi-agency working has been understood in terms of 'what works', looking at systems and communication, rather than in terms of the complex politics around professional roles and relationships. The perspectives of parents and young people on how services should work with them has been ignored or ineffectively included. In the Special Educational Needs and Disability (SEND) Code of Practice (DfE, 2015) there is acknowledgement that parents and children should be 'involved' in decision-making. Decisions are positioned, however, as arising from the expertise of the professionals, with family involvement being more about agreement rather than input. In this chapter, misconceptions of multi-agency working are traced through some key policy developments, leading to different kinds of thinking that might take us in other directions. We present an understanding not of multi-agency working per se, but focus on relationships and power, of and between professionals, practitioners, young people and their families. There is a need to organise services in a way for the different knowledges of all involved to have agency, is adaptive and flexible recognising parents have changing and differing kinds of needs and should be in a position to negotiate their own preferred identities. Professionals would aim to be 'privilege-cognisant' in challenging normative practices. It places the professionals in a range of roles. Instead of understanding what professionals do as enacting a kind of composite expertise around a child, relationships with agencies are, if they are working well, seen as supporting the child and their parents in actively becoming the kinds of young people and families they are seeking to be. However, too often the convergence of conflicting interests, given the last decade of austerity, does not make this easy to achieve.

Multi-agency working: do we have to use that term?

It is worth unpacking what we mean by 'multi-agency working' and how we propose to talk about it. Disabled children and their families find themselves interacting with a number of different professionals. There may be a need to consult professionals who occupy different roles in health, education, social care and other areas. It is not usually the case that families consult with a single professional – many meet, over time, with a considerable number. Where more than one practitioner or agency is involved there is invariably the question of what kinds of roles are carried out and what kinds of communication are needed in order for them to work effectively with the family. Or, to state this another way, that 'multi-agency' working can happen in a range of ways, and the manner of such working is experienced by the disabled child and family in a variety of ways, some helpful, some less so. Although we will use the term 'multi-agency' in this chapter, we are not just concerned with the relationships between agencies and how they work together and will therefore aim to challenge certain assumptions. The very term 'multi-agency' working sets up a dynamic of the professionals vis-à-vis children and parents. The focus of this chapter is, therefore, on possibilities for the working relationships between children, young people, parents and professionals. This chapter will not just refer to children with disabilities, but, in addition, to their parents (subsuming carers) or families, in recognition of the role played by all members of a family in each other's lives and of the particular role that parents of disabled children are often required to play in the lives of their child (Mittler and McConachie, 1983; Sandow, 1994a; Gascoigne and Wolfendale, 1995; Wolfendale, 2004). Also, the use of the word child or children will refer to both children and young people.

Multi-agency jigsaw: composite expertise

The call for agencies to work together – and for them to work better together towards a range of goals – is not new. The focus has not, of course, always been solely on the needs of disabled children. For example, the Plowden Report (HMSO, 1967) saw partnership between professionals as crucial to the solution of the problem of 'social disadvantage'. The same solution, was evident in The Court Report (HMSO, 1976) looking at the health needs of all children:

> The real cause of educational failure may lie in the individual's psyche or physical health or in the environment of home, school or society. To disentangle the strands is beyond any single expertise. Medical, social and psychological advice have therefore to be available if the child is to receive the best education that can be offered, and a full team approach with the teacher will sometimes be essential. (HMSO, 1976: section 10.39)

Such thinking goes back even further as demonstrated in an early review, known as the Summerfield Report, of the way educational psychologists operate, encompassing work with disabled children: 'No one discipline can be expert in all aspects of a child's life and the contributions of colleagues trained in the field of psychiatry, psychology, education and the social sciences must all be used effectively, each accepting the competence of his colleagues in their own field' (DES, 1968: section 2.34).

An assumption underlying much past but also present policy and legislation in health, education and social care is that the high level of complexity of problems for some children (not specifically referring to disabled children) has meant that solutions do not lie within any single discipline: that different disciplines make unique contributions.

What we see in these earlier policy developments is the evolution of a model of multi-agency working that has continued to the present. It is a model of differing contributive expertise. This takes a jigsaw approach to the individual concerned, seeing the person as separate parts all with differing needs to be met from the contrasting expertise, skills and knowledges of people from different professional backgrounds. It is the enduring presence of such a rationale that this chapter challenges as having contributed significantly to the failure to make noteworthy headway in improving the ways that agencies work together for and with disabled children and their families.

There is, of course, an obvious face validity to such a 'composite expertise' rationale. It seems clear that there is, in fact, a range of different professional identities, each with arguably dissimilar knowledges and skills, able to help in a number of ways. It follows that working together is reliant on each professional being able to communicate their particular perspectives with respect to the client. Problems in multi-agency working are, therefore, about improving the delivery of services and evolving new systems, and in particular about improving communication. Such conclusions are, indeed, often the outcome of discussions or evaluations in this area (Capper et al, 1993; Kendrick, 1995; Roaf and Lloyd, 1995; Dyson et al, 1998; Easen et al, 2000; Atkinson et al, 2001; Lloyd et al, 2001; Wigfall and Moss, 2001; Roaf, 2002; Stead et al, 2004; Townsley et al, 2004; Brown and White, 2006). However, conceptualising multi-agency working in terms of 'composite expertise' obscures complexities, ambiguities and powerful competing interests in relationships between agencies and between them and the people with whom they work. Relationships between professionals, and between them and clients are viewed in logical and linear ways. In particular, there is a failure to acknowledge the practices of professionals as having meaning and contributing to the socio-political construction of the identities of children and their families.

If we start to look at multi-professional working through more political lenses, policy developments over the last few decades might yield key understandings. We look at four areas of policy, first at the genesis of 'special educational needs' through the 1981 Education Act before considering, second, the inclusive education movement. We follow this by looking at the major multi-agency reforms brought by the ECM agenda. Our fourth area is further legislative change brought by The Children and Families Act 2014, and the SEND Code of Practice 2015, that put in place a new approach to the educational assessment and provision for children with special educational needs or a disability, that of education, health and care assessments and plans. We then consider, for each policy area, the roles in which parents and children have been placed with respect to the professionals, and at the implications of such relationships, before concluding with some considerations and challenges for more effective relationships. This is a reminder that we are not just looking at 'multi-agency' working as often understood, as what the professionals do and how they communicate and work together, but we are interested moreover in the roles, practices, relationships and politics of professionals, children with disabilities and their parents, and indeed the wider community.

Warnock: special educational needs

The 1981 Act, which arose from the Warnock Committee (1978), can be seen to have brought multi-agency working to the heart of the statutory assessment of 'special educational needs'. Such involvement of different agencies had not previously been to the same extent a feature of assessment. This Act took away previous labels given to children, a clear signal to remove from educational practice the particular kind of deficit thinking associated with these labels. In their place was put the concept of 'need', and in particular 'special educational needs'. Russell (1992) saw the 1981 Education Act as forcing professionals to work together around their differing assessment of need. The increased working together appeared to be a step forward, and indeed it did provide improved involvement and accountability in decision-making for a range of professionals. This arguably was progress for disabled children (for those who were given such an assessment), in that the expertise of different professionals was now available in a way that could potentially assist in finding out what was needed within the educational context and making appropriate provision. There was also a possibility that parents might be more involved in assessment since the Warnock Report was one of the first policy documents to herald parents as partners with professionals (Warnock, 1978).

However, we would not conceptualise the increase in multi-professional involvement as synonymous in any simple way with progress. 'Special educational needs', its concepts, assessment and independent tribunal all assume an 'individual' and (once again) 'deficit' focus. Attributes understood as internal constructions are assessed and are the basis on which decisions of need and school placement are made. The medical model of disability was invoked, focusing attention away from disability as a construction of society (Barnes, 1981; Oliver, 1996; Shakespeare, 2006) and positioning professionals (not parents) as those who hold relevant expertise. Assessment, intervention and school placement seemed analogous with squeezing differently fashioned pegs into identically shaped holes. There were also 'notions of individualism and progress, combined with a conviction that science was the key to human betterment' (Fisher and Goodley, 2007: 66). Critique of the educational context, and an investigation of what should change in that context, was avoided. Similarly obscured was debate into the relationship between socio-economic status, poverty and disability, a relationship we know has long existed (Blackburn et al, 2010; Tomlinson, 1982; Sloper, 1999). Significantly, we know that the Warnock Committee was directed away from considering the relationship between poverty and special educational needs (Dyson, 2005).

And what was the impact on the role and relationship possibilities for professionals, disabled children and their parents? 'Need', it seemed, provided a way to argue entitlement. Like motherhood and apple pie, 'need' is not easy to contest. However, need also holds value-laden assumptions and seems to convey notions of empiricism, authority, universality and objectivity. The term appears as something intrinsic to children, rather than ' "needs" as extrinsic to children ... "needs" as a cultural construction' (Woodhead, 1991: 42). Various writers (Edwards, 1978; Fulcher, 1989; Solity, 1991; Wood; 1994; Norwich, 1995) have provided a critique of the currently constructed notion of 'special needs'. As defined in the legislation, special need is a relative concept, defined in relation to educational context and local provision (DfE, 2015). According to the Code of Practice in England (DfE, 2015), a pupil is defined as having special needs if they have a learning difficulty that requires provision to be made, a circular argument. Provision is to be compatible with efficient education for other pupils in the same context. This leads to unresolved ambiguities in practice of decision-making about individual children. The lack of a clear definition (its circularity, need being what is needed) and the absence of engagement with the politics of need, was a vacuum into which stepped a massive expansion in the number and range of professionals involved (Galloway, 1994), eager to respond to statutory demands to measure and describe the different jigsaw pieces of a child. This refers, of course, to the requirement for psychological, medical and educational advice, required to make decisions about whether to create a statement of special educational needs. Thus the different reports giving alternative perspectives on special needs seemed more an expression of 'professional ownership, in which medical and educational definitions classify what can be special and who can claim a need' (Corbett, 1993: 549).

The main role of a multi-disciplinary assessment appeared to be to 'provide an arena for these negotiations' (Galloway et al, 1994: 151). The needs of clients seemed to be 'negotiated between professionals, as well as between professionals and their "client" in pursuit of a range of professional, political and pragmatic objectives' (Galloway et al, 1994: 151). It is as if we had created a complex process to describe the emperor's new clothes, then found that that process was problematic, but then continued to spend time making the process work, while all the time not realising that even if it is made less problematic it may well fail to deliver what is needed.

In conclusion, therefore, multi-agency working was created and became, itself, a problem that forever after needed to be addressed: the collaborative process and how to make it work became the challenge, rather than addressing the nature of the system and context that created the need for collaborative processes to be set up. There was (drawing on ideas from activity theory) a runaway quality (Engestrom, 2008). It (multi-agency working) obscured other solutions and failed to secure effective educational provision for children with disabilities. We need to make clear at this point that we are not talking here about the intentions of professionals. The first author was working in the 1990s as an educational psychologist. It appeared to be the intention of all those she came across, more generally confirmed in literature (Norwich, 1993; Galloway et al, 1994), to improve educational experiences for children with disabilities. What we are referring to here are the ways that practices and structures can work against the intentions of those involved to unanticipated outcomes. We next discuss whether matters improved as the focus changed towards inclusion?

Inclusive education

The second area considered is that of inclusive education, which has been emerging since the 1980s. Inclusive education is variously defined as to do with the kind of schooling placement for a child (mainstream vs special) or more widely and critically, 'as a process of increasing the participation of pupils in, and reducing their exclusion from, the cultures, curricula and communities of their local schools, not forgetting, of course, that education involves many processes that occur outside of schools' (Ainscow, 1999: 218).

With significant impetus from some parents and professionals, and a strong emerging international lobby (the Salamanca Statement, UNESCO, 1994) an inclusion policy imperative started to emerge in the late 1990s with a programme for action and curriculum guidance (Dyson, 2005). In 2001, a Special Needs and Disability Act extended protection on grounds of disability to children in school. At the same time, the Ofsted framework incorporated evaluation of the inclusiveness of schools. Inclusive education, its policies and practices, provided a significant change to the aims and focus of much multi-agency work. It changed the kinds of things that professionals expected to achieve in assisting children with disabilities and their parents with matters to do with schooling, and it heralded an increase in multi-agency teams.

Inclusive education has required a departure from the 'known and familiar' and a critique of disabling practices and structures that has not always been easy. However, it has not been fully achieved (Frederickson et al, 2004; Dyson, 2005; Riddell, 2009). It is contentious, resisted by some parents and professionals, under-resourced (though is arguably resource neutral), fails to be achieved for certain groups of young people (Visser and Stokes, 2003), is countered by the standards agenda (the focus on school attainments) and once again is not successful in tackling the more underlying socio-economic problems of the families of disabled children.

On the other hand, the effect of the inclusive education movement has been a shift in the context in which needs are assessed. While inclusion could take an individual deficit focus and assess what was needed in order to support a child in mainstream, it opened the way to more debate about the context of education and the extent to which it is disabling. It therefore enabled a more social model of disabilities to become part of discussions about education. It heralded a critique of the school setting in order to bring about a mainstream placement. It was and is still a challenge to the deficit assumptions of the 1981 Act as it focused on looking at how mainstream school can change to accommodate the needs of the disabled child. One might expect, therefore, less of a focus on deficits. Our impression, one of the authors having been employed as an educational psychologist in a local educational context for parts of the 1980s and 1990s, is that inclusion also brought an increase in the consideration of abilities and personal strengths. This enabled the edging away from the primacy of individual problems and needs. There was, consequently, more attention given to seeking the child's views. Partnership with parents and a consideration of the views of the child were now good practice in assessments (DFES, 2001). Integration of the social model into concepts of inclusion meant that there was a step away from the professionals holding all the expertise, towards acknowledging the experiential expertise held by parents and children. The concept of 'special educational needs' did not call for wider analysis of schools (such as school improvement or pedagogy, see Dyson, 2005), whereas the concept of inclusion presupposed such an analysis. There was an assumed critique of professional role that left a space for lobby groups – including the demands of individual parents. With inclusive education, the relationships between children with disabilities, their parents and professionals seemed tangibly different. However, there remained considerable frustrations for parents in obtaining the services and placements that they were looking for.

Interagency reorganisation: ECM

New Labour in the millennium instigated policy developments that had further consequences for the shape of the relationships between professionals, children with disabilities and their families. The ECM (HMSO, 2003) agenda brought major changes in the way services are structured and organised over the last decade. The overall aim was to improve the social care, education and health of all children. A structural and financial rearrangement of different agencies, particularly education and social care, was at the heart of these changes. There was a concerted effort for more joined-up thinking and working, reflected in structural changes to services. Professionals were increasingly organised into multi-agency teams. The headline aims for children were those of: being healthy, staying safe, enjoying and achieving, making a positive contribution and economic wellbeing. These became guiding principles for health, social and educational services, including schools. Such principles were to be fully compatible with 'inclusive education' in the requirement that 'raising standards in schools and inclusion must go hand in hand' (DfES, 2004: 36). There was also an obligation to ensure that every child 'has the chance to fulfil their potential by reducing levels of educational failure, ill health, substance abuse … neglect, crime and anti-social behaviour among children and young people' (HMSO, 2003: 11).

What were the implications and effects of the ECM agenda on multi-agency working with children with disabilities? Surely having more integrated multi-agency teams and a focus on improving multi-agency working could only be good? The long-awaited call by parents that the services offered to them should be more 'joined-up' seemed, in the ECM agenda, to be within reach. Being joined-up was to mean the achievement of less stressful negotiation of the involvement of different services, decreasing the time to engage a range of practitioners and reducing the need to repeatedly give information (Thomas, 1978; Sandow, 1994b; Roaf and Lloyd, 1995; Dessent, 1996). Key worker roles, as a way to achieve more joined-up services, were indeed central to the changes brought about by the ECM agenda, supported by new developments such as the Common Assessment Framework and the 'team around the child'. However, parents of children did not, it appears, experience services as more seemless (Abbott et al, 2005b). The key worker role lacked consistency (Greco and Sloper, 2004) – key workers rarely held the professional prestige that came with deep and specific expertise – and was not widely available to parents (Townsley et al, 2004; Abbott et al, 2005a; Slade et al, 2009).

There was indeed an increase in various kinds of provision that opened up some opportunities for disabled children and their families, such as within Sure Start and Children's Centres and in extended schools and services (Cummings et al, 2005, 2007, 2010; Anning et al, 2006; Stobbs, 2008). A range of interesting and creative projects were developed. However, the needs of disabled children were to an extent overlooked. One reason was the complexity of changes in local authorities that have followed from the ECM agenda (Council for Disabled Children, 2009). The needs of disabled children (and other groups) were overshadowed, we would claim, by the attention required to improve child safe-guarding and protection. This was perhaps not surprising given the origin of the ECM Agenda in the tragic death of Victoria Climbié, attributed in part at least to the failure of children's and social services to work together to prevent it. Furthermore, while there was some evidence that professionals themselves experienced improvements as a result of increased multi-agency working (Abbott et al, 2005a), research suggests that there was not a commensurate experience of improvement on the part of children and their families. On the contrary, families seemed to continue to experience a range of unmet needs (Townsley et al, 2004; Abbott et al, 2005a, 2005b; Goodley, 2007; Slade et al, 2009).

Acknowledgement of the relative failure of the ECM agenda to impact on the lives of children with disabilities was suggested by the launch of separate initiatives to focus on their needs. For example, 'Aiming High for Disabled Children' (AHDC), a joint DfES and HM Treasury report in May 2007 on improving services for disabled children committed the government to a 'transformation programme' for the delivery of services for disabled children and their families in England from 2008 to 2011 (HM Treasury, 2007). Other major initiatives had to make separate calls to make sure that disabled children came within their orbit. For example, the Council for Disabled Children (2009) played a role in trying to ensure that disabled children were catered for within the extended schools and children's centres initiatives, both key to the ECM agenda. Initial indications from pilot projects (personalisation, individual budgets, person-centred planning) suggested that elements of AHDC had the potential to offer improved multi-agency services for disabled children (Department of Health, 2010). However, they were likely to work well on the assumption that funding would continue beyond the pilot projects.

Another problem was the systemic medical model implicit in the whole edifice of the ECM agenda (Todd, 2007). The key vehicle for achieving the five positive outcomes, with the two overarching tenets of prevention and protection, was through the effective offering of services. This could be termed a 'service delivery' emphasis. Effective delivery seemed to be understood in terms of services being offered early enough in places easily accessible to children and families (that is, in full service extended/integrated schools), delivered by people with the correct skills (workforce reform), and with a graded response so that services were both universal and targeted. There was a well-articulated aim to organise services 'around the child, young person, or family, rather than the existing professional functions' (DfES, 2004). While this seemed all well and good, the focus was again on the individual as in some way needing to be fixed rather than how problems are produced within a context. It was the professional who does the fixing and it was, once again, most often a deficit focus. The composite expertise model was repeatedly in evidence. There were, therefore, contradictory messages for the relationships between children, parents and professionals. On the one hand, improvements were expected given the far-reaching nature of changes that are focused on making multi-agency working work better, but on the other hand, the systemic medical model that was implicit to the changes, strengthened the roles of professionals and arguably made it more difficult for partnership relationships to happen between children, parents and professionals.

Given the advances in multi-agency working expected as a result of the ECM agenda, if improvements were going to happen for children with disabilities and their families, it would happen now. However, it seemed this was not the case.

The story so far

To conclude this far, the increase in professional involvement in the lives of disabled children post-Warnock, the reorganisation of professionals into multi-agency teams as inclusive education came to the fore, and the increasing attention on ways for professionals to work better together, in ECM, did not seem to have been experienced by children and their parents as making a noticeable and positive impact on their lives. We know that there has long been evidence of the dissatisfaction of parents of children with special educational needs and disabilities with many educational services and, within this, of the roles of professionals (Thomas, 1978; Piper and Howlin, 1992; Sandow, 1994b; Townsley et al, 2004; Council for Disabled Children, 2009). Such views have not changed greatly throughout three very different policy developments that have been considered. Indeed Goodley (2007: 8) found 'Parents generally struggle more with coming to terms with fragmented service provision than the "disabilities" of their children'. There have been few attempts to evaluate multi-agency working from the perspective of children. However, we do have some evidence that children have valued some of the contact with professionals for the support provided (Tolley et al, 1998), but have generally not been put in a position where they understood professional roles or how decisions were reached. The main meaning for children of decisions taken about them seemed to be about blame or punishment (Galloway et al, 1994; Armstrong, 1995).

Education health care assessment and plans

The Children and Families Act (2014) introduced a process that combined the reports of professionals, the parents and the child into a single document that aims to describe not just needs but strengths and needs in a multi-disciplinary and holistic way, and to include the child's own perspective. Local authorities are now required to seek the views of parents and children to contribute their perspectives alongside the formal assessments of various agencies and professionals. Such obligations aimed to address the fragmentation of services, enable the provision of more joined-up services and embody a strengthening of the role of children and families' views in decision-making. This was, in principle, a step towards acknowledging the expertise of parents and children – consulting on the services required and how the Local Offer could work.

We cannot know whether the ambitions for the education health care assessments would have been achieved had they not been hampered by a decade of austerity and the consequent public sector cuts. Challenges have been many. Parents increasingly go to court to require local authorities to carry out an assessment or to issue a plan that recognises their child's educational needs. Most special educational needs and disability tribunals find in favour of the parent (often having waited many months for a hearing), but many parents lack time, money and knowledge to take this course of action. At the same time as stringent cuts to council budgets, there has been a rising demand for education health care assessments, and with no additional funding from central government. Cuts to school budgets and the provision of teaching assistant time has also meant a lack of school capacity to make adequate special educational provision. There are also doubts about the quality of education, health care plans with many varying in detail and quality, focusing on difficulties (rather than including strengths) and unconvincing in their inclusion of children's views (Palikara et al, 2018; Parsons et al, 2021). It seems, then, that the intention to work with family expertise has probably defaulted to privileging professional expertise with the involvement of families becoming about agreement rather than input and incorporation of ideas into the plan.

In more recent time as well as the decades of the past, multi-agency working has consistently been constructed in terms of 'composite expertise'. This appears to have meant that improvements were focused on finding ways to enable the expert to do their work more effectively, or to communicate better with other professionals – or the wholesale and complex reorganisation of local authorities. The solution has been technocratic, managerial and administrative, to find out 'what works' in order to do more of this, and less of what does not work. However, such an analysis mitigates against alternative, more political and critical, understandings of what happens between parents, children and professionals. It is to these that we turn next.

Constructing identities, positioning roles and knowledge

If the subject matter was uncontested, it is possible that a model of composite expertise might 'work'. However, questions (for example) about disability, need, educational provision and health concerns are rarely in the domain of certainties. They deal with aspects of experience that are socially constructed and contested. Even accepting Shakespeare's (2006) critical realist model of disability (that is, the understanding that impairments need to be seen also to be biological reality rather than solely socio-cultural interaction) the implications for provisions still depend upon the cultural constructions of, for example, education. Roles are unequal in terms of who has permission to speak, to claim knowledge, and when and about what, with the professional usually given the leading role. Our attention is therefore drawn to consider different permissions to name and make decisions about what is contested. The dominant individualised, medical model, or deficit focus of the professional gaze, calls for the expert and mitigates against the involvement of parents and children. The experiential expertise of parents and children holds little sway in a medical model. This has unintended outcomes. Professional practices together 'form an intricate social process which turns on a series of critical decisions initiating gradual but perceptual changes in a child's social status and leading ultimately to the elaboration of a social role' (Partlett, 1991: 229). McDermott (1996) shows how this can happen in a discussion of the way a child 'is acquired' by a learning difficulty (rather than the other way around). Other authors similarly show practice as social achievement:

> Once this category is attached to a child, those around him or her 'view the child's behaviour as symptoms rather than as expressions

of his or her unique personality'. (McLaughlin, 2005: 286, quoting Malloy et al 2002)

Objectivist inquiry had produced standardised cultural accounts which tended to subsume the divergent and paradoxical aspects of social living into categories of normalized order. (Danforth, 1995: 137)

In freezing the image, observational data – already multiply transformed – are set down and become part of the child's history and record. These then become the currency of interchange between professionals ... little tradition of professionals' challenging one another's judgement. (Partlett, 1991: 229)

It is clear from these quotes that practice is constructive of identities – of children and young people, but also of the parents and even, less obviously, of professionals. The professional role has been one of ownership, placed to define identities of special need, problem or difficulty and even of skill or resource. What is implicit is a kind of fixing of the identity claims made by professionals, such that once achieved they are difficult to change.

While the professional role has been one of ownership, active in making identity claims on behalf of children, those same children and their parents have been positioned as passive recipients. This assumed passivity has been the headline story of their role vis-à-vis professionals, alongside other different and contradictory roles and evidence of active engagement in their own lives. There is a tension, then, between how families are positioned as consumers of services in the SEN Code of Practice (DfE, 2015) but, on the other hand, positioned by professionals as passive and non-expert.

The child has been generally positioned as the 'absent special guest' (Todd, 2007) in all multi-agency decision-making about children with disabilities. Professional intentions in this area have changed over the last 30 years to bring the child more to the fore. As a result there has been an increase in consultation with children about services, and the involvement of young people in decision-making about their own educational provision (Hobbs et al, 2000) to the extent that this has now been incorporated into the current SEND Code of Practice (2015) and Education, Health and Care Plan process. However, much of this activity has been described as tokenistic and naively executed (Arnot and Reay, 2007; Whitty and Wisby, 2008; Sales and Vincent, 2018), and dependent on the beliefs, skills and context of the professionals involved (Sales and Vincent, 2018; Sharma, 2021). Professional agendas have continued by and large to drive the questions asked of children in the task of obtaining children's views (Todd, 2007), failing therefore to engage the agency of children. Assumed passivity is challenged by observation of children, showing them to be active in the construction of their own identities (White, 2007). Allen demonstrated the ways that children choose to step both inside and out with respect to their disabled identities as they make sense of the lives they actively engage within: 'One of them got a punishment and Laura didn't, because she's visually impaired. So Laura spoke up and said, "I'd like one too – there's no point in treating me differently because I don't like that"' (Allen, 1999: 63).

Parents occupy simultaneously a number of roles and positions in relation to professionals, alongside an assumed homogeneity. Such positioning is subject to complex trends and discourse, including those from, for example, educational policy, our understandings of disability, childhood, the family, and ideas about professional role. Parents are positioned as passive helper to the professional, but also as partner, information receiver, consumer and advocate. These exist concurrently and in ways that do not always produce intended and helpful outcomes. 'Passive helper' was dominant in the 1980s (Barton and Moody, 1981; Mittler and McConachie, 1983; Topping, 1986), but seems fully in evidence even in today's integrated services (Townsley et al, 2004; Hodge and Runswick-Cole, 2009), despite the rhetoric (since Warnock) of partnership that has been vocally claimed for the relationship between parents and professionals. This is reflective of the way parent partnership more generally is positioned by schools: parents are often seen as working in service of the school's agenda, rather than bringing their own interests and expertise – they are expected to fit in with and support what professionals determine is the most appropriate provision (Jay and Rose, 2023). Partnership is conditional and not accessible equally to all (Reay, 2004). It is not to be had for those required to supply their child to professionals or those who are 'sent for and told' Tomlinson (1981). Even in special schools, parents said, 'their children were not wanted because they didn't have the right sort of special need' (Duncan, 2003: 346). Partnership has had unintended outcomes in the past, disempowering by co-opting parents into the professional viewpoint (Galloway et al, 1994; Armstrong, 1995). The financial challenges for local authorities that have led to delays in education, health care assessments and insufficient funds to make necessary educational provisions have further compromised notions of partnership. Instead, parents are obliged to take a more adversarial role by using the tribunal to seek educational support and provision that their child needs.

The growing neo-liberalism of the 1980s has had client and patient now renamed consumer. Societal strikes on the professional role (that is, increasing accountability) has brought the advocate model, with expectations that parents will be asked their views and make demands about service quality (Bastiani, 1987; Sandow et al, 1987; McCarthy, 1991; Armstrong, 1995). In such a context, the existence of powerful pressure groups behind certain types of special educational need has led to advantages for some parents (not all) in terms of securing scarce educational resources (Riddell et al, 1994: 342). And this trend continues long post millennium.

The notion of parents as passive recipients of services has been challenged by evidence that they are active in response to disability, 'actively involved in conceptualizing and enacting care with their (disabled) babies' (Goodley and Tregaskis, 2006: 643). As with children, there is evidence that parents seek both to step into a narrative of disability for their child, but also at other times outside this narrative:

> Every second of his day, I was trying to teach him something. Everything had got a target about it. ... but, recently I've thought 'just love him'. I can't keep chasing that normal, normal. I feel I've done so much to try and make him normal. I just can't keep that up. I need to accept him as he is and enjoy him as he is. (Fisher and Goodley, 2007: 76)

> They seek to ensure that their child does not become contained, categorized, subjectified within a diagnosis; a false home disallowing other possibilities for the child's progress. (McLaughlin and Goodley, 2008: 327)

The complex politics by which children and parents are often silenced, is also reductionist about professional role. For example, the educational psychologist variously sees themselves as partner, advocate, informed facilitator, researcher, theorist, problem solver and listener, to name a few (Sykes et al, 2008). In a critical analysis of partnership, the educational psychologist saw her role as 'bleaching the arena of blame' (Todd, 2000). We do not have space to discuss the role complexities of other professionals likely to be working with disabled children. However, such professional identities are a long way from taking the lead in constructing identities or from standing in the way of partnership. Once again, to unravel such politics is not simply about improving structures or communication between different professional groups. These roles are obscured by the normative social practices and identity achievements of, for example, assessment and intervention.

Conclusion: 'Privilege-cognisant' professional to facilitate active involvement

To avoid another 40 years in which well-meaning and hard-working professionals struggle to work effectively, and to remove the need for the great effort of parents to secure services and provision, a change of direction is needed. Professionals need to start to engage with practice as politics and as a social and identity-forming achievement. There should also be a focus on the relational between each of professionals, parents and children.

As to the exact form that such a relational focus should take, the problem for commissioners of services is that a political analysis does not seem to lead to clear definitions of 'what works' and 'best practice'. Our analysis suggests, however, certain aspects that might need to be present. An exploration with children and families together to evolve local services would be a good place to start, bearing in mind what we know, as discussed earlier in this chapter, about the political pitfalls of partnership and consultation. The first author's PPC (people practice context) model of partnership (Todd, 2007) suggests the need for a critique of practice, and an evolution in the role of the professional. Professionals should aim to be 'privilege-cognisant' (Bailey, 2008) to challenge and uncover normative practices. This means that they need to have awareness of the privilege that a professional role brings and of the impact that this sense of privilege can have on others, particularly the families they are working with. Professionals therefore need to be able to step into the expert role when required but to abandon it at other times in favour of what Fisher and Goodley (2007: 68) refer to as 'the philosophy of the present and becoming'. Similarly:

> The parent–professional relationship needs to be fluid, able to respond to changing perspectives and shifting perspectives as parents and professionals engage with new experiences and influences. Those professionals who engage with parents as guides, experts on their children who can identify the skills as well as the deficits, are trusted and well received. It is the professionals who are willing to learn about the child, rather than those who want only to know about the 'disability', who are able to work effectively as partners. (Hodge and Runswick-Cole, 2009: 654)

It is the professional responsibility to make the first move to create a space where all knowledges, those of children, parents and professionals, are not just stated but have agency. Professionals therefore need to facilitate the active involvement of children and parents. Specialised professional expertise of course plays an important and necessary role in working with children with special educational needs or a disability, but there is also a need to develop and reconceptualise professional roles to encompass relational expertise. Professionals need the ability to reflect on positionality, to view their own and others' expertise from different perspectives, and to hear, work with and integrate families' thinking into support mechanisms. But crucially, relational approaches are likely to fail given a decade of austerity and pared back services that show little sign of change. Local inclusion panels are attempting to address some of the shortcomings in the education, health care assessments and plans by more agile decisions to make short-term alternative provision for children.

References

Abbott, D., Townsley, R. and Watson, D. (2005a) 'Multi-agency working in services for disabled children: what impact does it have on professionals?', *Health and Social Care in the Community*, 13: 155–163.

Abbott, D., Watson, D. and Townsley, R. (2005b) 'The proof of the pudding: what difference does multi-agency working make to families with disabled children with complex health care needs?', *Child and Family Social Work*, 10: 229–238.

Ainscow, M. (1999) *Understanding the Development of Inclusive Schools*, London: Falmer.

Allen, J. (1999) *Actively Seeking Inclusion: Pupils with Special Needs in Mainstream Schools*, London: Falmer Press.

Anning, A., Cottrell, D.M., Frost, N., Green, J. and Robinson, M. (2006) *Developing Multiprofessional Teamwork for Integrated Children's Services*, Buckingham: Open University Press.

Armstrong, D. (1995) *Power and Partnership in Education*, London: Routledge.

Arnot, M. and Reay, D. (2007) 'A sociology of pedagogic voice: power, inequality and pupil Consultation', *Discourse: Studies in the Cultural Politics of Education*, 28: 311–325.

Atkinson, M., Wilkin, A., Stott, A. and Kinder, K. (2001) Multi-agency Working: An Audit of Activity. LGA Research Report 17, Slough: NFER.

Bailey, A. (2008) 'Locating traitorous identities: towards a privilege cognizant white character', in A. Bailey and C. Cuomo (eds) *The Feminist Philosophy Reader*, New York: McGraw-Hill.

Barnes, C. (1981) *Disabled People in Britain and Discrimination: A Case for Anti-discrimination Legislation*, London: Hurst.

Barton, L. and Moody, S. (1981) 'The value of parents to the ESN(S) school: an examination', in L. Barton, and S. Tomlinson (eds) *Special Education: Policy, Practices and Social Issues*, London: Harper and Row.

Bastiani, J. (ed) (1987) *Parents and Teachers 1: Perspectives on Home-School Relations*, Windsor: NFER-Nelson.

Blackburn, C.M., Spencer, N.J. and Read, J.M. (2010) 'Prevalence of childhood disability and the characteristics and circumstances of disabled children in the UK: secondary analysis of the Family Resources Survey', *BioMedCentral Pediatrics*, 10: 1–12.

Brown, K. and White, K. (2006) Exploring the Evidence Base for Integrated Children's Services. Edinburgh: Scottish Executive Education Department.

Capper, C., Hanson, S. and Huilman, R.R. (1993) 'Community-based interagency collaboration: a poststructural interpretation of critical practices', *Journal of Educational Policy*, 9: 335–351.

Corbett, J. (1993) 'Postmodernism and the "special needs" metaphors', *Oxford Review of Education*, 19: 547–554.

Council for Disabled Children (2009) *Every Disabled Child Matters. Disabled Children and Health Reform*, June 2009, London: National Children's Bureau.

Cummings, C., Dyson, A., Papps, I., Pearson, D., Raffo, C. and Todd, L. (2005) *Evaluation of the Full Service Extended Schools Project: End of First Year Report*, London: DfES.

Cummings, C., Dyson, A., Muijs, D., Papps, I., Pearson, P., Raffo, C. et al (2007) *Evaluation of the Full Service Extended Schools Initiative: Final Report. Research Report 852*, London: DfES.

Cummings, C., Dyson, A., Jones, L., Laing, K. and Todd, L. (2010) *Extended Services Evaluation: Reaching Disadvantaged Groups and Individuals. Thematic Review*, London: Department for Children, Schools and Families.

Danforth, S. (1995) 'Towards a critical theory approach to lives considered emotionally disturbed', *Behavioural Disorders*, 20: 136–143.

Department of Health (2010) *Person Centred Planning*, March 2010, London: Department of Health.

DES (1968) *Psychologists in Education Services. Report of a working party appointed by the Secretary of State for Education and Science: the Summerfield Report*, London: HMSO.

Dessent, T. (1996) 'Meeting special educational needs: options for partnership between health, education and social services', in Special Educational Needs Policy Options Group (ed) *Policy Options for Special Educational Needs in the 1990s, Seminar Paper 6*. Tamworth: NASEN.

DfE (2015) *Special Educational Needs and Disability Code of Practice: 0 to 25 Years*, London: DfE.

DfES (2001) *Special Educational Needs Code of Practice*, London: DFES.

DfES (2004) *Every Child Matters: Next Steps*, London: DfES.

Duncan, N. (2003) 'Awkward customers? Parents and provision for special educational needs', *Disability and Society*, 18: 341–356.

Dyson, A. (2005) 'Philosophy, politics and economics? The story of inclusive education in England', in D. Mitchell (ed) *Contextualising Inclusive Education: Evaluating Old and New International Perspectives*, London: Routledge.

Dyson, A., Lin, M. and Millward, A. (1998) *Effective Communication between Schools, LEAs and Health and Social Services in the Field of Special Educational Needs*, London: DFEE.

Easen, P., Atkins, M. and Dyson, A. (2000) 'Inter-professional collaboration and conceptualisations of practice', *Children and Society*, 14: 355–367.

Edwards, J. (1978) 'Comment on Warnock. 1. Is the concept of "need" justified?', *Association of Educational Psychologists Journal*, 4: 44–45.

Engestrom, Y. (2008) The Future of Activity Theory: A Rough Draft, ISCAR 2008 – Ecologies of Diversities: The developmental and historical interarticulation of human mediational forms. ISCAR 2008 conference, San Diego, California, USA.

Fisher, P. and Goodley, D. (2007) 'The linear medical model of disability: mothers of disabled babies resist with counter-narratives', *Sociology of Health and Illness*, 29: 66–81.

Frederickson, N., Dunsmuir, S., Lang, J. and Monsen, J. (2004) 'Mainstream-special school inclusion partnerships: pupil, parent and teacher perspectives', *International Journal of Inclusive Education*, 8: 37–57.

Fulcher, G. (1989) *Disabling Policies? A Comparative Approach to Educational Policy and Disability*, London: Routledge.

Galloway, D. (1994) 'The role of consultants in reviewing provision for special educational needs: cautionary tales', *Evaluation and Research in Education*, 8: 97–107.

Galloway, D., Armstrong, D. and Tomlinson, S. (1994) *The Assessment of Special Educational Needs: Whose Problem?*, Harlow: Longman.

Gascoigne, E. and Wolfendale, S. (1995) *Working with Parents as Partners in SEN*, London: David Fulton.

Goodley, D. (2007) Parents, Professionals and Disabled Babies: Identifying Enabling Care: Non-Technical Summary (Research Summary). ESRC End of Award Report, RES-000-23-0129, Swindon: ESRC.

Goodley, D. and Tregaskis, C. (2006) 'Storying disability and impairment: retrospective accounts of disabled family life', *Qualitative Health Research*, 16: 630–646.

Greco, V. and Sloper, P. (2004) 'Care co-ordination and key worker schemes for disabled children: results of a UK-wide survey', *Child: Care, Health and Development*, 30: 13–20.

HMSO (1967) The Plowden Report Children and their Primary Schools. A Report of the Central Advisory Council for Education (England). London: HMSO.

HMSO (1976) Fit for the Future. Report of the Committee on Child Health Services, London: HMSO.

HMSO (2003) *Every Child Matters*, London: HMSO.

HM Treasury (2007) Aiming High for Disabled Children: Better Support for Families, May 2007, London: HM Treasury and DfES.

Hobbs, C., Taylor, J. and Todd, L. (2000) 'Consulting with children and young people: enabling educational psychologists to work collaboratively with children and young people', *Educational and Child Psychology*, 17: 107–115.

Hodge, N. and Runswick-Cole, K. (2009) 'Problematising parent-professional partnerships in education', *Disability and Society*, 23: 637–647.

Jay, T. and Rose, J. (2023) *Parental Engagement and Out-of-School Mathematics Learning: Breaking Out of the Boundaries*, Bingley, UK: Emerald Publishers.

Kendrick, A. (1995) 'Supporting families through inter-agency work: youth strategies in Scotland', in M. Mill, R.K. Hawthorne and D. Part (eds) *Supporting Families*, Edinburgh: HMSO.

Lloyd, G., Stead, J. and Kendrick, A. (2001) Hanging On in There: A Study of Inter-agency Work to Prevent School Exclusion in Three Local Authorities, London: National Children's Bureau.

McCarthy, T. (1991) 'Children with special educational needs: parents' knowledge of procedures and provisions', *British Journal of Special Education*, 18: 17–19.

McDermott, R.P. (1996) 'The acquisition of a child by a learning disability', in S. Chaiklin and J. Lave (eds) *Understanding Practice: Perspectives on Activity and Context*, Cambridge: Cambridge University Press.

McLaughlin, J. (2005) 'Exploring diagnostic processes: social science perspectives', *Archives of Disease in Childhood*, 90: 284–287.

McLaughlin, J. and Goodley, D. (2008) 'Seeking and rejecting certainty: exposing the sophisticated lifeworlds of parents of disabled babies', *Sociology*, 42: 317–335.

Mittler, P. and McConachie, H. (1983) *Parents, Professionals and Mentally Handicapped People: Approaches to Partnership*, London: Croom Helm.

Norwich, B. (1993) 'Idelogical dilemmas in special needs education: practitioners' views', *Oxford Review of Education*, 19: 527–546.

Norwich, B. (1995) 'Statutory assessment and statementing: some challenges and implications for educational psychologists', *Educational Psychology in Practice*, 11: 29–35.

Oliver, M. (1996) *Understanding Disability: From Theory to Practice*, Basingstoke: Macmillan.

Palikara, O., Castro, S., Gaona, C. and Eirinaki, V. (2018) 'Capturing the voices of children in the education health and care plans: are we there yet?' *Frontiers in Education*, 3. doi: 10.3389/feduc.2018.00024

Parsons, S., Ivil, K., Kovshoff, H. and Karakosta, E. (2021) '"Seeing is believing": exploring the perspectives of young autistic children through digital stories', *Journal of Early Childhood Research*, 19: 161–178.

Partlett, M. (1991) 'The assessment of hearing-impaired children', in D. Schon (ed) *The Reflective Turn: Case Studies In and On Educational Practice*, New York: Teachers College Press, pp 213–232.

Piper, E. and Howlin, P. (1992) 'Assessing and diagnosing developmental disorders that are not evident at birth: parental evaluations of intake procedures', *Child: Care, Health and Development*, 18: 35–55.

Reay, D. (2004) 'Educational and cultural capital: the implications of changing trends in education policies', *Cultural Trends*, 13: 73–86.

Riddell, S. (2009) 'Social justice, equality and inclusion in Scottish education', *Discourse: Studies in the Cultural Politics of Education*, 30: 283–296.

Riddell, S., Brown, S. and Duffield, J. (1994) 'Parental power and special educational needs: the case of specific learning difficulties', *British Educational Research Journal*, 20: 327–344.

Roaf, C. (2002) *Co-ordinating Services for Included Children: Joined Up Action*, Buckingham: Open University Press.

Roaf, C. and Lloyd, C. (1995) *Multi-agency Work with Young People in Difficulty*, York: Joseph Rowntree Foundation.

Russell, P. (1992) 'Boundary issues: multidisciplinary working in new contexts – implications for educational psychology practice', in S. Wolfendale (ed) *The Profession and Practice of Educational Psychology*, London: Cassell.

Sales, N. and Vincent, K. (2018) 'Strengths and limitations of the Education, Health and Care Plan process from a range of professional and family perspectives', *British Journal of Special Education*, 45(1): 61–80.

Sandow, S. (1994a) 'They told me he would be a vegetable: parent's views', in S. Sandow (ed) *Whose Special Need? Some Perceptions of Special Educational Needs*, London: Paul Chapman.

Sandow, S. (ed) (1994b) *Whose Special Need? Some Perceptions of Special Educational Needs*, London: Paul Chapman.

Sandow, S., Stafford, D. and Stafford, P. (1987) *An Agreed Understanding? Parent-Professional Communication and the 1981 Education Act*, Windsor: NFER-Nelson.

Shakespeare, T. (2006) *Disability Rights and Wrongs*, London: Routledge.

Sharma, P. (2021) 'Barriers faced when eliciting the voice of children and young people with special educational needs and disabilities for their Education, Health and Care Plans and Annual Reviews', *British Journal of Special Education*, 48(4): 455–476.

Slade, Z., Coulter, A. and Joyce, L. (2009) Parental Experience of Services for Disabled Children. DCSF-RR147August 2009, London: BMRB Qualitative.

Sloper, P. (1999) 'Models of service support for parents of disabled children. What do we know? What do we need to know?', *Child: Care, Health and Development*, 25: 85–99.

Solity, J.E. (1991) 'Special needs: a discriminatory concept?', *Educational Psychology in Practice*, 7: 12–19.

Stead, J., Lloyd, G. and Kendrick, A. (2004) 'Participation or practice innovation: tensions in inter-agency working to address disciplinary exclusion from school', *Children and Society*, 18: 42–52.

Stobbs, P. (2008) Extending Inclusion: Access for Disabled Children and Young People to Extended Schools and Children's Centres: A Development Manual, Nottingham: Council for Disabled Children.

Sykes, G., Todd, L., Carson, S., Dhir, G. and Gilbert, S. (2008) Clarifying and Developing the Role of the EP in Relation to All Aspects of Parent and Carer Partnership, Advocacy and Training. Executive Summary, DECP Parent Partnership Working Party Report, Leicester: British Psychological Society.

Thomas, D. (1978) *The Social Psychology of Childhood Disability*, London: Methuen.

Todd, E.S. (2000) The Problematic of Partnership in the Assessment of Special Educational Needs. PhD Thesis: Newcastle University.

Todd, L. (2007) *Partnerships for Inclusive Education: A Critical Approach to Collaborative Working*, London: Routledge.

Tolley, E., Girma, M., Stanton-Wharmby, A., Spate, A. and Milburn, J. (1998) *Young Opinions Great Ideas*, London: National Children's Bureau.

Tomlinson, S. (1981) *Educational Subnormality: A Study in Decision Making*, London: Routledge and Kegan Paul.

Tomlinson, S. (1982) *A Sociology of Special Education*, London: Routledge and Kegan Paul.

Topping, K. (1986) *Parents as Educators: Training Parents to Teach Their Children*, London: Croom Helm.

Townsley, R., Abbott, D. and Watson, D. (2004) *Making a Difference? Exploring the Impact of Multi-agency Working on Disabled Children with Complex Health Care Needs, Their Families and the Professionals Who Support Them*, Bristol: The Policy Press.

UNESCO (1994) The Salamanca Statement and Framework for Action on Special Needs Education, Paris: UNESCO.

Visser, J. and Stokes, S. (2003) 'Is education ready for the inclusion of pupils with emotional and behavioural difficulties: a rights perspective?', *Educational Review*, 55: 65–75.

Warnock, M. (1978) Report of the Committee of Enquiry into the Education of Handicapped Children and Young People, London: HMSO.

White, M. (2007) *Maps of Narrative Practice*, London: Norton.

Whitty, G. and Wisby, E. (2008) 'Whose voice? An exploration of the current policy interest in pupil involvement in school decision-making', *International Studies in Sociology of Education*, 17: 303–319.

Wigfall, V. and Moss, P. (2001) More than the Sum of its Parts? A Study of a Multi-agency Child Care Network? London: National Children's Bureau.

Wolfendale, S. (2004) Getting the Balance Right: Towards Partnership in Assessing Children's Development and Educational Achievement, Discussion paper commissioned by DfES, London: DfES. www.teachernet.gov.uk/workingwithparents.

Wood, K. (1994) 'Towards national criteria for special educational needs: some conceptual and practical considerations for educational psychologists', *Educational Psychology in Practice*, 10: 85–92.

Woodhead, M. (1991) 'Psychology and the cultural construction of "children's needs"', in M. Woodhead, P. Light and R. Carr (eds) *Growing Up in a Changing Society*, London: Routledge, Open University.

4

Disabled students in higher education: what progress has been made over the last 30 years?

Sheila Riddell and Elisabet Weedon

Introduction

The past 30 years have seen significant progress with regard to the inclusion of disabled students in higher education. Part 4 of the Disability Discrimination Act, passed in 1995, was amended by the Special Educational Needs and Disability Act 2001, which inserted new provisions with regard to the duties of schools and other educational establishments to disabled students. The Disability Discrimination Act was subsequently incorporated into the Equality Act 2010. Since 2001, universities have been obliged to avoid discrimination against disabled students by making reasonable adjustments and avoiding less favourable treatment. From this point, disabled students had enforceable rights to reasonable levels of support, rather than being dependent on the goodwill of staff and students. As we discuss below, participation rates of disabled students in higher education have improved rapidly and this group now make up around 15 per cent of all UK higher education students, and 17.5 per cent of first year, full-time, first degree students (HESA, 2022). Nonetheless, many problems remain, including unequal rates of participation by students with different types of impairment; higher drop-out rates and poorer degree outcomes for some groups; difficulties in accessing support; and challenges relating to social and academic inclusion. As reported in earlier research (Riddell et al, 2005a; Fuller et al, 2009; Hector, 2020), once admitted to a particular course at college or university, disabled students still have to engage in a daily struggle to access buildings, course materials and examinations. Developing friendships, building wider social networks and negotiating identity may also prove hugely challenging.

While progress has been made in relation to the inclusion of disabled students in higher education, progress may have stalled or even reversed. A report funded by the Disability Commission noted:

> Some of the HEPs (higher education providers) and disability practitioners who have contributed evidence to this inquiry have

described a perception that awareness of and legislation on the rights of disabled people weakened after the Equality Act (2010) took the place of the Disability Discrimination Act (DDA). There is also a fairly widespread perception that disabled people are at the bottom of the list of equality and diversity priorities. Some stakeholders perceive this to have happened partially because of the DDA and the Disability Rights Commission being amalgamated into a larger equality legislation and organisation, removing the specific focus on the rights of disabled people. Other contributors to our evidence suggested that the Equality Act is perceived as lacking teeth or not being enforced properly when it comes to the rights of disabled students. (Hector, 2020: 10)

Addressing the under-representation of students from less advantaged backgrounds has topped the political agenda for some years (Riddell et al, 2015a, 2015b, 2018; Hunter Blackburn et al, 2016). By way of comparison, little attention has been paid to disability and its inter-connections with social deprivation, sex and ethnicity. In addition, as noted by the Disability Commission, the increase in the number of protected characteristics specified in the Equality Act may lead to different groups vying for attention and funding. Finally, the resourcing of additional provision remains complex, with support funded either through the Disabled Students Allowance or university central funds. As discussed further later, there are different views about whether the future focus should be on support for the individual student or institutional support for all.

Fair representation and public presence (Phillips, 1998) remains a key aspect of equality. We therefore begin with an overview of patterns of participation by disabled students in higher education, using survey and administrative data to explore rates of participation by disabled students over time, their social profile in terms of type of difficulty, sex and social class and employment outcomes. Finally, we outline future policy directions signalled by government and relevant agencies. In conclusion, we consider the extent to which policy for disabled students may still be regarded as a success story, and the challenges which remain.

The social profile of disabled students in higher education

Participation rates

Over recent decades, participation in higher education has increased across the UK, despite the shifting of costs from the state to individual students.[1] During this period, there has also been a steady growth in the proportion of disabled people within the wider student population. In 1994/95, disabled students made up 3.5 per cent of all undergraduates, rising to 6 per cent in 2002/

Figure 4.1: Proportion of disabled students in the UK undergraduate student population

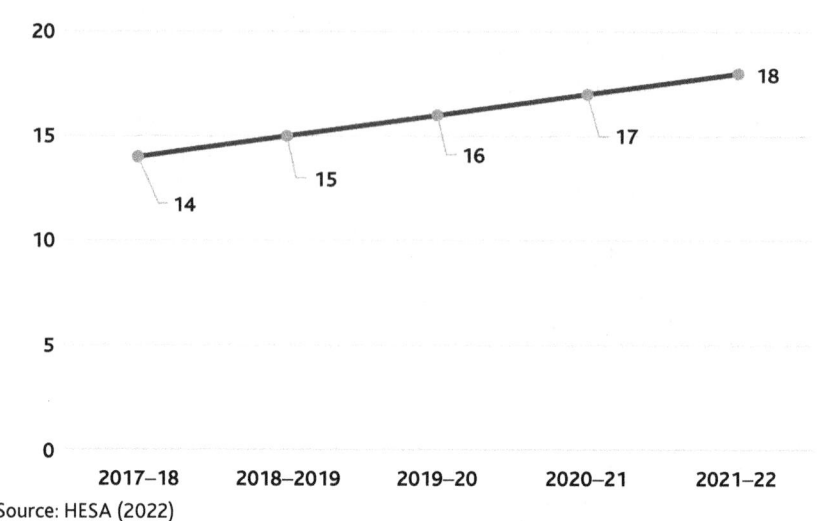

Source: HESA (2022)

03. By 2014/15, the proportion of disabled students had doubled, reaching 6 per cent of the total, and by 2021/22, 18 per cent of all undergraduate students disclosed a disability (see Figure 4.1). This accounts for more than a five-fold increase over a 30-year period, and is likely to reflect both a material growth in higher education participation by disabled people, but also a greater willingness of students to disclose disabilities while at university.

This rapid growth inevitably raises questions about what would count as fair representation, although it is clear that administrative and survey data provide very different estimates of the rate of disability in the wider population. According to the Family Resource Survey, 8 per cent of children in the general population and 19 per cent of working-age adults reported a disability in 2019/20. Scottish Government statistics show that disabled children make up around 4 per cent of the school population, although a much higher proportion, about a third of all children, are considered to have additional support needs. The Department for Education reckons that about 15 per cent of children in England have special educational needs. Clearly, measuring disability in any population is far from straightforward, since the criteria used vary and identification is based on both self-report and normative judgements.

Disabled Students Allowance (DSA) claimants

Although the proportion of students who self-declare as disabled has increased, the proportion who receive the DSA is much lower and has remained relatively stable over time (see Figure 4.2). Differences between

Figure 4.2: Proportion of disabled students in receipt of DSA by jurisdiction, 2015–21

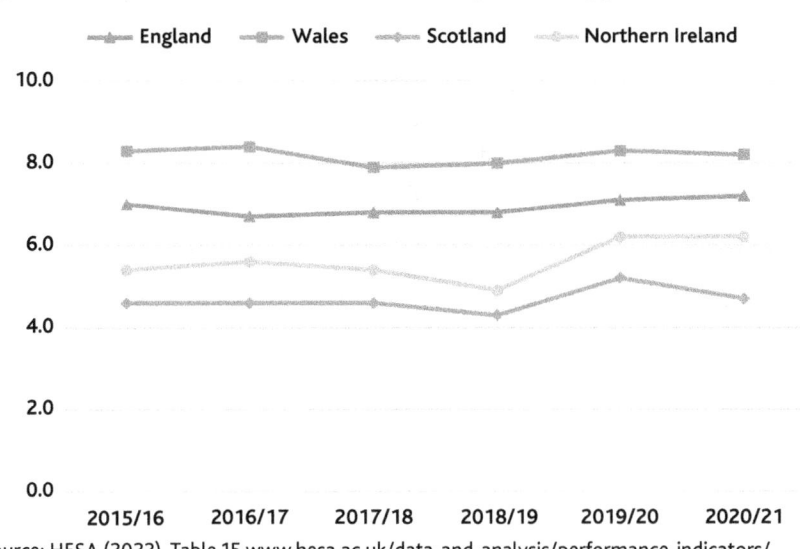

Source: HESA (2022), Table 15 www.hesa.ac.uk/data-and-analysis/performance-indicators/widening-participation/table-c

the four UK jurisdictions have remained similar. The lower and declining uptake of the DSA in Scotland may be due to a number of factors, such as lack of awareness of the benefit or stricter application of qualification criteria.

Figure 4.3 shows type of impairment as a proportion of all impairments reported by disabled students between 2016/17 and 2020/21. These data are drawn from University Central Admissions Service (UCAS) forms which are completed by applicants at the start of the admissions process. Prospective students are requested to indicate whether they consider themselves to be disabled, and if so, which category or categories most accurately reflects their difficulties. The categories are couched in language which might be seen as consistent with the medical model of disability, focusing on the nature of the person's impairment. More traditional terms, such as autistic spectrum disorder, are used in place of newer terminology such as neural diversity, which might be preferred by some students. The purpose of the data is to provide universities and external agencies with information about patterns of participation and the nature of institutional support required which may change over time. Individual students are not asked to show any medical or psychological evidence at this point, although this is required when a student applies for the DSA.

Type of impairment

Over the last five-year period, there has been a substantial change in the type of impairment disclosed by students, with some categories growing

Figure 4.3: UK domiciled undergraduate enrolments by type of impairment 2016–17 and 2021–22

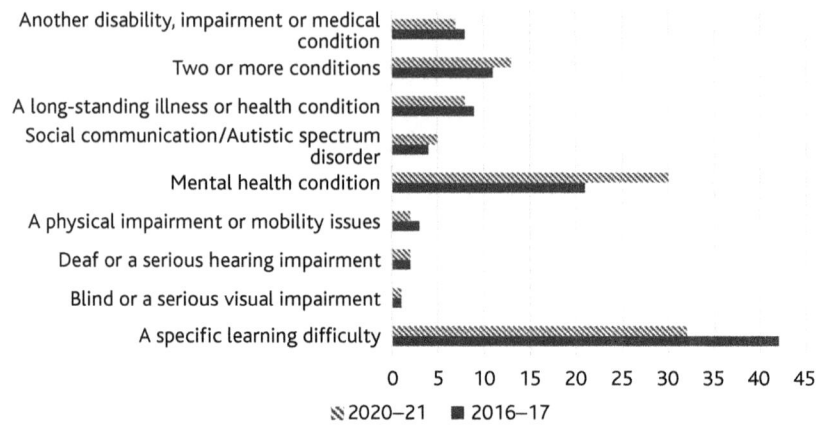

Source: HESA (2016-17, 2020-21, 2021-22), DT051, Table 15, www.hesa.ac.uk/data-and-analysis/students/table/15

and others declining. Overall, normative difficulties, such as visual and hearing impairments, as well as physical impairments and mobility issues, continue to be low incidence, and there appears to be a slight relative decrease in these categories as a proportion of the total. Specific learning difficulties continues to be the most frequently reported disability, although the overall proportion of students in this group has declined. By way of contrast, the proportion of students with mental health problems has increased.

Sex

Figure 4.4 shows the proportion of male and female students within each category. Overall, women make up 56 per cent of the non-disabled student population, but a much higher proportion of all disability categories apart from autistic spectrum disorder. There is an equal proportion of men and women among those who are blind or who have a serious visual impairment. The difference between women and men is greatest in the mental health difficulties category, where three quarters of all individuals reporting this disability are women.

It is evident that the sex ratio of university students is markedly different from that of the school population, where two thirds of those identified with SEN in England or ASN (additional support needs) in Scotland are boys (Riddell, 2020). Disparities in sex ratios may reflect material difference in the occurrence of particular conditions, but also the willingness of male and female applicants to disclose an impairment, which varies over time

Figure 4.4: UK domiciled undergraduate enrolments by type of impairment, no disability and sex, 2021–22

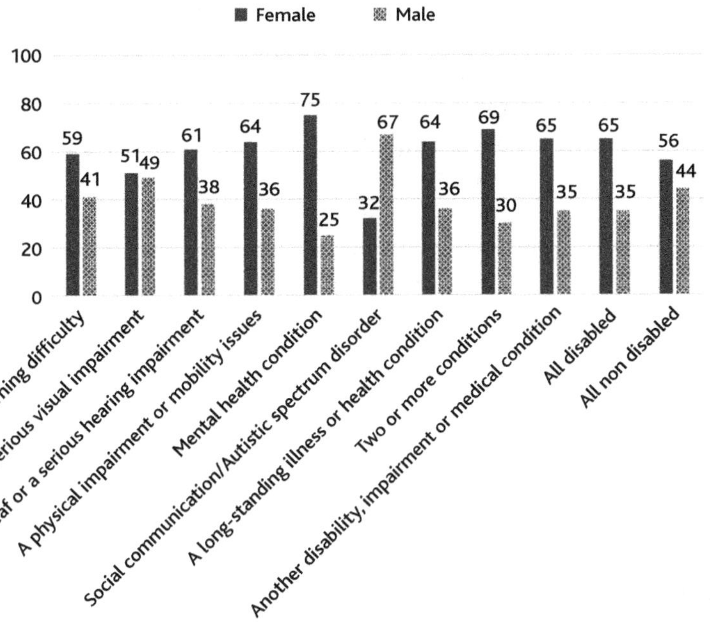

Category	Female	Male
A specific learning difficulty	59	41
Blind or a serious visual impairment	51	49
Deaf or a serious hearing impairment	61	38
A physical impairment or mobility issues	64	36
Mental health condition	75	25
Social communication/Autistic spectrum disorder	32	67
A long-standing illness or health condition	64	36
Two or more conditions	69	30
Another disability, impairment or medical condition	65	35
All disabled	65	35
All non disabled	56	44

Source: HESA (2021–22), DT051, Table 15, (note students identifying as other have been omitted as the overall proportions are less than 1 per cent), www.hesa.ac.uk/data-and-analysis/students/table-15

and place. For example, earlier research showed that boys were more likely to be diagnosed with specific learning difficulties/dyslexia in both school (Riddell, 2020) and in university (Riddell et al, 2005a). While boys continue to dominate the dyslexia category in schools, the reverse is true at university level. Our research showed that, in 2005, most disabled students were male on account of the predominance of men in the largest category, specific learning difficulties/dyslexia (Riddell et al, 2005a). By way of contrast, most disabled students are now female because of the greater willingness of women to disclose a disability in general, and mental health difficulties in particular. This disproportionality has been little researched, although it is clearly important to understand the underlying economic, social and cultural factors.

Social class

The social class profile of disabled students is also of interest. Riddell et al (2005a) commented that, based on analysis of HESA data, in post-92 institutions there were no marked differences in participation by students from different social class backgrounds as measured by parental occupation,[2] but those in pre-92 institutions were more likely to come from higher social class backgrounds. Weedon (2019) analysed the social class background of disabled and non-disabled students by parental occupation (see Figure 4.5). The data show that across the piece, university students are more likely to come from relatively advantaged backgrounds, but 53 per cent of disabled students come from managerial/professional backgrounds compared with 50 per cent of non-disabled students. Of students with mental health problems, 55.7 per cent come from professional/managerial backgrounds, suggesting that in socio-economic terms they are a more advantaged group than the wider university population. Again, there is a marked contrast with the school population, where the majority of children identified as having SEN/ASN come from less socially advantaged backgrounds (Riddell, 2020). As is the case in relation to disproportionalities relating to sex, there has been little research exploring social class disproportionalities among the disabled student population.

Transition from higher education to the labour market

Across the population, employment rates for all higher education graduates are much higher than those who lack higher level qualifications (see Figure 4.6, drawn from a House of Commons Research Service report authored by Powell, 2021). In March 2019, 89 per cent of non-disabled graduates were in employment, compared with 63 per cent of people with no qualifications, an employment gap of 26 per cent. By way of comparison, across all qualification levels the employment rate of disabled people is lower, but is even more strongly associated with level of qualification. Three quarters of disabled people with a degree are in employment, compared with only a fifth of those with no qualifications, an employment gap of 55 per cent. For a small number of disabled people, for example, those with very complex physical and learning difficulties, employment in the open labour market may not be possible, although supported employment is an option for virtually everybody (Riddell et al, 2001). However, the benefits of degree-level qualifications for disabled people are evident, suggesting that further expansion of higher education is probably desirable for the entire population, but for disabled people in particular. At the same time, there is clearly a need to investigate and address the lower employment rates of disabled graduates compared with non-disabled graduates. In addition, the low employment rates of people without qualifications needs to be addressed as a matter of social justice, with particular attention paid to the exclusion from employment of disabled people with no qualifications. Although equality legislation has attempted to prohibit discrimination in all areas of life, much greater efforts are needed to achieve an inclusive labour market.

Disabled students in higher education

Figure 4.5: Disabled students by type of impairment and socio-economic background compared to non-disabled students, percentages

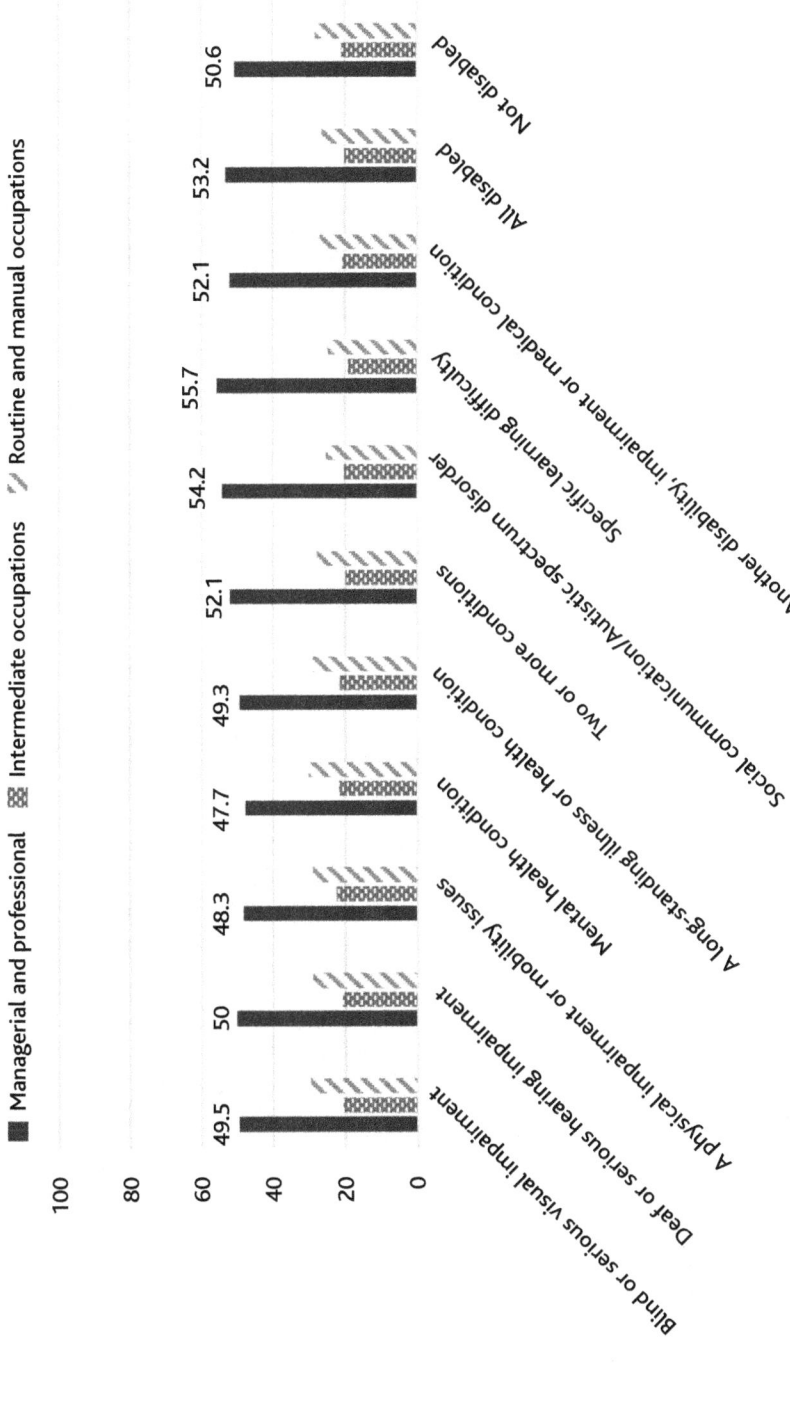

Source: HESA Student Record 2011/12 to 2014/15. Copyright Higher Education Statistics Agency Limited 2016

Figure 4.6: Employment rates of disabled and non-disabled people and gaps by highest qualification level, 2019

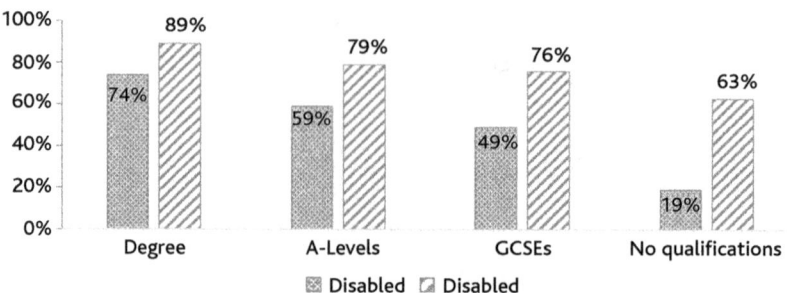

Source: House of Commons Library Briefing Paper Number 7540, 24 May 2021

Using data from the HESA Graduate Outcomes Survey conducted in 2021, Allen and Coney (2022) analysed the employment status of disabled and non-disabled graduates. All UK graduates were requested to complete the survey 15 months after graduation, and the report compares the outcomes of the disabled and non-disabled graduate population. The relationship between employment status and different graduate level qualifications (first degree, postgraduate (taught), postgraduate (research)) was explored. Across the three levels of graduate qualification, non-disabled graduates were more likely to be in employment than disabled graduates. For all graduates, there was an employment advantage in having postgraduate qualifications, but again the benefit was slightly less for disabled compared with non-disabled graduates (see Table 4.1).

The survey also investigated the employment outcomes for graduates with different types of difficulty. As shown in Table 4.2, people with autistic spectrum disorder have much worse employment outcomes than other disabled graduates, with only 36.4 per cent in employment, whereas those with specific learning difficulties have the best outcomes in terms of labour market participation.

Drawing together the findings from the analysis of administrative and survey data, it is evident that a growing proportion of students are disclosing a disability when they apply to university, but a much smaller proportion claim the DSA which is intended to offset some of the additional costs incurred by disabled students. There has been a major increase in the proportion of students disclosing a mental health difficulty, but the proportion of those with visual and hearing impairments and physical difficulties has remained fairly constant, while the inclusion of those with significant learning difficulties is still at an experimental stage. Marked disproportionalities exist in relation to gender and social class. Despite rising rates of participation, disabled students have worse labour market outcomes than non-disabled students. Nonetheless, particularly

Table 4.1: Outcomes of disabled and non-disabled graduates (by qualification level), percentages

	First degree: no known disability	First degree: disabled	Postgraduate taught: no known disability	Postgraduate taught: disabled	Postgraduate research: no known disability	Postgraduate research: disabled
Full-time employed	60.4	53.2	66.9	56.4	66.4	60.6
Part-time employed	9.5	12.0	9.6	12.7	9.0	11.4
Further study*	18.2	19.0	14.8	17.4	15.9	16.2
Other**	5.1	6.4	3.8	5.8	5.1	6.5
Unemployed	5.1	6.4	3.2	4.7	2.3	4.2

Notes: * Further study includes full-time, part-time or employment + further study. ** Other includes voluntary or unpaid work, travel, caring for someone or retired.
Source: Allen and Coney (2022)

for disabled graduates, the benefits of degree-level education are clear, since only 13 per cent of disabled people with no qualifications are in employment.

In the following sections, we consider some dilemmas in the identification and categorisation of disabled students and related issues concerning funding models.

Conceptual issues and dilemmas

The assessment of disability

Central to the thinking of the disability movement in the UK is the social model, which draws a key distinction between impairment and disability. Whereas the medical model emphasises individual deficits, the social model is based on the assumption that the economic, social and political environment in which people live their lives plays a critical part in determining their degree of social inclusion or exclusion. Inclusive environments based on universal design principles are able to mitigate or eradicate the effects of impairment. The social model has been much discussed, with some feminist critics suggesting that there may be dangers in ignoring or minimising the impact of mental or physical pain in people's lives (Crow, 1996; Meekosha, 1998). In addition, Thomas and Corker (2002) argued that disability should not be seen as the sole defining element in an individual's identity, but should be recognised as one of a number of strands of identity including gender, race, sexual orientation and age. These do not exist in separate compartments and therefore cannot be seen in isolation from disability politics. Papers in the collections by Riddell and Weedon (2006) emphasised the social relativism

Table 4.2: Graduate outcomes by disability type for first degree graduates

	Full-time employed	Part-time employed	Further study*	Other**	Unemployed
Blind/visually impaired	47.5%	13.9%	20.5%	9.2%	7.6%
Deaf/hearing loss	55.2%	11.5%	18.0%	8.3%	5.0%
Physical/mobility issues	46.8%	9.8%	22.3%	11.2%	8.8%
Mental health conditions	49.6%	13.0%	19.7%	9.1%	7.6%
Long-standing condition	55.3%	11.1%	19.7%	7.6%	5.9%
Two or more disabilities	42.4%	12.4%	21.9%	13.7%	7.5%
Autism	36.4%	17.2%	21.1%	11.8%	12.2%
Specific learning difficulties	58.6%	11.3%	17.4%	7.3%	5.1%
Other disability/condition	52.6%	12.3%	19.5%	8.6%	6.3%
No known disability	60.4%	9.5%	18.2%	6.0%	5.1%
1st degree disabled	53.2%	12.0%	19.0%	8.6%	6.4%

Notes: * Further study includes full-time, part-time or employment+ further study. ** Other includes voluntary or unpaid work, travel, caring for someone or retired.
Source: Allen and Coney (2022)

of disability. Disability is not a fixed condition, but is always constructed and experienced within a given social context and changes over the life course. The mutability of disability as a construct is evident, for example, in the fluctuating conditions which are reported by students. Over recent years, there may have been an increase in young people's psychological distress due to a number of factors including the COVID-19 pandemic, the negative effects of social media, the anomic nature of higher education and competitive economic pressures. At the same time, there may be a greater willingness across society to recognise and disclose mental health difficulties, possibly as a result of high-profile individuals acknowledging their own mental health struggles.

Tensions between medical and social models of disability are not simply academic talking points, but have a bearing on the way in which disability policy is constructed across many areas, including higher education. Although the social model is strongly advocated, the way in which disability is assessed is still based to a large extent on medical model thinking, with categories linked to individual deficits. It has been argued that current support systems do not sufficiently embody the principles of the social model of disability and universal design (Hector, 2020; Quinn, 2021; The Holmes Report, 2022). Quinn (2021), in a review of Edinburgh University's Student Disability Service, argues that students should be encouraged to self-identify as disabled and use any label which they think reflects the nature of their difficulties. Rather than wasting time on assessments which place the onus on the student to prove their disability, the university should listen to the student's own account of their learning needs and have support systems in place reflecting the principles of inclusive curricula. Simple measures should be implemented routinely, such as providing reading lists in advance; ensuring that all information is accessible on screen readers; using microphones in classes routinely; and ensuring that pre-recorded lectures are clearly captioned and available to students in a timely manner. Quinn's report also suggests that the Student Disability Service should be refocused to meet the needs of all students who have difficulty in learning for whatever reason (for example, care leavers), focusing more on a social model which empowers students and staff through inclusive practices.

As indicated in the reports referred to in the previous paragraph, the idea of universal design is widely accepted in the university sector, if not consistently practised. Although there would undoubtedly be advantages in moving away from bureaucratic assessment processes, there are also pitfalls related to the year on year increase in the number of students disclosing a disability. The problems associated with an ever-expanding population of disabled students, described by the sociologist Sally Tomlinson (2017) as the manufacture of inability, is illustrated in the Scottish school system. The proportion of the school population identified as having ASN has increased from 4 per cent in 2005 to more than 30 per cent in 2021. At the same time, the proportion of children with a statutory support plan[3] has decreased from 3 per cent of the school population in 2005 to 0.1 per cent over the same period. In addition, resources for ASN have failed to keep pace with the expanding population. Consequently, while children from poorer backgrounds are much more likely to be identified as having ASN compared with children from more advantaged backgrounds, the opposite pattern pertains in relation to the allocation of statutory support plans to children identified as having ASN (Riddell, 2020).[4] Boys from socially disadvantaged backgrounds are particularly over-represented in the stigmatised category of social emotional and behavioural difficulties, and are least likely to receive a formal support plan. The problem of expanding student numbers without a commensurate expansion of resources is likely to be a problem for universities as well as schools.

Funding models and their implications

There are ongoing discussions concerning the merits of individual versus institutional funding models which are linked to debates around formal assessment versus self-identification. As noted earlier, universities operate a dual system, with some funds channelled to the individual student via the DSA, while other support is resourced centrally, drawing on awards by funding bodies in relation to the number of disabled students within each institution. Overseas students, whose numbers have increased over recent years, particularly in the pre-92 sector, are not entitled to apply for the DSA, and many home students disclose a disability but either do not apply for the DSA or are not deemed eligible. Under the Equality Act, universities have a legal duty to make reasonable adjustments for all students, irrespective of whether they are domiciled in the UK or overseas.

Criticisms of the DSA include the fact that assessments may be lengthy and intimidating, giving students the impression that they have to 'beat the system' (Quinn, 2021). In addition, DSA assessments use formal medical and psychological categories of impairment and are therefore seen to be informed by a medical, rather than a social, model of disability. On these grounds, Quinn's review of the University of Edinburgh's Student Disability Service suggests that there should be a disengagement from the DSA model, instead funding all students from central resources.

By way of contrast, the Report into the Disabled Students' Allowance (DSA) by Lord Holmes, published in 2022, describes it as 'a gem of a policy', which, when it works well, supports students with a disability to thrive in education. The Holmes Report acknowledges the drawbacks of the policy, including overly bureaucratic assessment processes and time lags between assessment and the arrival of promised funding packages. However, in his view the DSA should be retained and improved rather than scrapped.

Clearly, there is a need to resolve the evident tensions between individual and institutional funding models. For many years, research has pointed to the downsides of the DSA, not just in relation to assessment issues but also concerning the burden placed on a student in managing their own support, which may include hiring assistants and purchasing specialised equipment (Riddell et al, 2005a). However, there are also many upsides to the DSA, including allowing the student some degree of autonomy in organising their support package. In this way, the DSA has similar upsides and downsides to direct payments made to disabled people by local authorities. This mode of service delivery has attracted widespread approval from the disability movement on the grounds that it empowers the disabled person to purchase and control their own support package, rather than leaving these to be centrally determined in a paternalistic manner (Priestley et al, 2007; Riddell et al, 2005b). There are also problems with shifting away from the DSA towards institutional support, a model that might work reasonably well in more affluent pre-92 institutions, but might well pose a problem for less well-endowed post-92 institutions which generally have a higher proportion of students with a range of support needs. There is a danger that the level of support offered to disabled students would be increasingly determined by the wealth of the institution they attend, amplifying existing social inequalities. One of the advantages of the DSA is that awards are not influenced by the nature of the institution, but by the student's assessed need, which has an equalising effect on funding levels between pre- and post-92 institutions.

Looking to the future: managerialism and widening access

In this section, we consider the measures which are being put in place to encourage participation by disabled students in higher education, as well as improving their university experience and post-university outcomes. Across the UK, since the early 1980s, the principles of New Public Management have been applied to universities, so that institutional autonomy is tempered by the achievement of targets specified in outcome agreements approved centrally as a condition of government grant. In England, the Office for Students, founded in 2018, acts as the regulator and competition authority for the higher education sector and has responsibility for widening access. In Scotland, Wales and Northern Ireland, responsibility for widening access rests with the Funding Councils. Since 2006, universities have also been required to produce equality schemes, establishing milestones and targets to chart institutional progress towards greater equality for disabled staff and students. Managerialist methods have thus been used to provide both sticks and carrots to the promotion of equality for disabled students. In general terms, the setting of targets may have positive consequences in terms of focusing institutional attention on areas of strategic importance including widening access, but may also lead to minimal compliance, the skewing of institutional priorities and the erosion of public trust (Riddell, 2018).

In England, the Office for Students, in 2021, specified the groups which it considers to be underrepresented in higher education, including students from areas of low higher education participation, low household income or low socio-economic status; some black, Asian and minority ethnic students, mature students; disabled students; care leavers; carers; people estranged from their families; people from Gypsy, Roma and Traveller communities; refugees; children from military families. It is noted that in 2020/21, there was a difference of 1.1 percentage point between the proportion of disabled and non-disabled students getting a First or 2:1. It is noted that this gap narrowed between 2010/11 and 2020/21, and the target is to eliminate the gap entirely. This target illustrates some of the potential weaknesses of the general approach. There is no consideration of what is driving this apparent improvement in disabled students' outcomes and how it relates to the expansion of the disabled student population and the changing social characteristics of the group. A more challenging target might be to increase participation by students with more severe learning difficulties or boys from socially disadvantaged backgrounds who have been categorised as having social, emotional and mental health difficulties at school.

In Scotland, targets have been set relating to some, but not all, aspects of widening participation. In its final report titled A Blueprint for Fairness, the Commission for Widening Access recommended that by 2030, students from the 20 per cent most deprived backgrounds should represent 20 per cent of all entrants to higher education, with interim targets charting progress towards this goal. The Scottish Government accepted this recommendation, which now features prominently in all university Outcome Agreements and in Scottish Funding Council statistics (2021). No targets have been set in relation to other equality indicators, and the Commissioner for Fair Access noted the difficulties of establishing targets for fairer access by disabled students, not least because of the lack of reliable and consistent data (CoWA, 2021). He drew attention to the discrepancy in the proportion of students disclosing a disability (which has rapidly increased) compared with the proportion claiming the DSA (which has remained relatively stable before decreasing over the past five years). The Commissioner also commented on differences between institutions in claiming the DSA, varying from 17.4 per cent at the Glasgow School of Art, to 1.5 per cent at the University of the West of Scotland, an institution with a much higher proportion of students from socially disadvantaged backgrounds. These discrepancies are also evident in terms of students disclosing a disability when applying to university. For example, in 2019, 15.8 per cent of students at the University of St Andrews disclosed a disability, compared with only 6 per cent at the University of Glasgow.

To summarise, in terms of future policy developments, central government appears to be committed to a managerialist approach, expecting universities to set targets for widening access which conform with centrally identified policy priorities. However, targets tend to focus on areas which can be easily measured, and the validity of the statistics used to measure progress is often insufficiently interrogated. Targets tend to focus on social characteristics in isolation from each other, and pay little attention to intersectionality. There appears to be little awareness of the social construction of disability, and categories are reified, an approach which may well be incompatible with the social model of disability. This is not to imply that target-setting has no place in improving policy and provision, but the data and targets need to be carefully considered with an awareness of potential perverse effects in relation to the skewing of institutional priorities.

Conclusion

By way of conclusion, we briefly summarise some of the points made in earlier sections before turning to some of the perennial challenges arising in relation to the creation of an inclusive higher education system. The analysis of survey and administrative data in the first section of this chapter shows that more progress is needed to ensure that the social profile of disabled students reflects that of the wider population, a definition of fair participation that has been adopted by the European Higher Education Area (Riddell and Weedon, 2022). Compared with school pupils identified with SEN/ASN, disabled university students are more likely to be female and from socially advantaged backgrounds, and are also slightly more socially advantaged than the wider student population. The category which is expanding most rapidly (mental health difficulties) is broadly non-normative. Students with learning disabilities, a large group in school, are virtually absent from universities, although across the world experimental projects are flourishing (O'Brien et al, 2019). This points to the need for intersectional analysis, recognising the strong association between disability, social class and other social variables.

Next, we discussed some of the unresolved and inter-related conceptual issues relating to the assessment of disabled students, the categories employed and competing funding models. These debates hinge on the relationship between medical and social models, and the difficulties in reconciling understandings of disability as a socially relational phenomenon with the perceived need for measurement and categorisation to decide who qualifies for additional support and on what grounds. These are not simply abstract issues, but are closely connected with issues of fairness in the allocation of resources (Riddell and Weedon, 2006).

The final section of the chapter focused on the approaches which are currently being adopted by the UK government and the devolved nations to improve the experiences and outcomes of disabled students. Managerialist approaches based on the use of hard indicators and targets have some benefits in focusing attention on policy priorities, but can easily be used in an uncritical way and fail to address issues which cannot be easily measured.

As we highlighted in our contribution to the earlier collection of essays edited by Haines and Ruebain (2011), there is much to celebrate in relation to the growing participation of disabled students in university. While the percentage and absolute number of disabled students in university has continued to increase, anxieties remain about whether sufficient additional resources are being allocated to meet growing need. This appears to be a perennial concern. In 1999, a report by the Heads of University Counselling Services noted that the growing number of students with mental health problems required much more intensive investment in support services, and that the expansion of higher education may have created a more anomic environment affecting the mental health and wellbeing of students (and staff):

> The fact of increasing numbers of both full-time and part-time students since 1992 has created a much busier, less personal study environment which requires that students possess great degrees of mental robustness and an ability to work independently. For many students, teaching staff are distant people to whom it is hard to gain access and it is possible for students to undertake their studies with few, if any, staff members being aware of their psychological well-being. In many cases, this is because the number of students on courses is very large and the amount of time that academic staff have available to interact with individual students is relatively small. (HUCS, 1999: section 16)

The systemic stresses referred to earlier are likely to increase in the future in light of the long-term impact of the pandemic and a range of associated social and economic disruptions. A survey conducted by Advance HE on behalf of the Disabled Students Commission (Borkin, 2021) found that 80 per cent of all respondents reported that COVID-19 had a negative impact on their mental health and wellbeing. Around 80 per cent of students experienced feelings of isolation and/or loneliness, a lack of motivation and increased stress levels. Students also reported pressures associated with taking less exercise, dealing with bereavement and living in unhealthy home environments. Rather than being a short-term phenomenon, the negative impact of the pandemic is likely to be felt for many years, as young people with damaged school experiences progress into university, leading to further expansion of the number of students with mental health difficulties. Staff, too, have experienced trauma as a result of the pandemic and ongoing disputes over pay and pension issues, and are perhaps in a less robust condition to meet the needs of their students. The position of disabled students has clearly improved over recent years, but there are likely to be huge challenges ahead with no guarantees of continued momentum.

Notes

[1] Tuition fees have increased markedly in the four jurisdictions of the UK since 2010. These are largely repayable by the individual student in England, Wales and Northern Ireland, but are paid by the state in Scotland. In all four jurisdictions, most students take out maintenance loans to cover living costs (Riddell et al, 2015a, 2015b, 2018).

[2] The National Statistics classification of occupations was used by HESA until 2017 to identify the socio-economic background of young students. It was discontinued as it was considered unreliable, partly because it was based on students' assessment of the occupation of the highest earning parent/carer in their family and also because data were missing for around 25 per cent of the students. Other measures of social background are now used, including the Scottish Index of Multiple Deprivation (SIMD) in Scotland and Participation of Local Areas (POLAR) in England.

3   Co-ordinated Support Plans (CSP) replaced Records of Need in Scotland under the terms of the Additional Support for Learning Act (2004). The CSP includes a formal assessment of need and a summary of the measures proposed by the local authority. Parents, young people and children aged 12–15 who have capacity must be involved in formal assessment and review, and may challenge decisions through the ASN Tribunal.
4   Riddell (2020) uses the SIMD, the Scottish Government's preferred measure of social deprivation. As noted by Paterson et al (2019), this measure is based on neighbourhood rather than individual data. Alternative measures of social deprivation, such as free school meals entitlement, are unreliable because all children in special schools receive free school meals.

References

Allen, M. and Coney, K. (2022) *What Happens Next? A Report on the Outcomes of 2018 Disabled Graduates*, Sheffield: Association of Graduate Careers Advisory Services (AGCAS).

Borkin, H. (2021) *Exploring the Impact of Covid-19 on Disabled Students' Experiences*. Published by Advanced HE on behalf of the Disabled Students' Commission.

Commission on Widening Access (CoWA) 2022 Report into the Disabled Students Allowance (DSA), London: House of Lords.

Crow, L. (1996) 'Including All of our lives: renewing the social model of disability', in J. Morris (ed) *Encounters with Strangers: Feminism and Disability*, London: Women's Press.

Fuller, M., Georgeson, J., Healey, M., Hurst, A., Kelly, K., Riddell, S., et al (2009) *Improving Disabled Students' Learning: Experiences and Outcomes*, London: Routledge.

Haines, S. and Ruebain, D. (eds) (2011) *Education, Disability and Social Policy*, Bristol: Policy Press.

Hector, M. (2020) *Arriving at Thriving: Learning from Disabled Students to Ensure Access for All*, London: Policy Connect Higher Education Commission.

HESA (2022) *Higher Education Student Statistics: UK, 2020–21*. www.hesa.ac.uk/news/25-01-2022/sb262-higher-education-student-statistics

The Holmes Report (2022) Report into the Disabled Students' Allowance (DSA), London: House of Lords, https://lordchrisholmes.com

HUCS (Heads of University Counselling Services) (1999) *Degrees of Disturbance: The New Agenda*, Rugby: BAC.

Hunter Blackburn, L., Kadar-Satat, G., Riddell, S. and Weedon, E. (2016) *Access in Scotland*, Edinburgh: The Sutton Trust.

Institute for Employment Studies (2015) *Understanding Provision for Students with Mental Health Problems and Intensive Support Needs*, HEFCE: Bristol.

Meekosha, H. (1998) 'Body Battles: body, gender and disability', in T. Shakespeare (ed) *The Disability Reader: Social Science Perspectives*. London: Cassell.

O'Brien, P., Bonati, M.L., Gadow, F. and Slee, R. (2019) *People with Intellectual Ability Experiencing University Life: Theoretical Underpinnings, Evidence and Lived Experience*, Brill: Leiden/Boston.

Paterson, L., Hunter Blackburn, L. and Weedon, E. (2019) 'The use of the Scottish Index of Multiple Deprivation as an indicator to evaluate the impact of policy on widening access to higher education', *Scottish Affairs*, 28(4): 414–433.

Phillips, A. (1998) *The Politics of Presence*, Oxford: Oxford University Press.

Powell, A. (2021) *Disabled People in Employment*, House of Commons Library Briefing Paper Number 7540, 24 May.

Priestley, M., Jolly, D., Pearson, C., Riddell, S., Barnes, C. and Mercer, G. (2007) 'Direct payments and disabled people in the UK: supply, demand and devolution', *British Journal of Social Work*, 37(1): 189–204.

Quinn, P. (2021) *Review of Student Disability Service*, Edinburgh: University of Edinburgh.

Riddell, S. (2018) 'Can the techniques of new public management be used to promote wider access to higher education?', in S. Riddell, S. Minty, E. Weedon, and S. Whittaker (eds) *Higher Education Funding and Access in International Perspective*, Bingley: Emerald Publishing.

Riddell, S. (2020) *Autonomy, Rights and Children with Special Educational Needs: Understanding Capacity across Contexts*, Switzerland: Palgrave Macmillan.

Riddell, S. and Weedon, E. (2006) 'What counts as a reasonable adjustment? Dyslexic students and the concept of fair assessment', *International Studies in Sociology of Education*, 16(1): 57–73.

Riddell, S. and Weedon, E. (2022) 'Promoting the Inclusion of socially disadvantaged and disabled students in European higher education', in I. Kushnir and E. Eta (eds) *Towards Social Justice in the Neoliberal Bologna Process*, Bingley: Emerald Publishing, pp 41–54.

Riddell, S., Baron, S. and Wilson, A. (2001) *The Learning Society and People with Learning Difficulties*, Bristol: Policy Press.

Riddell, S., Tinklin, T. and Wilson, A. (2005a) *Disabled Students in Higher Education: Perspectives on Widening Access or Changing Policy*, London: RoutledgeFalmer.

Riddell, S., Pearson, C., Jolly, D., Barnes, C., Priestley, M. and Mercer, G. (2005b) 'The development of direct payments in the UK: implications for social justice', *Social Policy and Society*, 4(1): 75–85.

Riddell, S., Minty, S., Weedon, E. and Hunter Blackburn, L. (2015a) 'Higher education and the Referendum on Scottish Independence', *Political Quarterly*, 86(2): 240–248.

Riddell, S., Weedon, E. and Minty, S. (2015b) *Higher Education in Scotland and the UK: Diverging or Converging Systems?* Edinburgh: Edinburgh University Press.

Riddell, S., Minty, S., Weedon, E. and Whittaker, S. (eds) (2018) 'Introduction', in *Higher Education Funding and Access in International Perspective*, Bingley: Emerald Publishing.

Scottish Funding Council (2021) *Report on Widening Access 2019–20*, Edinburgh: SFC.

Thomas, C. and Corker, M. (2002) 'A journey around the social model', in M. Corker and T. Shakespeare (eds) *Disability/Postmodernity: Embodying Disability Theory*, London: Continuum.

Tomlinson, S. (2017) *A Sociology of Special and Inclusive Education: Exploring the Manufacture of Inability*, London: Routledge.

Weedon, E. (2019) *Disabled students in Higher Education in the UK: social and other characteristics by type of impairment*, unpublished Working Paper, Edinburgh: CREID, University of Edinburgh.

5

Meeting the standard but failing the test: the case of children and young people with sensory impairments and access to assessments and qualifications

Caireen Sutherland and Martin McLean

In 2008, Miller, Cobb and Simpson wrote about the issues between assessment and attainment for children and young people who are deaf, have vision impairment (VI) or multi-sensory impairment (MSI). They examined the implications of an assessment system in England which effectively pulls in two directions.

While much remains challenging in the current system of assessment and attainment for children and young people with sensory impairment (SI), in 2023, what they achieve academically, one could argue, only gives us a small insight into their experiences in education.

This update will examine previous assertions made by Miller, Cobb and Simpson, including original extracts, in relation to the current situation. Additionally, we take a broader contextual look at education policy and changes and a glimpse at the holistic education experience for children and young people with SI.

Original chapter extracts

The following extract is taken from Chapter 8 in the first edition of this book, by Olga Miller, Rory Cobb and Paul Simpson.[1]

> This chapter takes as its focus issues around the relationship between the assessment and attainment of those children and young people who have special educational needs (SEN) and/or disabilities arising from hearing, visual or multi-sensory impairments. In particular, the chapter examines some of the implications of a system of assessment in England that pulls in two opposing directions. This is exemplified in the framework of government policy put in place by the Labour administration through the Every Child

Matters agenda (ECM), which stresses entitlement for all children and young people to universal services, against the thrust of other policies that push towards a system of setting and streaming based on ability, as determined by the outcome of a series of national tests and formal examinations.

One could argue that an approach based on setting and streaming is entirely appropriate in a society built around competition and that to argue otherwise is to undermine an education system that seeks to prepare young people for the stark realities of life in the 21st century. However, what is at the heart of any society is some form of engagement and participation. At a time of growing unemployment amongst young people in general and those with disabilities in particular, there is a danger that many young people will disappear from mainstream society and become lost in a growing underclass.

A number of these young people will not have thrived at school and may well have been assessed as having some form of SEN in combination with their disability and will certainly have had more than their fair share of difficulties. It is vital that the needs of these learners are understood by government before these young people give up all hope of ever gaining access to employment and lose the skills and independence needed to be successful.

Measuring attainment

Underlying much of this debate is the fundamental question of what do we mean by educational attainment? The OECD Glossary of Statistical Terms defines it as 'the highest grade completed within the most advanced level attended in the educational system of the country where the education was received'.[2] Attainment is expressed in terms of educational qualifications, which are recognised as a key enabler for obtaining employment. The Strategy Unit's research report Improving the Life Chances of Disabled People (Cabinet Office, 2005) demonstrates that over 40% of disabled people suffer some form of labour-market disadvantage because they have no qualifications.

The national framework for assessment is set by government. Public examinations are designed by awarding bodies according to the specifications laid down by Ofqual (the regulator) and are subject to the provisions of the 1995 Disability Discrimination Act [now superseded by the Equality Act 2010].

Educational attainment is measured through an assessment system that is firmly embedded in UK culture. This system depends largely on traditional pen and paper examinations, which are increasingly out of step with the technology that is so central to much of our work and leisure. There is a continuing belief that this approach acts as a leveller, placing all learners on the same footing and allowing them to be measured fairly against assessment objectives that are in some sense pure and universal. Yet, in truth, assessment only measures what we choose to think is important. As Stobart (2008, p 1) argues: 'Assessment does not objectively measure what is already there, but rather creates and shapes what is measured – it is capable of "making up people" '.

Historically, assessment systems have been designed around the needs of the majority, with access arrangements subsequently 'bolted on' to take account of minorities, such as disabled candidates. Tensions are clearly apparent in current attempts to move from this medically based model of disability to a social model where the needs and skills of different groups are embraced from the outset through a process of universal or inclusive design.

On balance, it appears that our current understanding of attainment data for learners with SEN generates far more questions than answers. Certainly the data that is currently provided by central government is insufficient to make sense of what is going on. At one level it may seem obvious why children with SEN attain less well than those without, but what this may really be telling us is that we are measuring everyone with the same blunt instrument. This is the old formative versus summative argument, that knowing what a child has achieved is only meaningful if it helps you to understand why. In addition, the complexity of the needs of many sensory-impaired young people makes summative assessment significantly less informative than for their peers as it fails to recognise key factors influencing raw results in attainment and thus conceals their real attainment.

An example of this difficulty is the new information and communication technology (ICT) Functional Skills qualification, which forms a compulsory part of the new Diploma and Apprenticeship framework. Functional Skills are described as 'practical skills that allow individuals to work confidently, effectively and independently in life'. ICT is a central tool in the lives of many blind and partially sighted learners, allowing them to access and manage information on equal terms with sighted people. It surely goes without saying that any test of functional ICT competence should build in an equal opportunity for visually impaired students to demonstrate their ICT skills and to do so on their own terms.

This is not the case however. The standards for the new qualification include an automatic expectation that being competent in ICT means using a mouse and working with graphics, so there is every chance that a blind student will not be able to pass it. The fundamental problem here is an assumption that everybody's functional skills have to be the same. If you are blind, the things you are going to do with technology and the way you do them will not be the same as a sighted person, because they will be looking at the screen and you will not. Providing you with reasonable adjustments is not the answer if there is no recognition of the impact of your disability in the standards themselves. It is not a question of lower, but different, expectations, which give credit for the many specialist ICT skills that a blind person may possess rather than penalising them for not being able to demonstrate those for which vision is essential.

This line of thought suggests that there may be instances where the concept of fully inclusive design may need to be refined by the development of alternative pathways to the same qualification, with a choice of units available to all candidates that provide a choice of tasks and working methods. The qualifications gained by disabled candidates would, therefore, be a more accurate reflection of their actual working methods, emphasising the importance of a policy of 'different but equal'. However, there is a danger that these alternative pathways might only be taken by disabled people, in which case qualifications including these units could be seen as less worthwhile than the 'standard' version. If so, this approach could end up reinforcing the difference between disabled and non-disabled people.

Arguably, therefore, anti-discrimination legislation has placed too much emphasis on equality rather than equity, with the result that disabled learners are always expected to achieve the same outcomes as their non-disabled peers even when it would sometimes make more sense to assess their skills in relation to outcomes that reflect the particular ways in which they learn and study. Additionally, as long as attainment is seen exclusively in terms of academic achievement it will never reflect the wider curriculum experience that schools are meant to be providing for their pupils under the (Government's) ECM (Every Child Matters) agenda. We might also question how effectively the access arrangements and reasonable adjustments discussed elsewhere in this chapter achieve their aim of removing disadvantage for learners with SEN and disability.

Are we effectively trying to fit square pegs into round holes? Here we need to make the point again that assessment is not an objective activity that exists above and outside the values of the society in which it takes place. Outside public examinations, classroom practice demonstrates a wide range of assessment processes. Assessment guidance is offered by government, including, recently, the concept of Assessment for Learning.

Assessment

The Secretary of State's Report on Progress towards Disability Equality across the Children's and Education Sector (DCSF, 2008) declares that a wider range of assessment strategies should help identify and celebrate the full range of learners' achievements, and states that Assessment for Learning should be firmly embedded throughout schools.

A successful school uses 'assessment for learning – using data to track, monitor and respond to individual pupil progress, and ensuring that progress informs next steps' (DCSF, 2009a). Linked to this is Assessing Pupils' Progress (APP) – a structured approach to teacher assessment developed by the QCDA in partnership with the National Strategies, and its use is also encouraged as it 'helps teachers to fine-tune their understanding of pupils' needs and tailor their planning and teaching accordingly' (DCSF, 2009b).

The National Curriculum Inclusion Statement underlines the importance of the wider purposes of assessment and sets out the requirement for teachers to adapt the curriculum as necessary by 'setting suitable learning challenges, responding to pupils' diverse learning needs and overcoming potential barriers to learning and assessment for individuals and groups of pupils'. This approach seems incompatible with that adopted in public examinations such as SATs and GCSEs where summative assessment is the key – indeed, coursework elements in GCSEs have recently been reduced or removed in many subjects in response to public concerns. Thus, unfounded public views have a direct influence on assessment policy, which in turn has a disproportionate effect on disabled students.

It is, of course, difficult to measure other more qualitative aspects of pupils' achievement such as those highlighted through the ECM publications (DfES, 2003), and to use them to form the basis for developing competition between schools. At present, performance is represented through what are characterised as 'league tables', which are seen by the government as providing information for parents and schools about the ranking of school success rates in terms of summative assessments. Consequently, examination results are given greater emphasis.

However, the previous government was aware of the problems inherent in relying too much on raw attainment results and intended to move to the collection of a limited number of wider measures, suggesting that 'we will develop a new School Report Card (SRC) for every school, which will provide a rounded assessment of school performance and enable parents and the public to make better informed judgments about the effectiveness of each school' (DCSF, 2009a). Even here, however, examination results will still be given prominence and a single grade for the school will emerge at the end allowing crude ranking to continue.

There is continuing pressure for further release of information including that related to disabled students and those with SEN. The view of the previous government was that low expectations prevail: 'for too long we have not set high enough ambitions for children with special educational needs' (DCSF, 2009d). This was echoed by Sarah Teather MP, Children's Minister for the Conservative–Liberal Democrat Coalition government, when launching the call for views on the SEN and Disability Green Paper: 'Children with special educational needs and disabilities should have the same opportunities as other children, but the current system is so adversarial that too often this doesn't happen'.[3]

The overarching approach to assessment in which disabled students are subsumed is influenced by notions of public accountability, which have recently assumed a more prominent position in the political world than ever before and are in danger of significantly overshadowing the formative purposes. In a letter to Lord Low (29 October 2009), Baroness Morgan (then Parliamentary under-Secretary of State for Children, Young People and Families) took up the issue around public confidence and qualifications in the following response:

> Although Ofqual's objective to secure public confidence in qualifications would ultimately be trumped by duties in the Equalities Bill, Ofqual, of course have to try to secure both. They will need to ensure that the qualifications system is accessible and that confidence in the system for all learners is maintained. That will not be easy, and Ofqual will not be able to do it alone.

Baroness Morgan went on to highlight the creation of advisory groups such as the 'Access Consultation Forum' where awarding bodies and disability groups come together to discuss these issues and advise Ofqual.

Other related developments may also have potentially positive consequences. The revised Ofsted framework (Ofsted, 2009) states that the school's equality and diversity grade, which would include assessment and provision for children with SEN and disability, will be a limiting factor. Schools that achieve an 'inadequate' grade in this area will be unlikely to get more than satisfactory for their overall grade, with those achieving 'satisfactory' unlikely to achieve more than 'good'. This should herald a greater concentration in mainstream schools on the appropriate assessment of the needs of disabled students, although the Ofsted judgement will depend on the ability and understanding of the inspectors themselves.

Evidence from the USA indicates that an undue emphasis on examination results and league tables has already had a negative effect on disabled children. For example, the requirements of the Individuals with Disabilities and Education Act (IDEA) in combination with the requirements of the No Child Left Behind (NCLB) legislation requires that each state must demonstrate that it has developed and implemented a single state-wide accountability system and that the test results of schools must be published. Furthermore, for a school to prove they have made sufficient progress, each group of pupils must reach or exceed the targets set by the state as measures of progress. Of particular relevance to this chapter is the requirement that not less than 95% of each group of pupils on the school roll is required to take the assessments with appropriate accommodations or alternative assessments in line with the IDEA legislation.

There are significant penalties in place for schools whose pupils do not meet the required targets. One of these penalties is the option for pupils to be transferred to another public school. Clearly, therefore, it becomes in the best interests of a school to keep the number of pupils covered by NCLB to a minimum. Ironically, what was intended as a safeguard for disabled pupils may have proved a disincentive for schools to accept such pupils and evidence suggests that, for example, deaf children who have not done well in public schools are now being 'shifted to schools for the deaf' (Marschark, 2007).

The outcome of public examinations is growing in significance and the importance of qualifications for disabled people cannot be overestimated; especially in view of the high rates of unemployment amongst this group – far greater than the rates for non-disabled people. Qualifications are essential in ensuring progression to suitable employment and higher education, for without skills and qualifications, today's young people will struggle to find meaningful work in the future. It is thus crucial that all barriers within examinations are removed.

As a response to the requirements of the 1995 DDA following its extension to general qualifications in 2007, government departments and several agencies are seriously endeavouring to address the issues of accessibility to examinations for disabled candidates. In its Single Equality Duty, the former government agency with responsibility for qualifications, the QCA, stated:

> This approach is applied through the equality impact assessment of QCA policies at the design stage, which allows us to see the potential barriers for disabled people early enough to remove or reduce them, so that the effect of the policy is not disadvantageous.

Many agencies have come to the view that the solution lies in the initial design of the qualifications, rather than relying entirely on post hoc adjustments such as the modification of carrier language or visual material in the original paper. In response to this, Ofqual has developed inclusion sheets, which are used to try to ensure that barriers are addressed and where possible removed at the point of qualification design. Awarding bodies and regulators have set up regular meetings – the Access Consultation Forum and Access to Assessment and Qualifications Advisory Group – at which they meet with professional associations and disability groups. Many issues raised by these groups have been addressed and this process of consultation is beginning to have a real influence on policy and practice. However, the continued existence of exemptions (where a section of a qualification is removed because it is inaccessible to some disabled students) raises concerns that truly inclusive qualifications will not be developed because an exemption can always be used as a last resort.

The accessibility of qualifications raises a number of issues. Governments of any political view are likely to be concerned not to appear to be watering down qualifications, and thus undermining public confidence in their integrity, by the application of reasonable adjustments. The Equality Bill [now Equality Act 2010] is a clear example of this, implying that reasonable adjustments for students are acceptable only as long as they do not undermine public confidence. The need for public education to ensure that the issues are understood and that accessibility for disabled candidates is not equated with 'dumbing down' by the public and employers is not mentioned.

Although there has been progress in many aspects of the provision of qualifications for disabled students, this chapter suggests that there is still a long way to go. It would be tragic if the system that should be designed to reward their achievements ultimately did no more than create additional barriers to their success.

A decade further on – increased attainment of qualifications but increased equity?

Jumping ahead to 2023 the issues raised by Miller, Cobb and Simpson still feel very pertinent. Our original authors objected to the excessive focus on exam results disadvantaging students with SI. It can be argued that nowadays exams are even more of a 'high-stakes' affair than they were back in 2008. The Coalition and Conservative Governments of 2010 to 2019 implemented significant reforms to GCSEs and A-levels in England. Coursework marks now have no or little weighting on qualification grades. Modular courses have been phased out and replaced by linear structures with exams at the end of courses. New, more challenging content was introduced with greater emphasis on accurate use of spelling, punctuation and grammar for some subjects.

When these changes were announced, many professionals supporting students with SI expressed concern. Many children and young people with SI have delayed language and communication development which can impact on executive functioning, in particular, working memory, which can make answering exam questions challenging. It was feared that a move towards assessment methods that depend even more greatly on memory skills would disadvantage children and young people with SI. It can be argued that the skills being assessed were not reflective of skills needed for work. When a wealth of facts and data is only a few mouse clicks away why is it necessary to memorise and recall huge amounts of information?

The pandemic years of 2020 and 2021 challenged the student assessment system even further. For reasons of public safety, exams were scrapped and replaced by teacher assessment. It was of little surprise to the authors of this chapter to see GCSE grades increase significantly for students with SI. While grades increased across the board for non-disabled students too, critically, there was a narrowing of attainment gaps. Those results may suggest that non-examination assessment is a fairer way of assessing the abilities of young people with SI. However, we also need to be cautious of reading too much into increased grades during the pandemic. Many teacher-assessed grades were determined from mock exam results and it therefore may not have been a sea-change in how young people are assessed but rather a continued heavy focus on exam results, albeit with greater flexibility around grading.

Miller, Cobb and Simpson outlined the picture of academic attainment for students who were 16 years old and deaf or had VI in 2008. For this chapter update, we have decided to focus on 2019 results due to the cancellation of the 2020 and 2021 exam series during the pandemic which skewed attainment results for these years. We will return, however, to methods of assessment during the pandemic later on in this chapter. Table 5.1 shows the proportion of English 16-year-olds achieving five GCSE passes or equivalent qualifications in 2008 and 2019 and the attainment gap between SI students and all students. It reveals a mixed picture – with pass rates having increased across all three groups but no progress in narrowing the attainment gap for young people with VI. While pass rates increased 10 per cent for deaf students, it was not matched by a 10 per cent decrease in the attainment gap because attainment also rose for all students. Some caution is needed when analysing the figures in the table because the MSI and VI cohorts are prone to fluctuation in attainment rates from year to year.

When attainment gaps are taken into consideration, it asks the question how much has really progressed for young people with SI over the past decade? The gap can be viewed with some disappointment. There were high hopes that newborn screening of deaf babies rolled out across the UK in the early 2000s would lead to a seismic change in outcomes. Early identification would mean earlier support for families in developing their child's language and communication. Improved language outcomes in the early years would,

Table 5.1: Proportion of English 16-year-olds achieving five GCSE passes or equivalent qualifications in 2008 and 2019 and the attainment gap between SI students and all students

Category	Proportion achieving five GCSE passes* 2008	Proportion achieving five GCSE passes* 2019	Attainment gap between cohort and all students 2008	Attainment gap between cohort and all students 2019
Deaf	37%	47%	23%	17%
MSI	25%	45%	35%	19%
VI	45%	46%	15%	18%
All students	60%	64%	–	–

Note: *Or equivalent vocational/technical qualifications at Level 2.

Source: UK Government website. Available at: https://explore-education-statistics.service.gov.uk/find-statistics/level-2-and-3-attainment-by-young-people-aged-19

in turn, lead to the attainment gap between deaf and hearing students being eradicated or at least made much narrower. However, progress has been limited. We believe it reasonable to question whether progress in closing gaps may have been held back by the changes to assessment outlined earlier.

One aspect of attainment that the original authors of this chapter did not explore was that of progress between the ages of 16 and 19. Government data suggest that the gap in attainment of GCSE-level qualifications between young people with SI and all young people is significantly narrower at age 19 compared with 16. This raises the question of whether many young people with SI have sufficient time to achieve the five GCSE benchmark by the age of 16. Given many SI young people have had a delayed start in their educational development, is it fair to assess them before they are ready? It can be argued there should be a shift away from the dominant narrative of how can we make sure more young people with SI pass their GCSEs at 16, to what will young people with SI need in terms of time to be ready to achieve GCSEs?

However, it has to be taken into consideration that the narrowing of gap at GCSE-level is in part attributed to achievement of vocational qualifications rather than just GCSEs. Most vocational qualifications are not achieved through passing high-stakes, end-of-course examinations. While there are access considerations to vocational course assessment, these generate considerably less discussion within stakeholder meetings run by the qualifications regulator, Ofqual. This may suggest that the more flexible approach, in general, to assessment for vocational qualifications, is advantageous to young people with SI. On the other hand, it may just be reflective of a cultural bias towards seeing academic qualifications as more critical for measuring success.

There appears to be an understanding among key stakeholders that there may have been an overemphasis on academic attainment at the cost of wider learning. In 2019, Ofsted released a revised inspection framework, moving away from data-heavy inspections and including a judgement based on the quality of education. The rationale behind this new judgement was to move away from statistics and data-laden inspections and instead gain a more holistic view of schools. Ofsted's clearer curriculum focus begins with conversations with the Senior Leadership Team about the curriculum before the actual inspection begins.

The Curriculum Framework for Children and Young People with Vision Impairment (CFVI) was launched in 2022 following a robust national consultation with professionals, families and young people across the UK. The Delphi research method was used to reach consensus over 18 months to finalise the form and content of the framework. This is the first national framework for children with VI in the UK, and its publication brings the UK into line with global colleagues who have had similar frameworks/curriculum for much longer. At present the CFVI does not have statutory status but it is being embedded into relevant national guidance and policy documents wherever applicable. The CFVI presents a framework of outcomes within 11 teaching areas and provides a common shared language to support better communication, purpose and ultimately support to enable children and young people with VI to access an appropriate and equitable education. The 11 teaching and learning areas identified in the framework clarify and define best practice support and are considered vital for children and young people with VI. Underpinning the framework is the 'access to learning – learning to access' model which reinforces/supports/embeds the approach that specialist support for young people with VI should focus on two key outcomes. That all children and young people should have fair and optimised access to education and have the opportunity to develop their own advocacy and independence (Hewett et al, 2022).

The skill areas covered across the 11 teaching areas are essential for a child/young person with VI to access not only everyday education but also exams and tests which are a deeply embedded, recognised measure of 'success' in our education system. Looking at only the attainment results for a child with VI is only part of the picture, it does not clearly indicate and illustrate the learning that has had to take place, with support and input from specialists, in order for a child with VI to learn to access the exam/test.

Measuring the learning of these essential skills is not something that is currently nationally recognised across all three sensory impairments, but if it were, would this provide us with a fuller picture of how children with SI are working and achieving?

A curriculum framework has been developed for deaf children and young people.[4] While it is not as extensive as the CFVI, it will put a helpful focus on wider learning that enables a deaf child to gain independence over time and better prepare for adult life. Additionally, a GCSE in British Sign Language (BSL) is in development. For deaf young people who use BSL, this new GCSE could be something of an equaliser, allowing their language skills to be recognised, even if only to the standard expected of Modern Foreign Language GCSEs. There was initially much resistance to the development of a BSL GCSE from the Department for Education, for BSL takes no written form. However, when the possibility of legal action loomed, the government backed down. This was a victory against an obstinacy that requires every GCSE, regardless of subject, to be assessed through reading and writing.[5]

Many of the issues raised by the original authors are still omnipresent, perhaps even more so than they were in the 2000s. Children and young people with SI are disadvantaged by a high-stakes examination system which does not recognise individual strengths and does not allow for students learning with different styles or pace. While successive education secretaries have paid lip service to the value of vocational education and practical skills, they remain obsessed with PISA (Programme for International Student

Assessment) rankings which measure attainment in maths, science and reading in different countries.

Nonetheless, there are shoots of optimism. The development of deaf and VI specific curriculums and a BSL GCSE acknowledging the specialist skills students with SI need to develop are positive steps. Additionally, there has been further formal attention to the accessibility requirements of assessments by the regulator Ofqual, who are producing guidance for awarding bodies on designing and developing accessible assessments.[6] This should help reduce the need for papers to have to be modified for language or to overcome obstacles to students with VI due to inappropriate use of images.

Interestingly, there have been growing calls in recent years for politicians to take a fresh look at the purpose of GCSEs and consider an alternative system of assessment and post-16 qualifications.[7] Since 2015 it has been compulsory to continue education until 18. If it is accepted that education for all should be continued until 18 then why such an emphasis on examinations at 16? Should those who are campaigning for GCSEs to be scrapped be successful, then it will be a valuable opportunity to address the lack of equity for young people with SI.

Notes

1. Some of the terminology used (for example, visual impaired) has changed since the original article was published. There are also references to defunct government policy and quangos. However, we have left the original wording of the chapter intact.
2. See the OECD website. Available at: http://stats.oecd.org/glossary/detail.asp?ID=742
3. www.education.gov.uk/childrenandyoungpeople/specialeducationalneeds/a0064387/childrens-minister-unveils-plans-for-education-of-sen-pupils
4. www.batod.org.uk/resources-category/specialist-deaf-curriculum-framework/
5. www.irwinmitchell.com/news-and-insights/newsandmedia/2018/august/major-boost-for-deaf-boys-sign-language-campaign-following-government-u-turn-jq-476239
6. www.gov.uk/government/consultations/consultation-on-designing-and-developing-accessible-assessments/outcome/guidance-on-designing-and-developing-accessible-assessments-decisions
7. https://news.sky.com/story/gcses-and-a-levels-should-be-scrapped-according-to-tony-blair-institute-report-12679568

References

Cabinet Office (2005) Improving the Life Chances of Disabled People, London: HMSO.

DCSF (Department for Children, Schools and Families) (2008) Secretary of State Report on Progress towards Disability Equality across the Children's and Education Sector. Available at: www.dcsf.gov.uk/des/docs/2008SecretaryofStateReport_a.pdf

DCSF (2009a) Your Child, Your Schools, Our Future: Building a 21st Century Schools System, London: TSO.

DCSF (2009b) National Strategies Progression Guidance 2009–2010. Available from: https://dera.ioe.ac.uk/id/eprint/2414/7/sen_prog_guid_0055309_Redacted.pdf

DfES (2003) Every Child Matters, London: HMSO.

Hewett, R., Douglas, G., McLinden, M., James, L., Brydon, G., Chattaway, T., et al (2022) Curriculum Framework for Children and Young People with Vision Impairment (CFVI): Defining specialist skills development and best practice support to promote equity, inclusion and personal agency. RNIB.

Marschark, M. (2007) *Raising and Educating a Deaf Child*, Oxford: Oxford University Press.

Miller, O., Cobb R., and Simpson, S. (2011) 'Meeting the standard but failing the test' in S. Haines and D. Ruebain (eds) Education, *Disability and Social Policy*, Bristol: Policy Press.

Ofsted (2009) Framework for the Inspection of Maintained Schools in England from September 2009. Available from: https://dera.ioe.ac.uk/id/eprint/10068/1/The_framework_for_school_inspection%5B1%5D.pdf

Stobart, G. (2008) *Testing Times: The Uses and Abuses of Assessment*, Abingdon: Routledge.

6

Exploring the intersection of race and disability in English schools

Valentina Migliarini and Chelsea Stinson

Introduction

In the autumn of 2020, the British Broadcasting Corporation (BBC) premiered *Small Axe*, a British anthology film series created and directed by Steve McQueen. The anthology focuses on the lives of West Indian (henceforth, Black or Black British)[1] immigrants in London from the 1960s to the 1980s. One of the films in the anthology, *Education*, is based on actual events of the 1970s, when some London councils followed an unofficial policy of transferring a disproportionate number of Black British children from mainstream education to schools for those then called 'educationally subnormal'.[2] The practice was exposed by Bernard Coard's 1971 pamphlet *How the West Indian Child Is Made Educationally Subnormal in the British School System*. The pamphlet explains that teachers and educationalists in British schools had a pervasive bias toward white children as inherently good and 'normal'. Instead, '[t]he [Black] children are made neurotic about their race and culture. Some become behaviour problems as a result. They become resentful and bitter at being told their language is second-rate, and their history and culture is non-existent; that they hardly exist at all except by the grace of whites' (2021: 32).

Coard's argument has been widely cited as a summary of the role of institutional racism in the intersection between race and ability in England (Gillborn, 2015; Rollock et al, 2015; Gillborn et al, 2016). His pamphlet exposed what many had been trying to disguise: from the early eugenicists and the origins of IQ testing, racism has been implicated in the history of education in England (Gillborn, 2008). Colonial racism shaped the context for the labelling of children of the Windrush generation as 'subnormal' and created the legacy of disproportionate discipline exclusion (Migliarini and Martin, under review), and identification of children from racialised backgrounds with emotional and behavioural categories of special educational needs (Coard, 1971, 2021). The attempts of successive governments to deny the existence of institutional racism have all but erased a language for discussing race, and its intersection with ability, in education. Intersectional analysis has at times been reduced to a fragmentation of categories of ethnicity and special educational need in administrative data. Yet, there is an urgent need to untangle these complex issues and to address the injustices that marginalised students face in the English education system up to today.

This chapter attempts to explore to what extent education policies and research take into account the intersection of ability and race in England. The purpose is to investigate how the education of Black and marginalised children has changed since Coard's publication, and whether his findings are still applicable today. We begin by positioning ourselves theoretically, by adopting the Disability Critical Race Theory (DisCrit) as a guiding and expanded framework (Annamma et al, 2022). We then use DisCrit as a lens to look at recent English disability policies and classifications, and to analyse whether these policies envision support for students living at the intersections of race and disability. We also explore what kind of contemporary research has covered this issue. The final part of the chapter focuses on a generative discussion on the need to centre more radically and authentically intersectionality in educational research, as well as in teaching and learning in contemporary England.

Theoretical framework

The segregation of Black British students in the 1970s due to white teachers' bias had disastrous consequences for their educational achievement, and life experiences. Since then, understandings of disability have changed over the years, but the racialisation of disability continues up to today. In this section, we present DisCrit as our theoretical positioning, which has been looking closely at the intersections of race and disability in the US and beyond (Annamma et al, 2022), and giving equal weight to these axes of oppression (Annamma et al, 2013; Connor et al, 2016).

In the contemporary context of special education in Britain and internationally, disability has been conceptualised through three lenses: the medical, the social, and the postmodern Disability Studies on which DisCrit builds. The medical model is driven by the imperative of 'healthy normalcy' (Watermeyer, 2013: 29), whose defining characteristic is the location of disability within the individual with biological impairments, ignoring macro-socio-political contexts of racism, ableism and other intersecting systems of oppression (Artiles, 2013). In contrast, the social model of disability affirms that disability is purely social – an oppression layered on top of impairment. Michael Oliver (1990), Britain's exponent of the social model, argues that impairment is not *part* of the body but is a *description* of the body. The social model of disability shifts the focus from the individual to the society as a whole and introduces discourses of accessibility and needs as rights. Translated into the context of education, this model pushed for changes of the system and structure of each school. The Disability Studies lens contradicts the social model by suggesting that the separation of impairment and disability is an illusion (Dolmage, 2018). From the Disability Studies' perspective, it is important to conceptualise disability and other identity markers as discursive constructions, with real material effects and value (Ferri, 2008; Leonardo and Broderick, 2011).

Disability Critical Race Theory

DisCrit exposes the fault lines in ableist and deficit-oriented perspectives of disability, to illustrate how disability interconnects with other socially constructed identities (for example, class, gender, race). DisCrit analyses ways in which both race and ability are socially constructed and interdependent, and how ability is distributed and withheld in schools and classrooms (Connor et al, 2016; Annamma, 2018). There are seven tenets of DisCrit that show the ways in which race and ability intersect; each tenet highlights why curriculum, pedagogy and relationships are conceptualised in hegemonic ways and how they can be reimagined in generative ways for students and teachers (Annamma and Morrison, 2018).

First, DisCrit focuses on how racism and ableism are endemic and interdependent in society. These mutually constitutive processes are systemic and interpersonal and are often rendered invisible to restrict notions of normalcy to the desired and to marginalise those perceived as 'different' in society and schools (Connor et al, 2016). Once a child is perceived and labelled as different from the norm (whiteness), they are then imagined as less capable in academic contexts (Annamma, 2018).

Second, DisCrit values multidimensional identities and troubles single notions of identities, such as race *or* disability. It acknowledges how experiences with stigma and segregation often vary based on other identity markers intersecting with race and disability (gender, language, class) and how this negotiation of multiply stigmatised identities adds complexities. Multiply marginalised students have a clearer sense of the mutually constitutive processes of oppression, and how these processes are visible within segregated or dysfunctional inclusive spaces.

Third, DisCrit rejects the understanding of both race and disability as primarily biological facts and recognises the social construction of both as society's response to 'differences' from the norm. Simultaneously, DisCrit acknowledges that these categories hold profound significance in people's lives, as it is evident in the marginalisation of Black and those students with disability labels, who are more likely to be segregated than their white peers with the same label (Fierros and Conroy, 2002).

Fourth, DisCrit privileges voices of multiply marginalised students and communities, traditionally missing in research (Matsuda, 1995).

Consequently, DisCrit recognises those who have been pushed outside of the educational endeavour through the discourse and practices of special segregated classrooms. DisCrit positions multiply marginalised students as knowledge-generators, capable of recognising interlocking oppressions and creating solutions to those systemic, interpersonal inequities.

Fifth, DisCrit considers how, historically and legally, whiteness and ability have been used to deny rights to those that have been constructed as raced and disabled (Valencia, 1997). Schools have historically functioned as spaces to sort and fix multiply marginalised children, curing them of their disability or problematic behaviour (Margolis, 2004). Through to the present day, multiply marginalised students – especially (im)migrant students – often attend under-resourced schools where they have limited access to qualified teachers, engaging curriculum and critical pedagogy (Fierros and Conroy, 2002). Even when attending resourced schools, students of colour are often kept out of advanced placement/gifted classes, where creative thinking is valued (DeCuir and Dixon, 2004).

Sixth, DisCrit recognises whiteness and ability as 'property', conferring rights to those that claim those statuses and disadvantaging those who are unable to access them (Adams and Erevelles, 2016). Thus, when students are positioned as less desirable, they are barred from access to engaging and accurate curriculum, culturally sustaining pedagogy, and relationships that are authentic (Leonardo and Broderick, 2011).

These tenets highlight the importance of resisting the existing state of education, which centres the ideal citizen and often segregates the unwanted into spaces less public (Erevelles, 2014). They also expose how multiply marginalised communities resist white supremacy in various ways. As such, work rooted in DisCrit commits to recognising the values and gifts of such communities (Annamma, 2018).

English disability policies and the evasion of race

In September 2014, the Special Educational Needs and Disability Code of Practice: 0 to 25 years, 2014 (Department for Education/Department of Health [DfE/DoH], 2015) came into force in response to what the House of Commons Education and Skills Select Committee (2006) identified as 'serious flaws in the SEN [special educational needs] system' and their declaration that 'the SEN system is failing' (Migliarini et al, 2022). The Code of Practice was presented, in the foreword from the Parliamentary Under-Secretary of State for Health and the Parliamentary Under-Secretary of State for Children and Families, as following 'extensive consultation' (DfE/DoH, 2015: 11) and as a response to the problems identified by the House of Commons Education and Skills Committee and the Audit Commission. By promising a system that was 'less confrontational' (DfE/

DoH, 2015: 11), the Code of Practice acknowledged that this had been a problem in the past (Migliarini et al, 2022). The two ministers promised early identification and assessment of special educational needs, full involvement of children and young people and their parents or carers, and raised aspirations through an increased focus on life outcomes, including employment and greater independence.

Given the political orientation that preceded the introduction of the policy, it comes as no surprise that the policy is evasive with notions of inclusion and intersectional identities. The then Conservative Prime Minister declared the party's intention to 'prevent the unnecessary closure of special schools and remove the bias towards inclusion' (HM Government, 2010: 29). This followed on from a substantial challenge to inclusive education from Mary Warnock (2005), the architect of inclusion (CSIE, 2005), who had pronounced it 'the most disastrous legacy of the 1978 report' (Warnock, 2005: 22). Warnock claimed that inclusion – her preferred term rather than inclusive education – was problematic, and argued that inclusion could damage children. Using unreflexive language, she argued that the 'Down's Syndrome girl' (Warnock, 2005: 35); the 'child who suffers from such disabilities as [asthma or epilepsy]; and autistic children who 'suffer all the pains of the permanent outsider' make a strong argument for special schools (Migliarini et al, 2022). At the time, David Cameron described Warnock's pamphlet as a 'stunning recantation' (Hansard, 22 June 2005, Col 825). Clearly, by 2010, Cameron had come to see inclusion as less than attractive.

Although Black British children continue to be disproportionately represented in categories of special educational needs (DfE, 2022) concepts of inclusive education and intersectional approaches to inclusive education never appear in the Code of Practice. There is mention of inclusive practice and a hint to the social model of disability in a reference to the UK government's commitment to the removal of barriers to learning and participation in education. The securing of the assumption of mainstreaming in law through the Code of Practice is underlined, with signposting more than once of guidance, in Chapter 1, relating to inclusive practice (Migliarini et al, 2022). Where the word inclusion is mentioned, it is expressed vaguely and as something that 'should', rather than 'must' be done.

Referring to the National Curriculum Inclusion Statement, the Code of Practice states that all children should have access to a broad and balanced curriculum, and calls for teachers to set high expectations for all pupils and to undertake lesson planning. However, with the spectre of exclusion never far away, especially for Black British children with SEND labels, the Code states: 'In many cases, such planning will mean that pupils with SEN and disabilities will be able to study the full national curriculum' (DfE/DoH, 2015: 94). The Code of Practice, coupled with the implementation of zero tolerance policies has rescinded efforts to reduce racial overrepresentation in discipline, claiming that these efforts usurp the rights of educators to remove problematic students from the classroom (DfE, 2019). Even though these policies claim to be detached from race, it is clear that these policies legitimise racist ideas of 'us' (white British individuals) and 'them' (marginalised communities) (Gillborn, 1995). These policies have resulted in the increased criminalisation of Black British students, as it impacts their academic success, with some UK teaching unions saying they are 'inhumane' tactics[3] (Addington, 2019). Hence, Black students labelled as having special educational needs or disabilities continue to be at risk of being excluded and being disciplined more harshly.[4]

The Code of Practice, just as other policies regulating students' behaviour, fails spectacularly as a policy on inclusion, but it may not have been intended as such. Hodkinson and Burch (2017) note that efforts to control the population through the promotion of the concepts of independence and 'safe educational spaces' have depleted activist movements and resistance to such discourse. They affirm that multiply marginalised students should resist the docility and dependency visited upon them by the Code of Practice and recognise the racialised character of zero tolerance policies.

Race, disability, and identity pluralism in education

In public, political and education discourses, 'race' and 'disability' are often treated as immutable, singular demographic categories. However, as the tenets of DisCrit affirm, these identities are dynamic and interdependent, with 'material and psychological impacts of being labelled as raced or dis/abled' which, in turn, further marginalise individuals and communities at their intersections (Connor et al, 2016: 19). Although the theoretical context of DisCrit emerged from American and indigenous North American conceptualisations and experiences of 'race' and 'racialised identity', Black British scholars, such as Hall (1980), whose conceptualisations and experiences of 'race' and 'racialised identity' emerged transnationally, attend to race and racism as 'plural'. That is, they urge us to understand and attend to the plurality and contextual qualities of racism. As such, we must imagine and trace similarities and differences in anti-racist, intersectional identity pluralism.

In the previous section, we outlined how educational policies in England have yet to effectively name and address educational wrongs and inequities enacted against Black British students at the intersection of race and disability, despite decades of being lived, documented and studied by British and Black British scholars, activists and artists following Coard's (1971) seminal publication. For example, Black British students continue to receive comparatively low grades on GCSE and A-level assessments and are overrepresented in special education programmes and/or less rigorous classes (see Gillborn et al, 2016; Strand, 2012).

Disproportionate outcomes for Black British students highlight a multidimensional problem that has been reflected by nations with similar racial, cultural and political dynamics for decades. For example, in the US, some of the earliest discussions of the overrepresentation of negatively racialised migrants in lower-tracked or segregated educational programmes emerged in the early 20th century (for example, Hollingworth, 1920). These historical documentations illuminate the surging prevalence of academic tracking and segregated special programmes as public education in the US gradually became more racially and linguistically diverse. The relegation of racialised migrants to special education or lower-tracked programmes echoed the subjective, imprecise process of snapshot diagnosis of migrants at immigration centres, where 'the insinuation of mental disability was conflated with a semiotics of exterior markers' and 'undesirable bodies were "raced" as nonwhite, or as disqualified whites' (Dolmage, 2018: 17). The negative racialisation and ability profiling of Black and/or migrant students in the US, especially among the poor and working classes, continued into the mid-20th century as use of intellectual functioning and learning disability labels in tandem with segregated educational programmes functioned as surreptitious tools to keep students from minoritised racial, socioeconomic and cultural backgrounds out of mainstream school spaces in the years following nationwide school desegregation (Ferri and Connor, 2004, 2005).

Drawing on Black British and American scholarship, it is clear that static, deterministic theories and discourses of race and disability have resulted in educational inequities for Black students and families across political borders. Thus, Paris and Alim (2014) have advocated for critical identity pluralism through critical culturally sustaining education which aims to support students' cultural and racial identities by understanding the 'traditional and evolving ways they are lived and used by young people' (p 91). Paris and Alim argue that 'rather than avoiding problematic practices or keeping them hidden beyond the White gaze, [pedagogy] must work with students to critique regressive practices ... and raise critical consciousness' (2014: 92). Using the example of Hip Hop pedagogy, they explain how extant policies and pedagogies do not support students across racial and cultural backgrounds to be culturally or linguistically flexible because they do not effectively deal with problematic student discourse and internalised hegemonic values. Paris and Alim explain, 'cultural and linguistic recombinations flow with purpose, [and] we need pedagogies that speak to this new reality' (2014: 92). Crucially, however, these veins of scholarship do not address ability and disability in concert and therefore do not adequately offer a fully intersectional perspective.

The concept of recognising and sustaining identity pluralism through educational policies and pedagogies which engage students' cultural knowledge and identity must converge with the concept of 'ability pluralism' put forth by Waitoller and King Thorius (2016) and DisCrit into a strong foundation for future directions for research focused on the experiences, outcomes and needs of Black British students and their families in British schools. First, educators and researchers must be able to understand and articulate culture and cultural differences in non-deterministic ways, but rather as dexterous, cross-pollinating elements which mediate our experiences across educational, social and political contexts. Second, educators and policymakers must understand their role in challenging internalised hegemonic values alongside students.

Conclusion

According to the Department for Education data,[5] currently 40 per cent of Black children in England achieve five good GCSEs, and yet Black Caribbean boys are three times as likely as other students to be permanently excluded. It seems to get worse when race intersects with disability: Black students are twice as likely to be identified with having special educational needs (Strand and Lindorff, 2018). In present times, the practice that Coard described as labelling Black children as 'educationally subnormal' and excluding them from mainstream education has been replaced by Alternative Provision[6] and Pupil Referral Units (PRU), which stand for education taking place outside of mainstream and special needs schools. According to the Institute of Race Relations,[7] Black Caribbean children labelled with special educational needs are educated in a PRU at almost four times the expected rate. Evidence submitted to the parliamentary education committee,[8] as well as the 2019 Timpson Review,[9] suggests that the disproportionality of Black disabled students in temporary and permanent school exclusions is due to slashed school budgets and government encouragement of schools implementing a 'zero tolerance' approach to behaviour.

These references and our analysis of current education policies and research in England show that sadly very little has evolved in relation to the education of Black and multiply marginalised students since Coard's publication in 1971. Despite such a pessimistic result, we conclude with the need for educational professionals to cultivate radical hope, and advocate for a reconceptualisation of education policy, practice and research through DisCrit, as an intersectional and interdisciplinary framework. DisCrit provides the unique opportunity to examine critically the ways in which disability and behaviour are traditionally imagined and responded to in education. DisCrit can help educators and teachers to reflect on the ways that Black and marginalised students are systematically oppressed, and on the ways that perceptions of and reactions to disability and behaviour have contributed to inequitable educational opportunities for these students. Without an explicit commitment to be aware of and address the intersections of race and ability, as well as intersecting oppressions, we argue that alternatives to exclusion will end up replicating previous colour-evasive policies and practices. Finally, DisCrit can help teachers and educators to adopt an understanding of how interlocking systems of oppression push students out of school and of the educational endeavour. This, in turn, provides the basis for engaging in enabling policies and practices.

Notes
1. To explore more in detail the history and the variation of the terms West Indians, Caribbeans and Black British please refer to: https://zakiyamckenzie.com/2020/09/04/caribbean-vs-west-indian-bame-vs-poc-whats-in-a-name/#page-content
2. www.theguardian.com/education/2020/nov/15/discrimination-at-school-is-a-black-british-history-lesson-repeating-itself-small-axe-education-steve-mcqueen.
3. www.theguardian.com/education/2019/apr/17/teaching-union-calls-zero-tolerance-school-policies-inhumane
4. www.allfie.org.uk/campaigns/disabled-black-lives-matter/
5. www.ethnicity-facts-figures.service.gov.uk/education-skills-and-training/11-to-16-years-old/a-to-c-in-english-and-maths-gcse-attainment-for-children-aged-14-to-16-key-stage-4/latest
6. https://assets.publishing.service.gov.uk/government/uploads/system/uploads/attachment_data/file/942014/alternative_provision_statutory_guidance_accessible.pdf
7. https://assets.publishing.service.gov.uk/government/uploads/system/uploads/attachment_data/file/942014/alternative_provision_statutory_guidance_accessible.pdf.
8. https://publications.parliament.uk/pa/cm201719/cmselect/cmeduc/342/342.pdf
9. https://assets.publishing.service.gov.uk/government/uploads/system/uploads/attachment_data/file/807862/Timpson_review.pdf

References

Adams, D.L. and Erevelles, N. (2016) 'Shadow play: DisCrit, dis/respectability, and the carceral logics', in S. Annamma, D. Connor and B. Ferri (eds) *DisCrit: Disability Studies and Critical Race Theory in Education*. New York, NY: Teachers College Press.

Addington, L.A. (2019) 'Black girls doing time for white boys' crime? Considering Columbine's security legacy through an intersectional lens', *Journal of Contemporary Criminal Justice*, 35(3): 296–314.

Annamma, S.A. (2018) 'Mapping consequential geographies in the carceral state: education journey mapping as a qualitative method with girls of color with dis/abilities', *Qualitative Inquiry*, 24(1): 20–34. https://doi.org/10.1177/1077800417728962

Annamma, S. and Morrison, D. (2018) 'DisCrit classroom ecology: using praxis to dismantle dysfunctional education ecologies', *Teaching and Teacher Education*, 73: 70–80. https://doi.org/10.1016/j.tate.2018.03.008

Annamma, S.A., Connor, D. and Ferri, B. (2013) 'Dis/ability critical race studies (DisCrit): theorizing at the intersections of race and dis/ability', *Race, Ethnicity and Education*, 16(1): 1–31. https://doi.org/10.1080/13613324.2012.730511

Annamma, S.A., Ferri, B.A. and Connor, D.J. (eds) (2022) *DisCrit Expanded: Reverberations, Ruptures, and Inquiries*, New York, NY: Teachers College Press.

Artiles, A.J. (2013) 'Untangling the racialization of disabilities: an intersectionality critique across disability models', *Du Bois Review*, 10(2): 329–347. https://doi.org/10.1017/S1742058X13000271

Centre for Studies in Education (2005) *News Digest*. June. Retrieved 3 March 2006, Available at: http://inclusion.uwe.ac.uk/csie/june05.htm

Coard, B. (1971) *How the West Indian Child Is Made Educationally Subnormal in the British School System* (1st edn), London: New Beacon.

Coard, B. (2021) *How the West Indian Child Is Made Educationally Subnormal in the British School System* (5th edn), Kingston: McDermott.

Connor, D.J., Ferri, B.A. and Annamma, S.A. (eds) (2016) *DisCrit: Disability Studies and Critical Race Theory in Education*, New York, NY: Teachers College Press.

DeCuir, J.T. and Dixon, A.D. (2004) '"So when it comes out, they aren't surprised that it is there": using critical race theory as a tool of analysis of race and racism in education', *Educational Researcher*, 33(5): 26–31.

DfE/DoH (Department for Education/Department of Health) (2015) Special educational needs and disability code of practice: 0–25 years. Statutory guidance for organisations who work with and support children and young people with special educational needs and disabilities. London: DfE/DoH.

Dolmage, J. (2018) *Disabled Upon Arrival: Eugenics, Immigration, and the Construction of Race and Disability*, Columbus, OH: The Ohio State University Press.

Erevelles, N. (2014) 'Thinking with disability studies', *Disability Studies Quarterly*, 34(2). https://doi.org/10.18061/dsq.v34i2.4248

Ferri, B.A. (2008) 'Changing the script: race and disability in Lynn Manning's weights', *International Journal of Inclusive Education*, 12(5–6): 497–509. https://doi.org/10.1080/13603110802377524

Ferri, B.A. and Connor, D.J. (2004) 'Special education and the subverting of Brown', *The Journal of Gender, Race, and Justice*, 8(1): 57–74.

Ferri, B.A. and Connor, D.J. (2005) 'Tools of exclusion: race, disability, and (re)segregated education', *Teachers College Record*, 107(3): 453–474. https://doi.org/10.1111/j.1467-9620.2005.00483.x

Fierros, E.G. and Conroy, J.W. (2002) 'Double jeopardy: an exploration of restrictiveness and race in special education', in D.J. Losen and G. Orfield (eds) *Racial Inequity in Special Education*, Cambridge, MA: Harvard Education Press, pp 39–70.

Gillborn, D. (1995) *Racism and Antiracism in Real Schools*. Open University Press.

Gillborn, D. (2008) 'Coincidence or conspiracy? Whiteness, policy and the persistence of the Black/White achievement gap', *Educational Review*, 60(3): 229–248. https://doi.org/10.1080/00131910802195745

Gillborn, D. (2015) 'Intersectionality, critical race theory, and the primacy of racism: race, class, gender, and disability in education', *Qualitative Inquiry*, 21(3): 277–287. https://doi.org/10.1177/1077800414557827

Gillborn, D., Rollock, N., Vincent, C. and Ball, S.J. (2016) 'The Black middle classes, education, racism, and dis/ability: An intersectional analysis', in D.J. Connor, B.A. Ferri and S.A. Annamma (eds) *DisCrit: Disability Studies and Critical Race Theory in Education*, New York, NY: Teachers College Press, pp 35–54.

Hall, S. (1980) 'Race, articulation and societies structured in dominance', in UNESCO (ed) *Sociological Theories: Race and Colonialism*, Paris: UNESCO, pp 305–345.

HM Government (2010) *The Coalition: Our Programme for Government*, London: Cabinet Office. Retrieved on 18 November 2020. Available at: http://programmeforgovernment.hmg.gov.uk/files/2010/05/coalition-programme.pdf

Hodkinson, A. and Burch, L. (2017) 'The 2014 special educational needs and disability code of practice: old ideology into new policy contexts?', *Journal of Education Policy*, 34(2): 155–173. https://doi.org/10.1080/02680939.2017.1412501

Hollingworth, L.S. (1920) *The Psychology of Subnormal Children*, New York, NY: Macmillan.

House of Commons Education and Skills Select Committee (2006) Special educational needs: Third report of session 2005, 2006 (Volume 1). Report, together with formal minutes. London: Stationery Office. Retrieved on 18 November 2020. Available at: https://publications.parliament.uk/pa/cm200506/cmselect/cmeduski/478/47809.htm

Leonardo, Z. and Broderick, A.A. (2011) 'Smartness as property: a critical exploration of intersections between whiteness and disability studies', *Teachers College Record*, 113(10): 2206–2232. https://doi.org/10.1177/016146811111301008

Margolis, E. (2004) 'Looking at discipline, looking at labour: photographic representations of Indian boarding schools', *Visual Studies*, 19(1): 54–78.

Migliarini, V., Allan, J., Van Hove, G. and De Schauwer, E. (2022) 'Legislation and Policy in Europe', in R. Tierney, F. Rizvi and K. Ercikan (eds), *International Encyclopedia of Education*, 4th edn, Amsterdam: Elsevier, pp 58–67.

Migliarini, V. and Martin (under review). 'Addressing discipline disparities of Black girls in English secondary schools', in E. Done (ed) *Theorising Exclusionary Pressures in Education*.

Matsuda, M. (1995) 'Looking to the bottom: critical legal studies and reparations', in K. Crenshaw (ed) *Critical Race Theory: The Key Writings that Formed the Movement*, New York, NY: New Press, pp 323–398.

McQueen, S. (Director) (2020) *Small Axe* [film anthology]. Turbine Studios/Lammas Park/EMU Films/BBC Film.

Oliver, M. (1990) *The Politics of Disablement: A Sociological Approach*, New York, NY: St Martin's Press.

Paris, D. and Alim, H.S. (2014) 'What are we seeking to sustain through culturally sustaining pedagogy? A loving critique forward', *Harvard Educational Review*, 84(1): 85–100. https://doi.org/10.17763/haer.84.1.982l873k2ht16m77

Rollock, N., Gillborn, D., Vincent, C. and Ball, S.J. (2015) *The Colour of Class: The Educational Strategies of the Black Middle Classes*, London: Routledge.

Strand, S. (2012) 'The White British–Black Caribbean achievement gap: tests, tiers and teacher expectations', *British Educational Research Journal*, 38(1): 75–101. https://doi.org/10.1080/01411926.2010.526702

Strand, S. and Lindorff, A. (2018) *Ethnic disproportionality in the identification of Special Educational Needs (SEN) in England: extent, causes and consequences*, University of Oxford: Department of Education.

Valencia, R.R. (1997) 'Conceptualizing the notion of deficit thinking', in R.R. Valencia (ed) *The Evolution of Deficit Thinking: Educational Thought and Practice*, London, UK: Routledge, pp 113–131.

Waitoller, F.R. and King Thorius, K.A. (2016) 'Cross-pollinating culturally sustaining pedagogy and universal design for learning: toward an inclusive pedagogy that accounts for dis/ability', *Harvard Educational Review*, 86(3): 366–389. https://doi.org/10.17763/1943-5045-86.3.366

Warnock, M. (2005) *Special Educational Needs: A New Look*. Impact No 11. The Philosophy Society of Great Britain, London.

Watermeyer, B. (2013) *Towards a Contextual Psychology of Disablism*, London: Routledge.

7

The hidden world of within-school exclusion

Rob Webster

The rise of 'unofficial' exclusions

Formal exclusion is a preventative or punitive sanction whereby a child or young person is removed from an educational setting for reasons connected to misbehaviour or rule breaking.[1] Headteachers in England can lawfully suspend a pupil from school for a fixed period and, in extreme instances, remove them from the school altogether via a permanent exclusion.

Excluded children and young people are often the most vulnerable children and young people. They are twice as likely to be in the care of the state, four times more likely to have grown up in poverty, seven times more likely to have special educational needs and disabilities (SEND), and ten times more likely to have recognised mental health problems (Gill, 2017).

Pupils with SEND account for a disproportionate number of suspensions and permanent exclusions. Official data show that rates for both types of exclusion have returned to pre-pandemic levels, with suspension rates around four times greater, and permanent exclusions about five times greater, for pupils with SEND, compared with those without SEND (DfE, 2024a). Separate data indicate exclusions for autistic pupils alone increased by 59 per cent between 2011 and 2016, compared with an overall exclusion rate of 4 per cent over the same period (Ambitious About Autism, 2018).

Schools cannot use formal exclusion procedures to remove pupils for reasons unrelated to breaches of behaviour. Yet in recent years, England has seen the emergence of a shadow system of unofficial exclusion. These are practices whereby pupils are 'managed out' of one setting, though often not into another (Nye, 2017). Again, pupils with SEND are much more likely to be the target of such action.

Perhaps the most well-known of these practices is off-rolling. Ofsted defines off-rolling as 'removing a pupil from the school roll without using a permanent exclusion, when the removal is primarily in the best interests of the school, rather than the best interests of the pupil. This includes pressuring a parent to remove their child from the school roll' (Owen, 2019).

Another example is pre-emptive exclusion. This practice ensures that pupils who, in the judgement of the school, are at risk of being off-rolled do not make it onto the roll in the first place. As a former Secretary of State for Education described it, pre-emptive exclusion occurs where 'parents looking at secondary schools are actively or in some way subtly discouraged from applying to a particular school for their child' (Hinds, 2018). Schools that pre-emptively exclude, instead encourage families to apply for a place at another local school with a good reputation for SEND provision. These settings have been labelled 'magnet schools' because of the way they attract disproportionate numbers of pupils with SEND (Worth, 2022).

The consensus is that unofficial exclusions are the by-product of England's high-stakes accountability system, in which pupils with SEND are viewed by some schools as a liability. Schools worry that these pupils' comparatively low academic achievement will have a drag effect on performance indicators, and that a dip in performance will result in a downgraded inspection rating or threaten a coveted league table position. The pressure this exerts on schools prompts some to game the system by jettisoning underachieving pupils (Norwich, 2014; Peacey, 2015; Mansell and Adams, 2016; Lehane, 2017; Nye, 2017; Long and Danechi, 2020).

The Education Policy Institute concluded that some of the 55,000 'unexplained' moves by pupils between schools in England over a five-year period could be attributable to schools 'trying to remove difficult children' (Coughlan, 2019). Despite denials, schools are known to off-roll pupils based on their anticipated and deleterious contribution to academic accountability measures (Ofsted, 2018a). But determining the extent of off-rolling is like detecting a black hole in space. There are no official data on this unofficial practice, so its presence must be inferred from distortions in the available local-level data.

An investigation by *The Times* newspaper, for example, found GCSE outcomes of more than 30,000 pupils were missing from results tables, despite these pupils appearing on school registers in the previous three years (*Tes*, 2018). Analyses by Ofsted (2018b) estimated that 30 per cent of 19,000 Key Stage 4 pupils who went missing (presumed off-rolled) in 2017/18 had SEND. The following year, it was 27 per cent overall, but the rates across local authorities ranged from 10 per cent to 58 per cent (Ofsted, 2020).

The decision to remove or not to admit pupils with SEND pits the school's self-interest against its moral purpose. For the school, unofficial exclusion is low risk, high reward. This may explain why there is an undefined, but seemingly sufficient number of mainstream settings in England open to using it as a school improvement strategy. Analyses by the Children's Commissioner for England (2019) found that just 10 per cent of schools were responsible for 88 per cent of all exclusions.

The low risk can be linked in part to political ambitions to create a fully trust-led system (DfE, 2022a); that is, to ensure that all schools are part of a multi-academy trust (MAT). During its tenure, the Conservative government (2010–2024) consistently pushed academisation as the most – indeed, the only – effective route to raising standards, to which there were only upsides for schools.

Unofficial exclusions are most common in secondary schools, 82 per cent of which are academies (DfE, 2024b). To fulfil its academisation agenda, the government disapplied academies and MATs from some aspects of accountability. For example, Ofsted were not permitted to scrutinise MATs to anything like the degree they are required to scrutinise local authorities (Ofsted, 2019).[2] These protections inadvertently provided the context and the cover for some academy leaders to manipulate school rolls, relatively free from challenge from a government mindful of undermining its flagship schools policy.

The high reward can be seen in terms of headline outcomes. Schools, for instance, 'benefit' from having pupils at risk of underachieving leave; 'their GCSE pass rates are higher than they would be if these children had stayed with them until the end of secondary school' (Children's Commissioner for England, 2017).

The high-stakes accountability environment in which schools and policymakers operate has, therefore, had much to do with intensifying a form of protectionism and incubating a convenient *omertà* to hold it in place. Little wonder then, that off-rolling has been called 'a national scandal' (Coughlan, 2019).

The quiet business of managing pupils 'away' from mainstream education

There is sufficient evidence to indicate that some schools in England act against the interests, and indeed the rights, of pupils with SEND, on the basis that some have learning needs deemed too complex to meet, and their attainment prospects are insufficiently flattering to the metrics by which schools are judged, to justify trying. It is of great concern that the education system has uncritically drifted towards legitimising exclusion as a response to the challenge schools face of including and teaching pupils with additional needs. It is important to say that there are pupils whose behaviour is connected to their needs, and also that having SEND does not mean removal from school is inevitable. Nevertheless, pupils with SEND are at much greater risk of official and unofficial exclusions than their peers.

Prior to a formal exclusion being issued, schools can, depending on the severity of the transgression, impose sanctions ranging from a detention to an informal exclusion (being sent home early 'to cool off' following a behaviour incident (DfE, 2022b)), to an internal exclusion (where a pupil is removed from the classroom to do their schoolwork in isolation elsewhere onsite (Titheradge, 2018)). These sanctions escalate, and as they do, so does the degree and the duration of the pupil's estrangement from the mainstream classroom, the teacher and their peers. Mercifully, the time-limited and relatively infrequent nature of these sanctions mean that the impact on learning is unlikely to be critical; although it could be, if used repeatedly as a punishment for persistent misbehaviour.

This chapter argues that there are parallel practices and patterns that, while neither determinative nor predictive, are markers of the trajectory toward an unofficial exclusion linked to academic underperformance. Specifically, the ways in which schools organise the inclusion and teaching of pupils with SEND are characterised by degrees of their marginalisation from the mainstream classroom, the teacher and other pupils. Beginning in primary schooling, arrangements that amount to within-school exclusion can essentially help to normalise the unofficial exclusions more synonymous with secondary mainstream education.

Even if they are never 'managed out' of mainstream education, there is evidence that pupils with SEND are quietly managed *away* from it. Schools rationalise these organisational arrangements in terms of creating an effective, differentiated teaching environment for pupils with SEND. Yet, as we will see, the separation and segregation this creates has an impact on pupils that is far from benign.

A fractured experience of schooling

The influential Australian academic, John Hattie (2002: 462), wrote that educational structures and the composition of the classroom appear 'less consequential than ... the nature and quality of instruction in the class'. He frames this position as 'attending to classroom organisation practices *versus* improving what happens once the classroom door is closed' [2002: 462, emphasis added]. This, however, is a false dichotomy. What happens inside the classroom is informed to an under-appreciated degree by the composition of the classroom. Teaching and learning are informed by, and emerge from, the combined effects of structural factors including: the size of the class; the way in which pupils are grouped for teaching; and the presence and behaviours of adults.

This concatenation of classroom factors and behaviours contributes to the 'structural exclusion' of pupils with SEND (Webster, 2022). The concept of structural exclusion is informed by an ecological approach, which conceives educational processes as being situated in hierarchically organised contexts, much in line with Bronfenbrenner's (1979) ecological systems theory model. The thesis advanced in this chapter is based on an extension of that framework, and states that within the microsystem of the school, there are smaller, nested contexts – classrooms and smaller groups of pupils organised within classrooms – that have distinct dynamics that impact the teaching and learning experience.

Crucially, these contexts differ for pupils with and without SEND, and the experiences the former group have of school are markedly different from those in the latter group. While the organisational arrangements put in place specifically for pupils with SEND are done so with the best of intentions, they create forms of within-school and within-class marginalisation, and lead to what Ruebain and Haines (2011) call a 'fractured experience of schooling'. What is more, the trade-offs involved have negative consequences for the pedagogical diet pupils with SEND receive and their learning outcomes.

This chapter considers three key elements of structural exclusion in primary schools and secondary schools: (i) the withdrawal of pupils with SEND from the mainstream classroom; (ii) class size and grouping; and (iii) the utilisation of classroom support assistants.

'Micro-exclusions': withdrawal from the mainstream classroom

Pupils with SEND are invariably low attainers academically. An everyday response to managing the attainment gap in primary schools is to put in place curriculum interventions designed to improve basic skills in literacy and numeracy. Some pupils (additionally) require support with developing their speech and language skills and/or require physiotherapy related to a physical or mobility need.

All such programmes/interventions are almost always delivered during a mainstream lesson, but not within a mainstream classroom. Instead, an alternative space is used. So, pupils with SEND often find themselves doing classwork outside the classroom. Removing these pupils from the lesson in this way is justified in terms of providing them with a quieter, less distracting environment in which to focus on their work. But it is also justified in the interests of the rest of the class, who might be 'held back', in some unspecified way(s), by the presence of a pupil(s) with SEND (Webster, 2022). The Italian academic, Simona D'Alessio (2011), refers to this form of separation from the classroom as 'micro-exclusions', mainly because of the way pupils with SEND are kept apart from their peers.

Another common feature of this practice is for schools to deploy teaching assistants (TAs) to deliver teaching and/or oversee learning. In England, withdrawal from the class appears to have increased considerably, over time. A survey of 300 primary teachers conducted by Croll and Moses (2000) found that two thirds of pupils with high-level SEND[3] were withdrawn from mainstream classrooms to work with a TA for an average 3.7 hours per week. Observational research conducted a decade later implies that the proportion of time these pupils spent being taught away from the classroom had as good as doubled to a day a week (Webster and Blatchford, 2013).

Withdrawal input from TAs is often referred to by those in schools as 'additional' support. However, it is not. It is an *alternative* to the teacher-led teaching they necessarily miss when working away from the classroom (Blatchford et al, 2012; Webster, 2022). Yet, as with the other two organisational approaches we consider in this chapter, perhaps what matters more is whether the intuitive appeal of withdrawing pupils with SEND from mainstream lessons for TA-led input makes a material difference to learning outcomes. When it comes to curriculum interventions, there is compelling international evidence that well-specified, well-structured (and generally commercially available) 'catch-up' programmes, delivered in small groups or on a one-to-one basis by trained TAs, can improve basic literacy and numeracy skills (Alborz et al, 2009; Sharples, 2016; Slavin, 2016; Nickow et al, 2020). Alternative 'homemade' programmes, however, tend to lack the structure of an off-the-shelf intervention or a bespoke schedule of work assembled by a specialist (for example, a speech and language therapist) (Webster and Blatchford, 2013), so outcomes are inconsistent (Webster, 2022).

Classroom composition: separation and segregation

Having considered the separation of pupils with SEND from the mainstream class, we turn next to the composition of the classroom itself, and how the arrangements put in place specifically for these pupils are a factor in their marginalisation from everyday education.

The commonplace organisational structures of schools and classrooms in England (and elsewhere) follow the assumption that teaching becomes more effective or efficient as the attainment range of a class is narrowed. One of the main justifications for smaller sized classes is that a lower teacher–pupil ratio allows those with the greatest academic need to receive more individual attention, in an environment in which they are better able to concentrate (Finn et al, 2003).

The average Key Stage 2 class size in English primary schools has remained relatively stable in recent years: 27.6–27.9 pupils (DfE, 2024b). As schools cannot easily create the physical space needed to increase the number of classrooms, class size reduction is largely unrealistic. Instead, it is the classroom environment that is modified for the purposes of ensuring pupils with SEND can receive individualised support. While most pupils tend to sit together (around tables) in mixed attainment groups, those with SEND are often split out and clustered together with similarly low-attaining classmates at a separate table. This forms the immediate environment in which they experience much of their learning. Consequently, compared with their peers, pupils with SEND experience less teaching in mixed attainment groups, and more teaching with pupils who are a lot like them (Webster and Blatchford, 2013).

In secondary schools, on the other hand, pupil cohorts are divided into classes at the year group level, again based on attainment. Most of these classes are roughly equal in size, except for the one composed of pupils with SEND, which is much smaller. Large-scale research conducted in 2015/16 by Blatchford and Webster (2018) found that the low attainment classes in which pupils with SEND were taught typically contained 16 pupils or fewer. In just over half of cases, they contained 12 pupils or fewer. The average attainment classes, meanwhile, contained at least 21 pupils. The pupil–adult ratios in each of these classes are different, too. Classes for low attainers have a teacher and at least one TA present, while TAs are seldom found in the larger classes for average attainers.

In secondary schools, this widespread organisational practice is known as setting. Among other things, setting obviates the need to withdraw certain pupils for 'catch-up' programmes, because those who are typically the target of such interventions are instead grouped together into smaller teaching units. Yet, the iteration of setting that Blatchford and Webster (2018) found in their study had, they concluded, more in common with 'streaming' or 'tracking' than setting. Streaming, where pupils are grouped by attainment for all subjects, was routinely found in UK schools in the 1950s and 1960s.

Schools are known to refer to setting and within-class grouping by attainment – or as it is often referred to, by 'ability'[4] – as a differentiation strategy (Deunk et al, 2015; Graham et al, 2021; Webster, 2022). It is an approach to structuring teaching that is hardwired into the culture and practice of English education. Yet the evidence in favour of it as an effective classroom context for learning remains elusive.

While homogeneous grouping has been shown to have some benefits for high-attaining pupils, it can be detrimental to the learning and self-confidence of average-attaining and low-attaining pupils (Boaler et al, 2000; Ireson et al, 2002; Kutnick et al, 2005; Taylor et al, 2016; Francis et al, 2017). Pupils educated in sets and groups for low attainers, which necessarily include those with SEND, are often provided with an impoverished curriculum and pedagogy, compared with their high-attaining peers (Kutnick et al, 2002; Hallam and Ireson, 2005; McGillicuddy and Devine, 2018). While pupils in high-attaining groups benefit from the positive affirmations of being top of the class, there is a corrosive effect on the emotional and behavioural outcomes (Papachristou et al, 2021), confidence and self-concept for those in what tend to be labelled the 'bottom' group (Peacock, 2016), where teachers' expectations of pupils are lower (Hargreaves, 2017; Francis et al, 2019). These negative associations with ability grouping have been found to apply specifically and acutely to the self-perception of pupils with SEND (Webster, 2022).

What is more, this way of organising teaching can widen the achievement gap between low attainers and their peers (Ireson and Hallam, 2009; Schofield, 2010), and entrench disadvantage, as there is little movement between year-level sets or (where observed) streams. Once placed in an ability group, pupils tend to remain there. As Stobart (2014) has shown, 88 per cent of four-year-olds placed in low-attaining groups were still there by the end of their schooling. Francis et al (2017) echo this, adding that progress or attainment seems to make little difference to whether a pupil transitions out of their group. This is odd for an organisational strategy ostensibly predicated on the meritocratic nature of setting, which implies a measure of porosity and movement of pupils between sets.

It does not necessarily follow that smaller classes and within-class groups for pupils with SEND ought to be composed exclusively or mostly of these pupils. But the evidence points to schools' extensive reliance on such grouping and their narrow social mix, especially in secondary schools. Viewed in the context of a steady reduction in breaktimes in secondary settings over time (Baines and Blatchford, 2019), the classroom becomes an important site for developing peer relations. This is especially true for those with SEND, as they tend to face greater social exclusion from formal and informal out-of-school contexts, such as recreational activities, sports clubs and meeting up with friends. Compared with their non-SEND peers, they have fewer opportunities to experience and derive social acceptance beyond school. In this sense, school may play a much greater role in the lives of those with SEND in terms of being and feeling included, as it is the one setting that they must routinely attend and where the basic conditions needed to foster a meaningful sense of belonging already exist.

Before we move on to the third organisational arrangement, it is worth pausing to review the coverage on micro-exclusions and classroom composition. Putting the evidence together, we can see that in primary schools, the everyday educational experience of pupils with SEND is epitomised by separation from the classroom, their teacher and their peers, while in secondary schools, there is a form of segregation in place, with pupils with SEND taught together in small homogeneous classes for low-attaining pupils, while their peers without SEND were taught in larger homogeneous classes. These arrangements, as we shall see, place considerable emphasis on the role of TAs to facilitate inclusion and mediate teaching.

TAs: their role and impact on learning

The long-term trend of including greater numbers of pupils with SEND in mainstream schools has been accompanied and assisted by an increase in the number of TAs. Education systems across the world have seen sizeable and sustained increases in TA numbers (Masdeu Navarro, 2015), but nowhere has this growth been more pronounced than in the UK. Over the two decades, the number of TAs in mainstream schools in England alone has more than trebled. TAs currently represent 37 per cent of the primary and infant school workforce, and 13 per cent of the secondary school workforce (DfE, 2024c).

School leaders report that one of the main reasons for the increase in TAs is that policies of including pupils with SEND would be impossible to implement without them (Blatchford et al, 2012). Testimonies from school staff and parents associate one-to-one TA support with the ability of pupils with SEND to 'manage' or 'survive' in a mainstream setting (Webster, 2022). A further indicator of the essentialness of TAs to inclusion, very much in line with the theme of this chapter, can be seen in evidence collated by the Children's Commissioner for England from 2013, which suggested 2.7 per cent of schools had sent children with high-level SEND home when their TA was unavailable.

Yet the presence and accompaniment of a TA means that the pupils in greatest need of teacher input end up 'spending a lot of their time in class with someone who [is] not a trained teacher' (Croll and Moses, 2000: 111). This picture was confirmed by the longitudinal Deployment and Impact of Support Staff (DISS) project, conducted between 2004 and 2009, which was designed to provide much-needed information on the utilisation and impact of TAs in the UK. It found that the intuitive benefits of having TAs in classrooms – in terms of allowing overstretched teachers to focus their time on the rest of the class, in the knowledge that the pupils who require the most support receive potentially valuable individual attention from TAs – led to TAs tightly orbiting pupils with SEND for much of the day. Essentially, the least qualified staff were assigned primary educator status for the pupils in most need (Blatchford et al, 2012).

An analysis of data from large-scale systematic observation studies of mainstream UK primary classrooms (carried out between 1976 and 2012) reveals the impact of the presence of TAs on the everyday educational experiences of pupils with SEND, over time (Webster, 2015). Pupils without SEND spent much more of their time as part of the whole-class audience, listening to the teacher teach, than they did in the 1980s and 1990s. Yet over this 36-year span, there had been virtually no change in the average amount of time pupils with SEND spent interacting in whole-class teaching contexts.

A key reason for this is likely to be the increase in time spent away from the classroom, which – as noted earlier – has become possible because of the rise in the number of TAs. But there is also a subtler form of separation that occurs within the classroom, which again seems only to affect pupils with SEND.

Analyses of extensive systematic classroom observation data reveal that the presence of TAs in the classroom and their interactions with pupils have a marked effect on the everyday experiences of those with SEND. During lessons, pupils without SEND barely interact with TAs, but those with SEND interact with TAs almost constantly. Blatchford et al (2012) found that TAs' interactions with pupils increase, and teachers' interactions decrease, with rising levels of pupil need. Further research by Blatchford and Webster (2018) involving pupils with high-level SEND found that one in five of the interactions that these pupils had in the primary classroom were with a TA. In secondary settings, the equivalent proportion was 15 per cent.

Crucially, what these data tell us is that pupils' interactions with TAs cut across, replace and reduce the opportunities they have to interact with their teacher and their peers. It amounts to a subtler form of separation during lessons, which we might call a 'nano exclusion'.

Again, the critical question is to what extent do high amounts of high intensity support impact on learning outcomes for pupils with SEND. The DISS project provided evidence of a qualitative, as well as quantitative, difference between the pedagogical contexts within which pupils with and without SEND were taught. Analyses of classroom interactions between teachers and pupils, and TAs and pupils, found that TAs were more concerned with task completion and correction than with learning, and acted reactively rather than proactively (Rubie-Davies et al, 2010). Also, TAs tended to close talk down, rather than open it up, as teachers do (Radford et al, 2011). Analyses of rich case study data from Webster and Blatchford's (2019) longitudinal study of pupils with high-level SEND led to the clear conclusion that the support provided by TAs amounts to a lower-quality pedagogical diet. That is, it was below the instructional quality one would expect from a teacher.

Returning to the DISS project, we see striking evidence of a troubling impact on academic outcomes. An analysis involving 8,200 pupils in mainstream primary and secondary schools assessed progress across English, mathematics and science for seven different year groups. In 16 of the 21 analyses (three core subjects across seven year groups), the results were in a negative direction. There were no positive effects of TA support for any subject or for any year group (Blatchford et al, 2012). Most troubling of all was that the magnitude of the effect was greatest for the pupils with high-level SEND. The relationship held even after controlling for pupil-level factors likely to be related to having TA support in the first place (for example, prior attainment; SEND status) (Webster et al, 2010). In a similar way, Klassen (2001) found that pupils who had a statement for a specific learning difficulty or dyslexia, and who were assigned TA support for literacy, made less progress than those who did not receive TA support.

The degrees of marginalisation and the lower-quality pedagogical diet that have been found to have a detrimental effect on learning outcomes of pupils with SEND are the real-world consequences of an under-theorised and unchecked drift over time towards a model of inclusion that relies almost exclusively on the employment and deployment of TAs. But there is an important caveat needed here, as there is a risk that matters are oversimplified, and that TAs are somehow miscast as 'the problem'. This is emphatically not the case. The DISS project authors concluded, it is the decisions made *about* TAs – and not the decisions made by TAs – that best explain both the lower-quality pedagogical diet and the results on academic progress.

From structural exclusion to structural inclusion

Hattie (2002: 449) may have a point when he says that 'Good teaching can occur independently of the class configuration or homogeneity of the students within the class', but the empirical evidence suggests that in the case of pupils with SEND, the odds of receiving 'good teaching' are markedly lower. This is because the concatenation of organisational arrangements outlined in this chapter conspire to create a different immediate learning environment for these pupils, compared with the one experienced by their peers without SEND. In this reading, there exists a form of within-school exclusion, structural in nature, which produces a very different experience of mainstream education for those with SEND. Indeed, we might question whether it is a mainstream education at all, or more an education in mainstream.

A key reason for this appears to be that the prevailing educational and political winds favour average and higher attaining pupils (those without SEND) and their outcomes. For all the policy narrative about inclusion and the importance of outcomes for pupils with SEND, the high-stakes accountability system in England does more to disincentivise inclusion than it does to reward schools for prioritising the needs of this group. A measure of the current situation is captured in Giangreco and colleagues' (2005) assessment from 20 years ago, that it is unlikely that a regime structured in this way, and which produces the sort of outcomes that it does, would be tolerated for pupils without learning difficulties.

Bringing about a more balanced and fairer education for pupils with SEND requires inclusively minded people acting in a coordinated way at every level of the system: from national policymakers, through leaders and decision-makers at the middle tier (that is, local authorities and MATs), to school leaders and classroom practitioners. In a word, inclusion is fundamentally about what Goddard (2019) pithily calls 'botheredness'. Transitioning from a system that structurally *ex*cludes to a system that structurally *in*cludes is a task of inestimable effort and value. So, how might this be achieved?

Let us consider three areas of reform: (i) addressing the perverse incentives within the accountability system that, in essence, makes exclusion the easier option for schools; (ii) broadening the palette of provisions and support for those with SEND, so the system is less dependent on TAs; and (iii) equipping teachers to teach pupils with SEND.

Incentivising inclusion

We need to go beyond holding schools to account for malign behaviours, such as off-rolling, to driving them out altogether. Indeed, policymakers must reform the accountability system so that such practices cannot emerge in the first place. A common suggestion is for Ofsted to rule that an overall grade for a school cannot exceed the grade it is awarded for its provision and outcomes for pupils with SEND. However, this may inspire different forms of game-playing.

A more constructive starting point would involve incentivising schools to become more inclusive. One suggestion stemming from a 2018 House of Commons Education Select Committee inquiry is for the government to 'introduce an inclusion measure or criteria that sits *within schools* to incentivise schools to be more inclusive' [emphasis added] (HoC, 2018). It is an interesting idea, but capturing values-based behaviour is tricky to do reliably (Booth and Ainscow, 2002). Schools would want assurances that the measure would be applied consistently across a range of settings and circumstances, and parents will need to know that it would tell them something meaningful about inclusion. It cannot rely on poor proxies for inclusion, such as a school's annual spend on SEND, or the proportion of time a pupil spends with a one-to-one TA.

It is also potentially limiting. The inclusion of pupils with SEND is not just about maximising their participation in school life. It means being accepted wherever that child or young person is. Inclusion is not a place across town to which you commute. As such, it has a relative dimension. To form a rounded assessment of the inclusiveness of any one school, one would need to know whether it is admitting its fair share of children with SEND from its local community. And for that, comparable data are needed on the inclusivity of its nearest schools. To make sense of a school's 'inclusion score', one would need to see how it matches up against its neighbours. A between-school measure would therefore offer more than a within-school measure alone.

There seemed to be some acceptance of this in the DfE's plans to publish local and national inclusion dashboards, in its 2023 SEND and Alternative Provision Improvement Plan. However, the pledge to publish school-level data on inclusiveness was quickly, and quietly, dropped. Instead, only local area metrics would be made available. However, at the time of writing (August 2024), inclusion dashboards have yet to emerge.

Broadening the palette of provisions and support

Educating pupils with a wide range of needs is challenging. It is a fact of school life that there will be occasions when the learning and development of some pupils with SEND requires a greater degree of individualisation, which is difficult to accommodate in the regular run of mainstream coverage without compromising the quality of one or both. As such, it becomes necessary at times to address the needs of such pupils somewhat independently of the rest of the class. The standpoint of this chapter is not that any or all forms of separation and segregation are unjust, unwarranted or harmful, but it is clear that the way in which the educational architecture is routinely arranged in mainstream settings to teach some pupils with SEND is problematic. In other words, it is less the existence of these structures that is the issue, but the extent and frequency of their use – and that is particularly true of TA support.

Reconfiguring the organisational elements of the everyday school and learning environment, and broadening the palette of provisions and support beyond the default setting of TA support, has the potential to make the overall learning experience more inclusive and less exclusive. Here are three areas for schools to consider.

First, secondary schools need to optimise their use of smaller classes by ensuring that lessons are taught by highly skilled, specialised teachers who are trained in effective approaches to: (i) teach pupils with SEND; (ii) maximise the advantages of teaching smaller size classes; and (iii) blend these with mainstream mixed attainment teaching. Relatedly, the (mainly primary school) practice of withdrawing pupils from the lesson to work outside the classroom for a curriculum intervention should be used far more judiciously. Guidance on this can be found in Webster et al (2021). The essential criterion for deciding on when to use small class or small group teaching has to be this: the coverage and input a pupil with SEND receives in that context must more than compensate for the time they spend away from mainstream teaching and curriculum coverage.

Second, the careful use of smaller teaching and learning contexts for including pupils with SEND is also connected to the need to improve the social mix in lessons. To increase opportunities for peer support, secondary schools could, for example, take the bold step of mixed attainment teaching, for at least some subjects. As a minimum, schools should adopt grouping strategies that mitigate the more harmful effects of streaming or 'hard' setting (Francis et al, 2017; Mazenod et al, 2018). In lessons, teachers should ensure pupils with SEND are not routinely grouped together for paired or group work, but have opportunities to interact, work with and learn from others.

Finally, schools must address the way in which the prevalence and presence of TAs has given teachers 'permission to withdraw', leaving TAs 'to get on with the task of inclusion' (Slee, 2012: 47). Inside three decades, TAs have become the mortar in the brickwork of schools; holding things together in numerous and often unnoticed ways (Webster et al, 2021). The COVID-19 pandemic revealed how pivotal TAs were in allowing schools to keep functioning, and to support pupils and families during lockdown. A survey of 9,000 UK TAs found that nine in 10 TAs were on site, enabling schools to stay open to vulnerable children and children of keyworkers, while continuing to provide individualised support to those with SEND and deliver targeted interventions (Moss et al, 2021). It is difficult to see how schools would have managed without them during this most turbulent and uncertain of times.

TAs, however, should be part of a wider, more balanced and coherent set of strategies to meet the needs of pupils with SEND – not the sole response. Elsewhere, colleagues and I have written extensively on what schools can do to repurpose the everyday opportunities TAs have for extended interaction with pupils (Webster et al, 2016, 2021; Bosanquet et al, 2021). Instead of replacing the teacher in an instructional capacity, TAs should be recast as scaffolding experts, supporting pupils to engage in learning and develop the skills to manage their own learning independently. The starting point for this is to acknowledge the teacher as the pedagogical expert in the room, and to recognise that TAs' skills and pupil outcomes are maximised when TAs support problem-solving *alongside* the mainstream curriculum. Training TAs in this approach has been shown to not only improve TAs' talk behaviours – greatly reducing the 'complete and correct' practices – but also have a positive impact on pupil engagement (Dimova et al, 2021).

Improving teachers' confidence and competence with SEND

Broadening the palette of provisions and support necessarily means also addressing the specific, longstanding failure to train teachers adequately on SEND. Every education system needs its teachers to be confident and competent in this area. Pupils at risk of exiting the school system, informally or formally, are 'rarely pushed out because schools do not want to help them; more often it is because their needs are so far outside the norm that schools, in their current form, are not equipped to support them' (Menzies and Baars, 2015: 13).

The evidence of teachers' knowledge deficit around SEND goes back decades. There is the persistent lack of pre-service training for teachers in England. Annual surveys of new teachers in England have consistently shown that following their initial teacher education (ITE) course, new teachers rank their confidence in teaching pupils with SEND as one of their least secure areas. Each of the last available surveys, covering 2015 to 2017, found that just over half of new teachers felt secure in this area of their practice (Pye et al, 2016; Ginnis et al, 2018). Incidentally, their confidence in knowing how to deploy TAs effectively ranks equally low.

In her 1978 landmark report on special education, Mary Warnock acknowledged that 'some 40 years will need to elapse' before the English education system is at a point where all teachers will have undertaken adequate SEND training as part of their initial training, and therefore have the requisite skills to teach pupils with SEND effectively (DES, 1978). That milestone was passed seven years ago, yet despite some progress, the pattern over the last four decades concerning the adequacy, quality and amount of training in SEND offered to pre-service teachers has been one of repeated missed opportunities. In his skilful assessments of the landscape, Hodkinson (2009, 2019) concludes that the rhetoric from successive governments on the position of SEND in ITE has come to sound 'like a scratched record'.

This chapter can only restate the essential need for the government to improve the coverage of SEND in ITE and in-service training, finally and firmly. As vital as ITE training is, the time teachers have to engage in professional learning remains necessarily limited. What, however, are generally more abundant in supply are opportunities to sit with a pupil, to get to know them, their needs, their talents, their aspirations, the things they like and can do, the things they find unfamiliar and tricky, the things that provoke their curiosity, and the things teachers can do to stimulate, challenge and include them. The message for schools then is to arrive at collective and shared views about how best to respond to the needs of pupils with SEND via everyday teaching.

The primacy of inclusion policy

It is reasonable to deduce from the recommendations above that there is much that schools can do to improve inclusive practice, regardless of what happens in terms of national policy. That said, the education system in England remains in urgent need of a comprehensive strategic plan for the inclusion of pupils with SEND. At the time of writing – one month after the July 2024 General Election – the trajectory of SEND and inclusion policy is uncertain. The newly installed Labour government has indicated it intends to take a 'community-wide approach [to] improving inclusivity' (Labour Party, 2024), although it is currently unclear what this entails.

The new government would be wise to accept the inheritance, incorporating learning from the ongoing implementation of the SEND Improvement Plan (DfE, 2023) into an updated strategy that commits to taking some ambitious steps towards making schools more inclusive. This could include a serious and sustained investment in specialist resourced provisions within mainstream schools to take the pressure off special schools, and an investigation into the impact of these units on facilitating pupils' inclusion in mainstream lessons.

Nearly five decades ago, the Warnock Inquiry report – the UK's most comprehensive review of SEND ever commissioned and completed – offered the government of the day 225 recommendations designed to improve the educational experiences, outcomes and life chances of children and young people with SEND. It is as cogent a case for mainstreaming pupils with SEND as it was when it was published in May 1978. Inclusion remains a serious policy. What is needed is a serious government willing to switch attention from exclusion to inclusion, and to do what is necessary to make it a reality.

Notes

1. At the time of writing, the official reasons a school can give for an exclusion are: physical assault, verbal abuse/threatening behaviour against a pupil or an adult; bullying; racist abuse; sexual misconduct; drug/alcohol related; damage; theft; and persistent disruptive behaviour (Coram Children's Legal Centre, 2024).
2. The Labour government has pledged to bring MATs into the inspection system (Labour Party, 2024).
3. In this chapter, the term 'high-level SEND' is used to distinguish, where appropriate, pupils whose needs are sufficiently complex to require an Education, Health and Care Plan (EHCP) or a statement (the predecessor to EHCPs) from the general population of pupils with SEND. Pupils with high-level SEND comprise 26 per cent of all pupils with SEND (DfE, 2024d).
4. Although setting is often referred to as organising pupils into 'ability' groups, this is rather misleading, because allocation is usually based on some measure of attainment. There is now a strong and commonly shared view that it can be misguided to assume pupils can be grouped on the basis of some underlying and fixed 'ability'.

References

Alborz, A., Pearson, D., Farrell, P. and Howes, A. 2009. *The Impact of Adult Support Staff on Pupils and Mainstream Schools*. London: EPPI-Centre, Social Science Research Unit, Institute of Education. Accessed 25 October 2021. https://eppi.ioe.ac.uk/cms/Default.aspx?tabid=2438

Ambitious About Autism. 2018. *We Need an Education*. Accessed 20 September 2022. www.ambitiousaboutautism.org.uk/sites/default/files/resources-and-downloads/files/we-need-an-education-exclusions-report.pdf

Baines, E. and Blatchford, P. 2019. *School Break and Lunch Times and Young People's Social Lives: A follow-up national study*. Final Report. London: UCL Institute of Education/Nuffield Foundation. Accessed 2 March 2022. https://bit.ly/3sIV5Z6

Blatchford, P. and Webster, R. 2018. 'Classroom contexts for learning at primary and secondary school: Class size, groupings, interactions and special educational needs', *British Educational Research Journal*, 44(4): 681–703. https://doi.org/10.1002/berj.3454

Blatchford, P., Russell, A. and Webster, R. 2012. *Reassessing the Impact of Teaching Assistants: How research challenges practice and policy*. Abingdon: Routledge.

Boaler, J., Wiliam, D. and Brown, M. 2000. 'Students' experiences of ability grouping: Disaffection, polarisation and the construction of failure', *British Educational Research Journal* 26(5): 631–48. https://doi.org/10.1080/713651583

Booth, T. and Ainscow, M. 2002. *Index for Inclusion: Developing learning and participation in schools*. Bristol: Centre for Studies on Inclusive Education.

Bosanquet, P., Radford, J. and Webster, R. 2021. *The Teaching Assistant's Guide to Effective Interaction: How to maximise your practice* (2nd edn), Abingdon: Routledge.

Bronfenbrenner, U. 1979. *The Ecology of Human Development: Experiments by nature and design.* Cambridge, MA: Harvard University Press.

Coram Children's Legal Centre (2024) Coram School Exclusions Hub, Accessed 6 January 2025. https://schoolexclusionshub.org.uk/young-people-and-families/

Children's Commissioner. 2013. *Always Someone Else's Problem.* London: Office of the Children's Commissioner for England. Accessed 24 September 2021. www.childrenscommissioner.gov.uk/resource/always-someone-elses-problem/

Children's Commissioner. 2017. *Briefing. Falling Through the Gaps in Education.* London: Office of the Children's Commissioner for England. Accessed 24 September 2021. https://assets.childrenscommissioner.gov.uk/wpuploads/2017/11/BRIEFING-Falling-through-the-gaps-in-education-CCO.pdf

Children's Commissioner. 2019. *Excluded Teens Are Often the Most Vulnerable – and They're Falling through the Gap.* London: Office of the Children's Commissioner for England. Accessed 5 August 2024. www.childrenscommissioner.gov.uk/2019/03/27/excluded-teens-are-often-the-most-vulnerable-and-theyre-falling-through-the-gap/

Coughlan, S. 2019. Warning over 'unexplained' school moves. BBC News. Accessed 6 December 2024. https://www.bbc.co.uk/news/education-47962294

Croll, P. and Moses, D. 2000. *Special Needs in the Primary School: One in five.* London: Cassell.

D'Alessio, S. 2011. *Inclusive Education in Italy: A critical analysis of the policy of integrazione scolastica.* Rotterdam: Sense Publishers.

DES (Department of Education and Science). 1978. *Special Educational Needs.* The Warnock Report. London: HMSO.

Deunk, M., Doolaard, S., Smale-Jacobse, A. and Bosker, R.J. 2015. *Differentiation within and across Classrooms: A systematic review of studies into the cognitive effects of differentiation practices.* Groningen: RUG/GION. Accessed 10 September 2021. https://bit.ly/3MjR4C9

DfE (Department for Education). 2022a. *The Case for a Fully Trust-led System.* London: DfE. Accessed 20 September 2022. https://assets.publishing.service.gov.uk/government/uploads/system/uploads/attachment_data/file/1076862/The_case_for_a_fully_trust-led_system.pdf

DfE (Department for Education). 2022b. *Suspension and Permanent Exclusion from Maintained Schools, Academies and Pupil Referral Units in England, including Pupil Movement. Guidance for maintained schools, academies, and pupil referral units in England.* London: DfE. Accessed 20 September 2022. https://assets.publishing.service.gov.uk/government/uploads/system/uploads/attachment_data/file/1101498/Suspension_and_Permanent_Exclusion_from_maintained_schools__academies_and_pupil_referral_units_in_England__including_pupil_movement.pdf

DfE (Department for Education). 2023. *Special Educational Needs and Disabilities (SEND) and Alternative Provision (AP) Improvement Plan: Right support, right place, right time.* London: DfE. Accessed 5 August 2024. https://assets.publishing.service.gov.uk/media/63ff39d28fa8f527fb67cb06/SEND_and_alternative_provision_improvement_plan.pdf

DfE (Department for Education). 2024a. *Suspensions and Permanent Exclusions in England. Academic year 2022/23.* London: DfE. Accessed 5 August 2024. https://explore-education-statistics.service.gov.uk/find-statistics/suspensions-and-permanent-exclusions-in-england

DfE (Department for Education). 2024b. *Schools, Pupils and their Characteristics. Academic year 2023/24.* London: DfE. Accessed 5 August 2024. https://explore-education-statistics.service.gov.uk/find-statistics/school-pupils-and-their-characteristics

DfE (Department for Education). 2024c. *School Workforce in England. Reporting Year 2023.* London: DfE. Accessed 5 August 2024. https://explore-education-statistics.service.gov.uk/data-tables/fast-track/22f8dc16-dfef-4558-a1f8-08dc6a923eb2

DfE (Department for Education). 2024d. *Special Educational Needs in England. Academic year 2023/24.* London: DfE. Accessed 5 August 2024. https://explore-education-statistics.service.gov.uk/find-statistics/special-educational-needs-in-england

Dimova, S., Culora, A., Brown, E.R., Ilie, S., Sutherland, A. and Curran, S. 2021. *Maximising the Impact of Teaching Assistants: Evaluation report.* London: Education Endowment Foundation. Accessed 7 October 2021. https://educationendowmentfoundation.org.uk/projects-and-evaluation/projects/maximising-the-impact-of-teaching-assistants

Finn, J.D., Pannozzo, G.M. and Achilles, C.M. 2003. 'The "Why's" of Class Size: Student behavior in small classes', *Review of Educational Research* 73(3): 321–368. https://doi.org/10.3102/00346543073003321

Francis, B., Archer, L., Hodgen, J., Pepper, D., Taylor, B. and Travers, M.-C. 2017. 'Exploring the relative lack of impact of research on "ability grouping" in England: A discourse analytic account', *Cambridge Journal of Education* 47(1): 1–17. https://doi.org/10.1080/0305764X.2015.1093095

Francis, B., Hodgen, J., Craig, N., Taylor, B., Archer, L., Mazenod, A., et al 2019. 'Teacher "quality" and attainment grouping: The role of within-school teacher deployment in social and educational inequality', *Teaching and Teacher Education* 77: 183–192. https://doi.org/10.1016/j.tate.2018.10.001

Giangreco, M.F., Yuan, S., McKenzie, B., Cameron, P. and Fialka, J. 2005. '"Be careful what you wish for …": Five reasons to be concerned about the assignment of *individual* paraprofessionals', *Teaching Exceptional Children* 37(5): 28–34. https://doi.org/10.1177/004005990503700504

Gill, K. 2017. *Making the Difference: Breaking the link between school exclusion and social exclusion*. London: Institute for Public Policy Research. www.ippr.org/publications/making-the-difference

Ginnis, S., Pestell, G., Mason, E. and Knibbs, S. 2018. *Newly Qualified Teachers (NQTs): Annual survey 2017*. London: DfE. Accessed 6 October 2021. www.gov.uk/government/ publications/newly-qualified-teachers-nqts-annual-survey-2017

Goddard, V. 2019. 'Swimming against the tide', in R. Webster (ed) *Including Children and Young People with Special Educational Needs and Disabilities in Learning and Life: How far have we come since the Warnock enquiry – and where do we go next?* Abingdon: Routledge, pp 59–62.

Graham, L.J., de Bruin, K., Lassig, C. and Spandagou, I. 2021. 'A scoping review of 20 years of research on differentiation: Investigating conceptualisation, characteristics, and methods used', *Review of Education* 9(1): 161–198. https://doi.org/10.1002/rev3.3238

Hallam, S. and Ireson, J. 2005. 'Secondary school teachers' pedagogic practices when teaching mixed and structured ability classes', *Research Papers in Education* 20(1): 3–24. https://doi.org/10.1080/0267152052000341318

Hargreaves, E. 2017. *Children's Experiences of Classrooms*. London: SAGE Publications.

Hattie, J. 2002. 'Classroom composition and peer effects', *International Journal of Educational Research* 37: 449–481. https://doi.org/10.1016/S0883-0355(03)00015-6

Hinds, D. 2018. 'Education secretary makes inaugural speech to children's services sector'. London: DfE. Accessed 6 August 2018. www.gov.uk/government/speeches/ education-secretary-makes-inaugural-speech-to-childrens-services-sector

HoC (House of Commons Education Committee). 2018. *Forgotten Children: Alternative provision and the scandal of ever increasing exclusions. Fifth report of session 2017–19*. London: HoC. Accessed 6 August 2018. https://publications.parliament.uk/pa/cm201719/cmselect/cmeduc/342/ 342.pdf

Hodkinson, A. 2009. 'Pre-service teacher training and special educational needs in England 1970–2008: Is government learning the lessons of the past or is it experiencing a groundhog day?' *European Journal of Special Needs Education* 24(3): 277–289. https://doi.org/10.1080/ 08856250903016847

Hodkinson, A. 2019. 'Pre-service teacher training and special educational needs in England, 1978–2018: Looking back and moving forward?' in R. Webster (ed), *Including Children and Young People with Special Educational Needs and Disabilities in Learning and Life: How far have we come since the Warnock enquiry – and where do we go next?* Abingdon: Routledge, pp 36–41.

Ireson, J. and Hallam, S. 2009. 'Academic self-concepts in adolescence: Relations with achievement and ability grouping in schools', *Learning and Instruction* 19(3): 201–213. https://doi. org/10.1016/j.learninstruc.2008.04.001

Ireson, J., Hallam, S., Hack, J., Clark, H. and Plewis, I. 2002. 'Ability grouping in English secondary schools: Effects on attainment in English, mathematics and science', *Educational Research and Evaluation* 8(3): 299–318. https://doi.org/10.1076/edre.8.3.299.3854

Klassen, R. 2001. '"After the statement": Reading progress made by secondary students with specific literacy difficulty provision', *Educational Psychology in Practice*, 17(2): 121–133. https://doi.org/10.1080/02667360120059337

Kutnick, P., Blatchford, P. and Baines, E. 2002. 'Pupil groupings in primary school classrooms: Sites for learning and social pedagogy?' *British Educational Research Journal* 28(2): 187–206. https://doi.org/10.1080/01411920120122149

Kutnick, P., Sebba, J., Blatchford, P., Galton, M., Thorpe, J., MacIntyre, H. and Berdondini, L. 2005. *The Effects of Pupil Grouping: Literature review*. Research Report 688. London: DfES. Accessed 31 March 2021. https://dera.ioe.ac.uk/18143/

Labour Party. 2024. Labour Party Election Manifesto. Accessed 5 August 2024. https://labour.org.uk/change/break-down-barriers-to-opportunity/

Lehane, T. 2017. '"SEN's completely different now": Critical discourse analysis of three "Codes of Practice for special educational needs" (1994, 2001, 2015)', *Educational Review* 69(1): 51–67. https://doi.org/10.1080/00131911.2016.1237478

Long, R. and Danechi, S. 2020. *Off-rolling in English Schools*. House of Commons Library Briefing Paper. London: HoC. Accessed 19 September 2022. https://commonslibrary.parliament.uk/research-briefings/cbp-8444/

Mansell, W. and Adams, R. 2016. 'England schools: 10,000 pupils sidelined due to league-table pressures', *Guardian*, 21 January. Accessed 30 April 2017. www.theguardian.com/education/2016/jan/21/england-schools-10000-pupils-sidelined-due-to-league-table-pressures

Masdeu Navarro, F. 2015. *Learning Support Staff: A literature review*. OECD Education Working Paper No. 125. Paris: OECD. Accessed 25 November 2020. https://doi.org/10.1787/19939019

Mazenod, A., Francis, B., Archer, L., Hodgen, J., Taylor, B., Treshchenko, A. and Pepper, D. 2018. 'Nurturing learning or encouraging dependency? Teacher constructions of students in lower attainment groups in English secondary schools', *Cambridge Journal of Education* 49(1): 53–68. https://doi.org/10.1080/0305764X.2018.1441372

McGillicuddy, D. and Devine, D. 2018. '"Turned off" or "ready to fly": Ability grouping as an act of symbolic violence in primary school', *Teaching and Teacher Education* 70: 88–99. https://doi.org/10.1016/j.tate.2017.11.008

Menzies, L. and Baars, S. 2015. *The Alternative Should Not Be Inferior: What now for 'pushed out' learners?* London: LKMCo/Inclusion Trust. https://bit.ly/3sH3BaQ

Moss, G., Webster, R., Bradbury, A. and Harmey, S. 2021. *Unsung Heroes: The role of teaching assistants and classroom assistants in keeping schools functioning during lockdown.* London: UCL. Accessed 1 April 2021. https://discovery.ucl.ac.uk/id/eprint/10125467

Nickow, A., Oreopoulos, P. and Quan, V. 2020. *The Impressive Effects of Tutoring on PreK–12 Learning: A systematic review and meta-analysis of the experimental evidence.* NBER Working Paper No. 27476. Accessed 1 August 2020. www.nber.org/papers/w27476

Norwich, B. 2014. 'Changing policy and legislation and its effects on inclusive and special education: A perspective from England', *British Journal of Special Education* 41(4): 403–425. https:// doi.org/10.1111/1467-8578.12079

Nye, P. 2017. 'Who's left: The main findings'. Blog. *Education Datalab*. Accessed 22 September 2021. https://ffteducationdatalab.org.uk/2017/01/whos-left-the-main-findings

Ofsted. 2018a. *Teachers' Awareness and Perceptions of Ofsted: Teacher attitude survey 2018 report.* London: Ofsted. Accessed 24 October 2021. www.gov.uk/government/publications/annual-teachers-survey

Ofsted. 2018b. *The Annual Report of Her Majesty's Chief Inspector of Education, Children's Services and Skills 2017/18.* London: Ofsted. Accessed 19 September 2022. https://assets.publishing.service.gov.uk/government/uploads/system/uploads/attachment_data/file/761606/29523_Ofsted_Annual_Report_2017-18_041218.pdf

Ofsted. 2019. 'Ofsted: Let us inspect multi-academy trusts (MATs)'. Blog. *Ofsted*. Accessed 20 September 2022. www.gov.uk/government/news/ofsted-let-us-inspect-multi-academy-trusts-mats

Ofsted. 2020. *The Annual Report of Her Majesty's Chief Inspector of Education, Children's Services and Skills 2018/19.* London: Ofsted. Accessed 19 September 2022. https://assets.publishing.service.gov.uk/government/uploads/system/uploads/attachment_data/file/859422/Annual_Report_of_Her_Majesty_s_Chief_Inspector_of_Education__Children_s_Services_and_Skills_201819.pdf

Owen, D. 2019. 'What is off-rolling, and how does Ofsted look at it on inspection?' Blog. *Ofsted*. Accessed 20 September 2022. https://educationinspection.blog.gov.uk/2019/05/10/what-is-off-rolling-and-how-does-ofsted-look-at-it-on-inspection/

Papachristou, E., Flouri, E., Joshi, H., Midouhas, E. and Lewis, G. 2021. 'Ability-grouping and problem behavior trajectories in childhood and adolescence: Results from a UK population-based sample', *Child Development* 93(2): 341–358. https://doi.org/10.1111/cdev.13674

Peacey, N. 2015. *A Transformation or an Opportunity Lost? The education of children and young people with special educational needs and disability within the framework of the Children and Families Act 2014*. Discussion paper. London: RISE. Accessed 1 October 2021. www.risetrust.org.uk/online-publications/53-send-2015

Peacock, A. 2016. *Assessment for Learning without Limits*. Maidenhead: Open University Press.

Pye, J., Stobart, R. and Lindley, L. 2016. *Newly Qualified Teachers (NQTs): Annual survey 2016*. London: DfE. Accessed 6 October 2021. www.gov.uk/government/publications/ newly-qualified-teachers-nqts-annual-survey-2016

Radford, J., Blatchford, P. and Webster, R. 2011. 'Opening up and closing down: Comparing teacher and TA talk in mathematics lessons', *Learning and Instruction* 21(5): 625–635. https://doi.org/10.1016/j.learninstruc.2011.01.004

Rubie-Davies, C.M., Blatchford, P., Webster, R., Koutsoubou, M. and Bassett, P. 2010. 'Enhancing learning? A comparison of teacher and teaching assistant interactions with pupils', *School Effectiveness and School Improvement* 21(4): 429–449. https://doi.org/10.1080/09243453.2010.512800

Ruebain, D. and Haines, S. 2011. 'Introduction', in S. Haines and D. Ruebain (eds) *Education, Disability and Social Policy*. Bristol: Policy Press, pp 1–6.

Schofield, J.W. 2010. 'International evidence on ability grouping with curriculum differentiation and the achievement gap in secondary schools', *Teachers College Record* 112(5): 1492–1528. Accessed 26 October 2021. www.tcrecord.org/Content.asp?ContentId=15684

Sharples, J. 2016. 'EEF blog: Six of the best – how our latest reports can help you support teaching assistants to get results'. Education Endowment Foundation. Accessed 17 April 2020. https://bit.ly/350FpY6

Slavin, R. 2016. 'Trans-Atlantic concord: Tutoring by paraprofessionals works'. Accessed 17 April 2020. https://robertslavinsblog.wordpress.com/2016/03/03/trans-atlantic-concord-tutoring-by-paraprofessionals-works

Slee, R. 2012. 'Inclusion in schools: What is the task?'. In C. Boyle and K. Topping (eds), *What Works in Inclusion?* Maidenhead: Open University Press, pp 41–50.

Stobart, G. 2014. *The Expert Learner: Challenging the myth of ability*. Maidenhead: McGraw-Hill/Open University Press.

Taylor, B., Francis, B., Archer, L., Hodgen, J., Pepper, D., Tereshchenko, A. and Travers, M.-C. 2016. 'Factors deterring schools from mixed attainment teaching practice', *Pedagogy, Culture and Society* 25(3): 327–345. https://doi.org/10.1080/14681366.2016.1256908

Tes. 2018. 'Schools "off-roll thousands to boost results"', *Tes*, 28 August. Accessed 22 September 2021. https://bit.ly/3IItQmY

Titheradge, N. 2018. 'Hundreds of pupils spend week in school isolation booths'. *BBC News*. 12 November. Accessed 22 September 2022. www.bbc.co.uk/news/education-46044394

Webster, R. 2015. 'The classroom experiences of pupils with special educational needs in mainstream primary schools – 1976 to 2012: What do data from systematic observation studies reveal about pupils' educational experiences over time?' *British Educational Research Journal* 41(6): 992–1009. https://doi.org/10.1002/berj.3181

Webster, R. 2022. *The Inclusion Illusion: How children with special educational needs experience mainstream schools*. London: UCL Press. Accessed 1 September 2022. www.uclpress.co.uk/theinclusionillusion

Webster, R. and Blatchford, P. 2013. 'The educational experiences of pupils with a statement for special educational needs in mainstream primary schools: Results from a systematic observation study', *European Journal of Special Needs Education* 28(4): 463–479. https://dx.doi.org/10.1080/08856257.2013.820459

Webster, R. and Blatchford, P. 2019. 'Making sense of "teaching", "support" and "differentiation": The educational experiences of pupils with education, health and care plans and statements in mainstream secondary schools', *European Journal of Special Needs Education* 34(1): 98–113. https://doi.org/10.1080/08856257.2018.1458474

Webster, R., Blatchford, P., Bassett, P., Brown, P., Martin, C. and Russell, A. 2010. 'Double standards and first principles: Framing teaching assistant support for pupils with special educational needs', *European Journal of Special Needs Education* 25(4): 319–336. https://dx.doi.org/10.1080/08856257.2010.513533

Webster, R., Russell, A. and Blatchford, P. 2016. *Maximising the Impact of Teaching Assistants: Guidance for school leaders and teachers* (2nd edn), Abingdon: Routledge.

Webster, R., Bosanquet, P., Franklin, S. and Parker, M. 2021. *Maximising the Impact of Teaching Assistants in Primary Schools: Guidance for school leaders*, Abingdon: Routledge.

Worth, D. 2022. 'The rise of SEND "magnet schools"', *Tes*, 12 January. Accessed 19 September 2022. www.tes.com/magazine/analysis/general/rise-send-magnet-schools

8

Social, emotional and mental health needs in educational settings: putting wellbeing into socio-relational context

Robin Banerjee

One of the key 'areas of need' identified in the 2001 Special Educational Needs Code of Practice[1] was 'behaviour, emotional and social development' (hereafter BESD), which was operationalised as follows: 'Children and young people who demonstrate features of emotional and behavioural difficulties, who are withdrawn or isolated, disruptive and disturbing, hyperactive and lack concentration; those with immature social skills; and those presenting challenging behaviours arising from other complex special needs' (p 87).

This was replaced in the 2015 Special Educational Needs and Disability Code of Practice[2] with some subtle but important differences in wording. The area of need was now worded as 'Social, emotional and mental health difficulties' (hereafter SEMH), and operationalised as follows:

> Children and young people may experience a wide range of social and emotional difficulties which manifest themselves in many ways. These may include becoming withdrawn or isolated, as well as displaying challenging, disruptive or disturbing behaviour. These behaviours may reflect underlying mental health difficulties such as anxiety or depression, self-harming, substance misuse, eating disorders or physical symptoms that are medically unexplained. Other children and young people may have disorders such as attention deficit disorder, attention deficit hyperactive disorder or attachment disorder. (p 98)

Of particular note is the way in which 'mental health' has been headlined as a core part of one primary area of need within the 2015 code of practice, whereas in 2001 those words only appeared in the context of noting the potential link between special educational needs and Child and Adolescent Mental Health Services. Over time, then, we have observed a much more explicit articulation of 'mental health' as underpinning social and emotional difficulties that may fall under the umbrella of Special Educational Needs and Disabilities (hereafter SEND), replacing the previous focus on 'behaviour' in the label for this area of need. In this short reflection, I will examine the concept of SEMH needs in the context of SEND, particularly considering the implications for the positioning of social and emotional learning (SEL) within educational settings, and adopting a *strengths-based, relational and universal whole-school* approach to the topic.

Let us start by noting that we are dealing here with a significant proportion of the children and young people recorded as having special educational needs. In the 2004 statistical release on this topic in England, from a population of around 8.3 million pupils, the proportion identified with BESD as their primary need was second highest in terms of both 'School Action Plus' (27 per cent of approximately 352,000 in this category) and 'Statement of SEN' (14 per cent of approximately 240,000 in this category).[3] The classifications of categories for SEND support in schools had changed following the new code of practice and so are not directly comparable, but the new SEMH label was also one of the most prevalent areas of need: in 2018, from a population of around 8.7 million, the proportion of pupils identified with SEMH as their primary need was third highest in terms of both 'SEN support' (18 per cent of approximately 1.3 million in this category) and 'Education, Health and Care Plan' (13 per cent of approximately 250,000 in this category).[4] Moreover, since the COVID-19 global pandemic, it seems that SEMH has become even more prevalent: in the 2023/24 academic year it remained the third most common area of need, representing 16 per cent of the now much larger group of approximately 400,000 pupils with 'Education, Health and Care Plans'.[5]

Approaching this issue from a different angle, and using different datasets, the overall proportion of children and young people aged 5 to 15 estimated to have a 'mental disorder', defined as causing significant distress or impairing functioning, was 10.1 per cent in 2004, rising slightly to 11.2 per cent when assessed in 2017.[6] The overall rate of mental disorders has since risen substantially to 17.4 per cent of 6–16-year-olds in 2021.[7] These figures on the prevalence of mental disorders clearly do not correspond in a precise way to SEND categories, but there is no doubt that the incorporation of social and emotional difficulties and mental health difficulties under the broad umbrella of SEND means that a very large number of children and young people are considered to require 'special' provision. This is already a matter of statutory requirements for the approximately 62,000 pupils with Education, Health and Care Plans who currently have SEMH as their primary area of need. But if the 17.4 per cent of youths estimated to have a 'mental disorder' were all formally identified as such within educational settings and deemed to require special provision in law, then we would be looking at well over a million children and young people.

In fact, the statistical trend is clearly towards more and more formal identification of mental health as a disability: whereas 2,500 UK applicants accepted into university courses had declared a disability related to mental health in 2011, this had increased more than tenfold to around 36,000 in 2023; overall figures for UK university students (at all levels of study) reporting a mental health disability had risen to well over 100,000 by 2021/22.[8] Students registered as having mental health disabilities are then entitled to 'reasonable adjustments' to teaching and assessments under the Equality Act 2010.

In summary, many different statistical indicators are telling us that a very large – and increasing – number of children and young people are considered to require special educational provision under the SEND Code of Practice and/or reasonable adjustments under the Equality Act 2010, because of some combination of social and emotional difficulties and underlying mental health problems.

Against this backdrop, it is particularly interesting to reflect on some of the conceptual complexities implicated in SEMH. Four interlinked questions that deserve attention are:

1. Can SEL provide a framework for, at least partly, understanding and responding to SEMH needs?
2. Can SEMH needs be understood as, at least partly, relational qualities of social groups and wider communities?
3. Should SEMH needs be addressed in terms of universal, whole-school approaches, beyond interventions directed at individuals?
4. Can we interpret SEMH needs as more than difficulties to be corrected, and instead as strengths that can be built through a relational approach to support human flourishing?

I will now briefly articulate my reasoning for answering each of these questions in the affirmative, drawing out the implications for policy and practice.

The centrality of SEL

There is a great deal of evidence – which continues to grow rapidly – demonstrating that what is now commonly referred to as 'social and emotional learning' (SEL) provides a critical foundation for supporting mental health through the lifespan. The Collaborative of Academic, Social, and Emotional Learning (CASEL), a leading multidisciplinary network of researchers and practitioners, defines SEL as 'the process through which all young people and adults acquire and apply the knowledge, skills, and attitudes to develop healthy identities, manage emotions and achieve personal and collective goals, feel and show empathy for others, establish and maintain supportive relationships, and make responsible and caring decisions'.[9] Over the last three decades, school-based programmes aimed at helping children to develop these skills have been recognised as potentially providing a bedrock for mental health, consistent with evidence that key areas of mental health difficulty are intimately connected with how youths make sense of and regulate their emotions and relationships in everyday social interactions with others. This argument applies whether we are considering emotional problems associated with internalising difficulties such as anxiety or depression, or the disruptive behaviour associated with externalising difficulties such as conduct disorder, oppositional-defiant disorder, or attention-deficit hyperactivity disorder (ADHD).[10]

In fact, over the last two decades, we have seen numerous examples of both individual and group intervention and prevention approaches to mental health difficulties that are fundamentally rooted in the promotion of social and emotional competencies. Indeed, much of the dominant NICE-recommended guidance for common mental health difficulties in young people has clear and obvious connections with the range of skills covered under the SEL umbrella.[11] Of course, SEL cannot possibly cover the full range of issues involved in our mental health – think about the use of medication in ADHD or psychosis, or the focus on detailed nutritional plans for those with eating disorders, for example – but in virtually all cases of mental health interventions, we can find at least some degree of attention to young people's understanding of themselves and others, their skills in managing social relationships, and/or their emotional coping strategies.

It is important to stress that these social and emotional competencies should be regarded as an integral part of the mental health issues, rather than simply as secondary aspects of 'underlying mental health difficulties such as anxiety or depression', as stated in the description of SEMH within the 2015 SEND Code of Practice. This empowers those working on SEL in educational contexts to act with the confidence that this work has the potential to reduce or even prevent mental health difficulties. It also makes us less likely to treat mental health difficulties as an intrinsic property of the individual, often to the point that it is seen as a stable, maybe even dispositional, quality of the person. Unfortunately, it is very easy to fall into the trap of separating out social and emotional competencies from mental health difficulties in this way: by the time young people are sitting standardised exams at the end of their schooling or subsequently undertaking assessments at university, the focus in educational policy in relation to mental health is often less about social and emotional skills development, and more about making reasonable adjustments for the disability as a feature – specifically a 'protected characteristic' – of the person, as demanded by legislation on equality.[12] This support for those with mental health disability of course is of critical importance, but the risk here is that we are missing the many additional opportunities available in educational settings to address the social and emotional skills that play such a crucial role in reducing mental health difficulties. Indeed, in the context of the increases in the prevalence of mental health difficulties in young people noted earlier, reconceptualising mental health as *fundamentally rooted* in social and emotional skills – not just *giving rise* to social and emotional problems – offers a powerful and scalable way forward in educational policy.

The socio-relational context of mental health

One concern people may have about the focus on SEL in mental health is that it may appear to lay the responsibility for mental health issues solely at the door of the individual suffering distress or other difficulties. After all, I have argued earlier that social and emotional competencies should be regarded as an integral part of the mental health issues, so one would be forgiven for assuming that the key task here is to identify what skills a given individual with mental health difficulties is lacking – for example, in self-awareness, emotional regulation or empathy – and then to apply some intervention to 'teach' those skills to the individual. However, such an interpretation misses a crucial part of what we know from child and adolescent psychology about the development of social and emotional skills, namely that they develop not within each individual child in isolation, but rather in a deeply relational context. That is to say, until we understand and respond to the network of social relationships within which each child is embedded – whether at home in the family, at school with adults and peers, or in the wider community – we have not fully addressed the skills development that needs to happen for supporting mental health.

This consideration of relational context is entirely in keeping with theoretical models of mental health difficulties and approaches to intervention. Social and emotional competencies are so powerful in understanding and addressing mental health issues precisely because they are intimately connected with the qualities of our social relationships. For example, those relational qualities could be the very reasons a child may be seriously distressed or anxious, and so working with a particular set of social relationships could be the critical factor in helping a child to develop the social and emotional competencies needed for reducing problematic behaviour. A good illustration of this can be found in Barrett's work on family treatment models for different kinds of mental health issues in children. Initial studies had shown that family discussion about ambiguous social situations had actually *increased* anxious children's tendencies to select maladaptive avoidant plans, and oppositional-defiant children's tendencies to select maladaptive aggressive plans.[13] Subsequent studies demonstrated that incorporating the family into cognitive-behavioural therapy led to significant benefits for clinically referred children.[14] The key here is that we are paying attention not just to an individual child's competencies in reasoning about themselves and others in the social world, but also to the relational context (in this case, the family) within which children are developing and practising those skills.

In the educational context, this same kind of understanding can be scaled up to consider all members of the school community. Most recently, our research group has been reviewing best practice in relation to the development of a whole-school approach to mental health in the context of the UK government's implementation of Mental Health Support Teams in England.[15] We found that in many educational settings, there was a mature recognition that work on mental health, and the SEL that supports it, is not simply about remediating difficulties in an individual child identified as having a disability, but also about engaging with the entire socio-relational context to create the conditions for nurturing the skills needed for mental health.

Universal as well as targeted work

The emphasis on a whole-school approach to supporting mental health is closely aligned with the focus on 'universal' provision for SEL and mental health among all learners in the school setting, complementing any 'targeted' work aimed at specific individuals deemed to be at elevated risk or already showing indicators of early mental health difficulties. It has long been recognised that it is not always easy to draw a clear dividing line between those who have a mental health 'disorder' and those who do not. In the vast majority of cases, there is no single fact that one can point to as an entirely objective and unambiguous statement of a person's mental health disability. Returning to the earlier definition of SEMH in the SEND Code of Practice, it was recognised that this label applies to a 'wide range of social and emotional difficulties' which could include 'becoming withdrawn or isolated, as well as displaying challenging, disruptive or disturbing behaviour'. Of course, we do have clinical diagnostic criteria (for example, the ICD, the *International Classification of Diseases*,[16] or the DSM, the *Diagnostic and Statistical Manual of the American Psychiatric Association*[17]) and any number of standardised scales with significant volumes of psychometric research to establish clinical thresholds. But, important and valuable as these tools may be, the fact remains that they simply offer us a consistent and reliable way to approach the identification of mental health difficulties that are considered to deserve clinical attention; none offers an absolute, categorical differentiation between those who have SEMH needs and those who do not.

Indeed, it has become increasingly recognised that support for mental health is relevant to all children and young people in a school and thus merits a universal provision, even while some children may be deemed to require additional targeted help, sometimes from experts with specialist training and expertise. This recognition lies at the heart of the whole-school approach to mental health discussed earlier, whereby support for the mental health of everyone in a given socio-relational context is recognised as playing a role in preventing, or at least reducing the likelihood of, mental health difficulties. In the context of promoting social and emotional competencies too, there is a long history of educational work to cultivate personal, social and health-related knowledge and skills: personal, social and health education (sometimes integrating relationships and sex education, citizenship, and/or economic education) has been a feature of school curricula in the UK and many other countries for decades. Indeed, in the most recent relaunch of the national curriculum in Wales, the Curriculum for Wales 2022, 'health and wellbeing' is listed as one of the core Areas of Learning and Experience (AoLEs), sitting on the same level as literacy, mathematics, science and humanities.[18] Similarly, in CASEL's model of SEL, the work on building skills in self-awareness, social awareness, relationships, motivation and responsible decision-making is typically framed as a universal provision that is situated within the context of classroom climate, school policies and practices, engagement with families and caregivers, and wider learning opportunities in the local community.[19] Crucially, in these models, any targeted work with specific individuals considered to require additional or more specialist support is understood to be aligned with a broader universal provision aimed at building the social and emotional competencies among all members of the given socio-relational context.

The journey to implement these kinds of integrated models of universal and targeted provision for SEL and mental health support is far from complete. In our research group's work in this area, Mental Health Support Teams' own self-assessments of the implementation of the whole-school approach noted very significant room for improvement, although there are clearly positive strides being made towards positioning work on mental health as core to the business of the whole school. In our recent Best Practice Review of whole-school approaches to mental health, we found variations along 17 dimensions of implementation (including levels of engagement of staff, governors, pupils and parents/carers, through to the collection and use of data to inform activity).[20] And in our most recent pilot work on developing a self-assessment toolkit for rating key outcomes relevant to mental health at a school or college level, we found preliminary evidence that variations in implementation were clearly and strongly related to variations in perceived outcomes.[21] This research has illuminated the fact that universal work, reaching all learners in a given setting, needs to be integrated with the targeted work addressing the needs of the most vulnerable individuals and groups. It also highlights the fact this work is not solely the domain of those with specialised responsibilities relating to health and wellbeing, but in fact is relevant to all members of the school or college community; indeed, it shines a light on how the wellbeing of staff members themselves is intimately related to the social and emotional experiences of the young people.

Taking a strengths-based approach

One other major consideration in this area relates to the opportunities that are afforded by a positive focus on growing health and wellbeing, as opposed to an emphasis on remediating illness and dysfunction. Arguably, much of the focus in the dominant discourse on children and young people's mental health has focused on the latter. That is very clear from the previously listed definition of SEMH in the 2015 SEND Code of Practice, which refers to 'social and emotional difficulties' in the first line and then to being 'withdrawn or isolated', and to 'challenging, disruptive or disturbing behaviour', 'underlying mental health difficulties' and 'disorders' in the subsequent sentences. Moreover, in the 2017 government green paper that paved the way for the establishment for Mental Health Support Teams, the opening paragraph highlights the prevalence of problems or difficulties: 'One in ten young people has some form of diagnosable mental health condition and we know that children with a mental health problem face unequal chances in their lives.'[22] However, in the past three decades, building on a diverse range of relevant disciplinary and interdisciplinary traditions, there has also been growing attention to a different, strengths-based approach to human development and mental health, with clear applications in both education and social care.[23] This offers the opportunity for a relational, universal and whole-school approach to SEMH that focuses on the qualities and experiences that will enable children and young people to flourish, and to experience wellbeing in a way that is far more than merely the absence of difficulties or disorders.

The emphasis on building upon strengths – within and between people – rather than remediating individual pathologies provides a distinctive method of addressing SEMH needs in children and young people. The still-maturing field of 'positive psychology' as applied to school settings has drawn our attention to the need for prevention and intervention work in educational settings to address social and emotional skills that promote wellbeing and flourishing for all, not just reducing distress for individuals labelled as having 'difficulties'.[24] Moreover, conceptualisations of wellbeing that involve *eudaimonia* – commonly thought to encompass having a sense of meaning, purpose and fulfilment – enable us to take a wider view to understanding the relational context of SEMH for all members of a school community. Even the starting point of assessing strengths in social and emotional skills, rather than deficits in mental health, offers a radically different perspective to educational practice in the area of SEMH.[25]

Importantly, it complements a growing recognition that social-contextual support for meeting basic human needs – for autonomy, competence and relatedness, according to self-determination theory – may be the crucial foundation for 'facilitating optimal function of the natural propensities for growth and integration, as well as for constructive social development and personal well-being'.[26] Specifically, recent work has integrated these concepts of basic need satisfaction with the concepts of SEL described earlier, positing that environments satisfying basic human needs foster the socio-emotional autonomous motivation needed for developing social and emotional competence.[27] This is in line with recent work from our research group, where we sought to understand the mechanisms by which participation in the creative arts appeared to be fostering wellbeing benefits for marginalised youths. Our results – from work involving music-making and drama – showed how the environmental qualities of creative arts activities supported basic need satisfaction, which in turn fostered self-development and a strong sense of social acknowledgement, ultimately interpreted as giving rise to an empowerment of the young people as active agents with positive aspirations for their own lives.[28]

These results raise key questions about how the qualities of the environments observed in the arts practice – opportunities for self-expression and freedom of choice, within a socially bonded community, together with a validation of competence with appropriate challenge – can be translated into the environment of a typical school environment, with its multiplicity of priorities and demands. This is likely to be a key direction of travel for future research on educational practices, underscoring the points made earlier about the need for a whole-school, universal approach to address SEMH. Specifically, the engagement of all members of the community in creating a health-promoting environment – including all adults as well as the children and young people – may be as important as, or indeed more important than, simply correcting an individual student's withdrawn, disruptive or otherwise challenging behaviour.

Last, but certainly not least, this kind of integrated, strengths-based model – one that is firmly rooted within a socio-relational approach – offers a way to resolve the longstanding tension between a focus on academic achievement and a focus on relationships and wellbeing in school settings. Contrary to the assumption that the amounts of school time and resource spent on these need to be traded off against each other, we now have well-established findings that interventions to promote SEL can have positive effects on performance on standardised academic assessments.[29] This fits with work from our own group showing that early social understanding is associated with higher levels of subsequent academic achievement, via improved social competence and peer relationships.[30] At the same time, we are accumulating evidence that basic needs satisfaction is related to academic achievement, including indirectly via increased behavioural engagement in the classroom.[31] Thus, it seems reasonable to predict that a strengths-based approach to social and emotional skills development, rooted in creating a social environment that meets the basic human needs of all those in the school community – both students and staff – could be a critical route to achieving benefits to all aspects of self-development, encompassing academic gains as well as growth in mental health and wellbeing.

These reflections imply that attention to SEMH needs in the context of the 2015 SEND Code of Practice should be positioned within a socio-relational context that places social and emotional skills at the centre, is focused on meeting basic human needs to build strengths rather than correcting deficits, and is aligned with a whole-school, universal approach that reaches every member of the school community. Crucially, this cannot be reduced to the implementation of a single curriculum programme or resource – it is essential to walk the walk, not just talk the talk, and that means modelling SEL skills in everyday teaching and reinforcing curriculum work with a supportive whole-school ethos.[32] But perhaps most importantly, it fundamentally shifts our focus on SEMH away from one that serves to separate out children and young people identified as having social and emotional difficulties or mental health disabilities; instead, any support provided to address such issues is understood to be part of a much bigger whole, one that meets the basic human needs of all members of the community and creates a health-promoting socio-relational context that enables every child and young person to flourish and achieve their potential.

Notes

[1] Department for Education and Skills (2001). *Special Educational Needs Code of Practice.* Retrieved from https://assets.publishing.service.gov.uk/media/5a7cac22ed915d7c983bc342/special_educational_needs_code_of_practice.pdf

[2] Department for Education (2014). *Special Educational Needs and Disability Code of Practice: 0 to 25 years.* Retrieved from https://assets.publishing.service.gov.uk/media/5a7dcb85ed915d2ac884d995/SEND_Code_of_Practice_January_2015.pdf

[3] Department for Education and Skills (2004). *Special educational needs in England, January 2004.* Retrieved from https://webarchive.nationalarchives.gov.uk/ukgwa/20130103143229mp_/http://media.education.gov.uk/assets/files/pdf/sfr442004v4pdf.pdf

[4] Department for Education (2018). *Special educational needs in England: January 2018.* Retrieved from https://assets.publishing.service.gov.uk/media/5b587d61ed915d0b63dfd3f3/SEN_2018_Text.pdf

[5] Department for Education (2024). *Special educational needs in England, Academic Year 2023/24.* Retrieved from https://explore-education-statistics.service.gov.uk/find-statistics/special-educational-needs-in-england

[6] NHS Digital (2018). *Mental health of children and young people in England, 2017.* Retrieved from https://digital.nhs.uk/data-and-information/publications/statistical/mental-health-of-children-and-young-people-in-england/2017/2017

[7] NHS Digital (2021). *Mental health of children and young people in England, 2021.* Retrieved from https://digital.nhs.uk/data-and-information/publications/statistical/mental-health-of-children-and-young-people-in-england/2021-follow-up-to-the-2017-survey

8. Lewis, J. and Stiebahl, S. (2024). *Student mental health in England: Statistics, policy, and guidance*. Retrieved from https://researchbriefings.files.parliament.uk/documents/CBP-8593/CBP-8593.pdf
9. CASEL (n.d.). *Fundamentals of SEL*. Retrieved from https://casel.org/fundamentals-of-sel/
10. Banerjee, R. (2023). Educational psychology: Research on developmental and social factors. In G. Davey (ed) *Applied Psychology*, 2nd edn, Oxford: Wiley, pp 327–354.
11. National Institute for Health and Care Excellence (2014). Antisocial behaviour and conduct problems in children and young people: Quality Standard QS59. Retrieved from https://www.nice.org.uk/guidance/cg158
12. Scope (n.d.). Reasonable adjustments in college and university education. Retrieved from https://www.scope.org.uk/advice-and-support/reasonable-adjustments-college-university/
13. Barrett, P.M., Rapee, R.M., Dadds, M.M. and Ryan, S.M. (1996). Family enhancement of cognitive style in anxious and aggressive children. *Journal of Abnormal Child Psychology*, 24(2): 187–203.
14. Barrett, P., Farrell, L., Dadds, M. and Boulter, N. (2005). Cognitive-behavioral family treatment of childhood obsessive-compulsive disorder: Long-term follow-up and predictors of outcome. *Journal of the American Academy of Child & Adolescent Psychiatry*, 44(10): 1005–1014.
15. Procter, T., Roberts, L., Macdonald, I., Morgan-Clare, A., Randell, B. and Banerjee, R. (2021). *Best Practice Review of Whole School Approach (WSA) within MHSTs in the South-East and East of England*. Retrieved from https://arc-kss.nihr.ac.uk/document-download/158-best-practice-review-of-whole-school-approach-wsa-within-mhsts-in-the-south-east-and-east-of-england-evaluation-report/file
16. World Health Organization (2019). *International Statistical Classification of Diseases and Related Health Problems* (11th edn). https://icd.who.int/
17. American Psychiatric Association (2022). *Diagnostic and Statistical Manual of Mental Disorders* (5th edn, text rev.). https://doi.org/10.1176/appi.books.9780890425787
18. Welsh Government (n.d.). *Curriculum for Wales*. Retrieved from https://hwb.gov.wales/curriculum-for-wales
19. CASEL (n.d.). *What is the CASEL Framework?* Retrieved from https://casel.org/fundamentals-of-sel/what-is-the-casel-framework/
20. Procter, T., Roberts, L., Macdonald, I., Morgan-Clare, A., Randell, B. and Banerjee, R. (2021). *Best Practice Review of Whole School Approach (WSA) within MHSTs in the South-East and East of England*. Retrieved from https://arc-kss.nihr.ac.uk/document-download/158-best-practice-review-of-whole-school-approach-wsa-within-mhsts-in-the-south-east-and-east-of-england-evaluation-report/file
21. Robinson, E., Ferrell, A., Macdonald, I., John, M., Randell, B., Procter, T. and Banerjee, R. (2023). *Evaluating the Impact of the Whole School and College Approach to Mental Health and Wellbeing: The Development and Pilot of the WSCA Outcome Self-Assessment Tool*. Retrieved from https://arc-kss.nihr.ac.uk/document-download/475-whole-school-college-approach-outcome-self-assessment-tool-full-report/file
22. Department of Health and Department for Education (2017). *Transforming Children and Young People's Mental Health Provision: A Green Paper* (p 3). Retrieved from https://assets.publishing.service.gov.uk/media/5a823518e5274a2e87dc1b56/Transforming_children_and_young_people_s_mental_health_provision.pdf
23. Kumar, P.A. and Mohideen, F. (2021). Strengths-based positive schooling interventions: A scoping review. *Contemporary School Psychology*, 25: 86–98.

    Toros, K. and Falch-Eriksen, A. (2021). Strengths-based practice in child welfare: A systematic literature review. *Journal of Child and Family Studies*, 30: 1586–1598.

[24] Seligman, M.E., Ernst, R.M., Gillham, J., Reivich, K. and Linkins, M. (2009). Positive education: Positive psychology and classroom interventions. *Oxford Review of Education*, 35(3): 293–311.

[25] Nickerson, A.B. and Fishman, C.E. (2013). Promoting mental health and resilience through strength-based assessment in US schools. *Educational and Child Psychology*, 30(4): 7–17.

[26] Ryan, R.M. and Deci, E.L. (2000). Self-determination theory and the facilitation of intrinsic motivation, social development, and well-being. *American Psychologist*, 55(1): 68.

[27] Collie, R.J. (2020). The development of social and emotional competence at school: An integrated model. *International Journal of Behavioral Development*, 44(1): 76–87.

[28] Ferrell, A., Levstek, M. and Banerjee, R. (in press). 'We Have a Voice. We Exist.': Value of Basic Needs Satisfaction for Well-Being and Goal Development in Inclusive Theater Spaces for Young People. *The Journal of Creative Behavior*, 57(4): 674–689.

Levstek, M. and Banerjee, R. (2021). A model of psychological mechanisms of inclusive music-making: Empowerment of marginalized young people. *Music & Science*, 4: 20592043211059752.

[29] Corcoran, R.P., Cheung, A.C., Kim, E. and Xie, C. (2018). Effective universal school-based social and emotional learning programs for improving academic achievement: A systematic review and meta-analysis of 50 years of research. *Educational Research Review*, 25: 56–72.

Durlak, J.A., Weissberg, R.P., Dymnicki, A.B., Taylor, R.D. and Schellinger, K.B. (2011). The impact of enhancing students' social and emotional learning: A meta-analysis of school-based universal interventions. *Child Development*, 82(1): 405–432.

[30] Lecce, S., Caputi, M., Pagnin, A. and Banerjee, R. (2017). Theory of mind and school achievement: The mediating role of social competence. *Cognitive Development*, 44: 85–97.

[31] Wang, Y., Tian, L. and Huebner, E.S. (2019). Basic psychological needs satisfaction at school, behavioral school engagement, and academic achievement: Longitudinal reciprocal relations among elementary school students. *Contemporary Educational Psychology*, 56: 130–139.

[32] Education Endowment Foundation (2021). *Improving Social and Emotional Learning in Primary Schools*. Retrieved from https://educationendowmentfoundation.org.uk/education-evidence/guidance-reports/primary-sel

Conclusion

David Ruebain and Steve Haines

As we thought about, debated, drafted and finalised the second edition of *Education, Disability and Social Policy* we found ourselves at the start of another significant political transition, with potentially major policy consequences.

The change of government to a Labour administration has brought with it a new manifesto commitment:

> Labour will take a community-wide approach, improving inclusivity and expertise in mainstream schools, as well as ensuring special schools cater to those with the most complex needs. We will make sure admissions decisions account for the needs of communities and require all schools to co-operate with their local authority on school admissions, SEND inclusion, and place planning.

This commitment is made against a backdrop of severe financial strain and 'utter disarray' in the system in England to support children with special educational needs (SEN), as reported by the Local Government Ombudsman.[1] A report for the Local Government Association revealed that resourcing the requirements of Education, Health and Care (EHC) plans has led to cumulative deficits in local authorities in England which at the time of writing stand at £3.2 billion and are projected to rise to £5 billion by 2026.[2] Meanwhile, the same report finds that in 2022/23, only 8 per cent of children and young people with EHC plans achieved the expected level in reading, writing and mathematics, a figure that has remained unchanged from 2016/17. If nothing else, this stagnation indicates a pressing need for a renewed focus on educational outcomes for students with SEN. It is clear that despite the effort of parents, professionals, public servants and politicians, and despite the promise of major reforms, incremental changes to the system are often failing to deliver for children with SEN while risking financial meltdown in local authorities.

It is worth taking a long view and reflecting on the transformation brought about by the Warnock Report (1978) which, along with preceding analysis and argument, recommended the precursor to the current framework of SEN support in the Education Act 1981. The 'jigsaw of provision' of the Special Educational Needs and Disability Act (2001) which amended Part 4 of the Education Act (1996) to make further provision against discrimination on grounds of disability in schools and other educational establishments, which followed the 1981 legislation, characterised the framework that our first edition commented on. Subsequently, the Children and Families Act (2014) sought to bring together education, health and care and set out a clearer 'local offer'. In our second edition, our authors again find that reforms have continued to lead to a variable and unsatisfactory system, out of step with the needs of young people and limited in its reach beyond resourcing need.

When we began drafting this edition, we identified a more inclusive ethos at the core of schooling. However, this desire for inclusion has invariably not been matched by sufficient incentives or resources from government. During the time between our editions the landscape of education in England has been significantly shaped by ever greater decentralisation, marketisation and privatisation; in turn resulting in a fragmented system where local authorities, academies, free schools and private providers operate with varying degrees of autonomy and accountability. One outcome of this is inconsistent support for young people, with resources and expertise unevenly distributed across different regions and institutions. In addition, accountability appears to override practices of inclusion in England (Daniels et al, 2019) rather than strengthen it. And again, the competitive nature of market-driven education has often served to marginalise those with additional needs, with schools distanced from local authorities and lacking the resources to invest in the necessary support infrastructure. In this context, the understandable loss of parental confidence in the SEN system has perhaps unduly driven the policy debate towards a focus on resourcing EHC plans rather than strengthening the mainstream system, to resolve the situation where parents are dissatisfied with, and in some cases contesting the support their children are receiving.

As editors, we initially anticipated that the second edition would serve as an update to the first. However, through extensive conversations and valuable feedback, we saw the need for a fundamental re-evaluation. There were critical areas that we had neglected in our first edition, such as the intersection of ethnicity and special educational needs, and the nexus of social, emotional and mental health with exclusions; crucial for a comprehensive understanding of SEN. These factors highlight the dynamic and evolving nature of the issues, necessitating continuous reflection and adaptation in policy and practice.

We believe that a new policy discourse is needed. One that develops an alternative understanding rooted in the wider context of education, social and health policy, ultimately based on human flourishing. The advent of a new government at least affords an opportunity for this re-evaluation. The movement of the SEN brief within the Department for Education from the Children's Minister to the Schools Minister signals a potential change in focus that could support this shift. We do not discount the positive intent of successive reforms to establish the universal right to education, put in place a framework of SEN support, extend the disability rights framework to education settings or seek to coordinate health and education services, but we do assert that in the context we now find there is a pressing need to take the next step to reimagine a system that emphasises outcomes, moving beyond resourcing need to ensuring that every child with SEN achieves their fullest potential.

The chapters in this second edition argue that the task ahead is not so much to build on the existing frameworks, but to learn from the progress and challenges and reframe how we consider the education of children with SEN. Returning to the right to education for disabled children set out in the 1981 Education Act, we need a shift in our collective thinking from SEN as a bureaucratic challenge to a question of educational equity, working in concert and not in conflict with standards in education. We advocate for a renewed focus to empower struggling local authorities, invest in the teaching workforce and review curriculum and assessment frameworks. These measures must include children with SEN, not as a post-hoc consideration or as part of a separate system, but as an integral part of the aims and purposes of education.

From our initial chapter on the history of segregated schooling to the final call for building strengths rather than correcting deficits for young people with social, emotional and mental health needs, we hope that this book stimulates reflection. We remain of the view that the core purpose of the SEN system must be to support inclusion rather than 'othering' and to find a way forward from the current scale of the challenge we should create an educational environment that recognises and nurtures the potential of every young person, regardless of their needs.

In conclusion, we urge the new administration to embrace this challenge, reframe the task ahead, and prioritise the outcomes of children with SEN. A community-wide approach and improving inclusivity could allow for young people to return to the centre. Ultimately, we hope for an inclusive, equitable and effective educational system for all.

Notes

[1] www.theguardian.com/education/article/2024/aug/04/special-educational-needs-system-england-utter-disarray-ombudsman-amerdeep-somal

[2] www.local.gov.uk/publications/towards-effective-and-financially-sustainable-approach-send-england

References

Daniels, H., Thompson, I. and Tawell, A. (2019) *After Warnock: The Effects of Perverse Incentives in Policies in England for Students With Special Educational Needs.* Frontiers in Education.

Labour Party (2024) Labour Party Election Manifesto. https://labour.org.uk/change/break-down-barriers-to-opportunity/

Warnock, M. (1978) Special educational needs: Report of the Committee of Enquiry into the Education of Handicapped Children and Young People, Cmnd 7212, London: HMSO.

Index

References to figures and photographs appear in *italic* type; those in **bold** type refer to tables.

A

A-Levels *82*, 101
ability, academic 9, 95, 109, 110, 113, 125–126
academisation 121
Access Consultation Forum 99, 100
Access to Assessment and Qualifications Advisory Group 100
'access to learning – learning to access' model 104
accessibility plans 32, 36
accountability 35–37, 120, 121, 129–130, 155
achievement, academic *see* attainment/achievement, academic
additional support 23, 33, 37, 76, 124
  Additional Learning Need 34, 38
  Additional Support Needs 37, 78, 85, 91n3
adjustments, reasonable
  Additional Learning Need 32, 33–34, 36
  and higher education 74, 86
  and SEMH 144, 145
  and sensory impairment 96, 97, 101
Advance HE 90
'Aiming High for Disabled Children' (AHDC) report 59–60
Ainscow, M. 57
Alice's experience 13
Allen, J. 64
Alternative Provision 2, 29–30, 114, 130
appeal, rights of 12, 27, 30, 32, 33, 35–36
Areas of Learning and Experience (AoLEs) 148
Assessing Pupils' Progress (APP) 97–98
Assessment for Learning 97
assessment of disability 83–85, 89, 95–101
  statutory assessment 21, 24, 26–27, 34, 54
assessment of need 2, 25, 55, 57–58, 91
assessment systems 23, 26, 94, 95–96, 101
assessment, teacher 97, 101
asylums 7, 11
attainment/achievement, academic 150
  and assessment of disability 95, 96–101
  and curriculum 104–105, 123, 125
  and DfE 104, 114
  and educational qualifications 95–97, 98, 99, 100–101
    and GCSEs 101, 105, 114
  and equality 97, 99
  and examinations 95, 98–99, 100, 101, 112–113
  and exclusion from education 120, 123, 125–126, 134n4
  and expectation of achievement 14, 98, 111, 125
  and Ofqual 99, 100, 103, 105
  and Ofsted 99, 103
  and Progress 8 28, 34, 39
  and race 112–113, 114
  and sensory impairment 94–97, 101, 102–104
  and United States 99–100, 113
attainment gap 101, 102, 103, 125–126
autistic spectrum disorder 78, *81*, 82, **84**, 119
auxiliary aids 32, 33

B

background, social 12, 55, 75
  and EHCPs 25, 27
  and exclusion from education 13, 119
  see also social class
Ball, Stephen 5
Banerjee, Robin 4–5, 142–151
Barrett, P. 146
behaviour modification 11
behavioural difficulties
  and exclusion from education 12, 119, 121–122
  and race 107, 114
  and SEMH 4–5, 142, 150
Best Practice Review 148
Black children 107
Blatchford, P. 127
Blatchford, P. and Webster, R. 125, 127
Blueprint for Fairness, Commission for Widening Access 88
Board of Education 11, 12
Booth, Cherie, Bush, Marc and Scott, Ruth 2
Borsay, Anne 1, 6–16
British Sign Language (BSL) GCSE 3, 104, 105
Bronfenbrenner, U. 122

C

Cameron, David 111
capability approach 2–3, 34
care, children in 119

Care Quality Commission (CQC) 26, 29
Carter Review of Initial Teacher Training 39
'catch-up' programmes 124, 125
characteristics, protected 75
charitable foundations 6–7, 8
Chief Medical Officer 13–14
Child and Adolescent Mental Health Services 142
Children and Families Act (CFA) (2014) xi, 2, 20, 21, 22–31, 36
  and Local Offers 23, 61, 155
children, disabled xiii–xiv, 79, 80
  involvement of 26, 66, 111
  and multi-agency working 56, 59, 63–64
  numbers of 20–21, 24–25, 58, 143–144
  Scotland 85, 91n3
  see also behavioural difficulties; family involvement; learning difficulties; mental health problems; parental involvement; relationships between professionals and families; sensory impairment (SI); students of higher education, disabled
children, 'ineducable' 9
children with SEND xi, 28, 29, 31, 35, 111, 130
  and exclusion from education 119, 121–123, 127–128
  high-level SEND 123, 127–128
Children's Centres 59
Children's Commissioner for England 4, 120, 127
children's rights 37
  see also disability rights approach; human rights
choice, parental 9, 29, 31
class size 122, 124, 125, 131
classroom composition 122, 124–126, 131, 134n4
Climbié, Victoria 59
Co-ordinated Support Plans (CSP), Scotland 34, 91n3
co-production 3, 23, 26, 30–31
Coard, Bernard 4, 107, 114
Cobb, Olga, Miller, Rory and Simpson, Paul 3, 94–101
cochlear implants 11
cognitive-behavoural therapy 146
Collaborative of Academic, Social, and Emotional Learning (CASEL) 144–145
Collaborative of Academic,Social, and Emotional Learning (CASEL) 148
Colony foundation, Cheshire 7
Commission for Widening Access, Blueprint for Fairness 88
Commissioner for Fair Access 88
Common Assessment Framework 59
communication in multi-agency working 54

community involvement 13, 14, 133
compassion 7
composite expertise model 53–54, 60, 62
Conservative government 101, 121
Conservative/Liberal Democrat Coalition 1, 101
Conservative Manifesto 1, 4
contact lenses 11
cooperation between statutory bodies 22, 26, 29–30, 36
Council for Disabled Children 59
courses, modular 101
coursework 98, 101
Court Report 53
COVID-19 3, 84, 90, 101, 131, 143
creative arts 150
criminalisation of black students 112
critical realist model of disability 62
Croll, P. and Moses, D. 123
Crowther, Neil 3
culture 107, 113, 114
curriculum 104–105, 123, 124, 125, 148
Curriculum for Wales 148
Curriculum Framework for Children and Young People with Vision Impairment (CFVI) 103–104

D

D'Alessio, Simona 123
Danforth, S. 63
Darwin, Charles, *On the Origin of Species* 7
David's experiences 15
decision-making, multi-agency 51, 55, 56, 61, 63
Delivering Better Value in SEND programme 26
Delphi research method 103
Department for Education (DfE) 30, 32, 35, 130
  and educational attainment 104, 114
  and numbers of disabled children/young people 23–24, 25, 76
Deployment and Impact of Support Staff (DISS) project 127, 128
'difference'/other xi, 109, 112
Diploma and Apprenticeship framework 96
Disability Commission 74, 75
Disability Critical Race Theory (DisCrit) 4, 108, 109–110, 114–115
Disability Discrimination Act (DDA) (1995) 16, 74, 75, 95
Disability Discrimination Act (DDA) (2005) 20, 32, 100
Disability Discrimination appeals 35
disability discrimination claims 27, 31
disability policies, English 110–112
disability rights approach 20, 33–39, 40

Index

disability rights legislation 20–40, 154–155
  and parental involvement 22, 23–24, 26–27, 28–29, 30
  see also Children and Families Act (CFA) (2014); Disability Discrimination Act (DDA) (1995); Disability Discrimination Act (DDA) (2005)
Disability Rights Task Force, Task Force Report 31–32
disability rights training 39
Disability Studies 109
Disabled Students Allowance (DSA) 75, 76–77, 82, 86–87, 88
disagreement resolution 22
discrimination 12–13, 15
  see also Disability Discrimination Act (DDA) (1995); Disability Discrimination Act (DDA) (2005); Equality Act (2010)
diversity 75, 99
Down, John Langdon 11
dyslexia 79, 128

E

Early Career Teachers (ECTs) 39
ecological systems theory model 122–123
Edinburgh, University of 86
Education Act (1870) 7–8
Education Act (1944) 8–10
Education Act (1981) 9–10, 12, 54–55, 156
Education Act (1993) 12
Education and Skills Select Committee, House of Commons 110–111
Education, Health and Care Plans (EHCPs) 23–29
  Additional Learning Need 33–34, 35
  and DfE 23–24, 25
  and First Tier Tribunal 22, 27
  and funding of EHCPs 25–26, 35, 154, 155
  and involvement of children/family 26–27, 63
  and LEAs 24, 25, 26
  and multi-agency working 61–62, 63, 64
  and numbers of disabled children/young people 24, 25
  and SEND Improvement Plan 29, 30
  and social background 25, 27
  and statutory educational provision 22, 23–27, 143
education, higher 3, 74–91, 143–144
  and Equality Act (2010) 74, 75, 86, 144
  and tuition fees 75, 90n1
  see also students of higher education, disabled
education, inclusive 10, 54, 57–58, 60, 111
  see also inclusive education
education, mainstream *see* schools, mainstream

Education Policy Institute 120
Education Select Committee, House of Commons 130
educational experiences, positive 13
educational psychologists 53, 56, 57, 65
emotional difficulties *see* social, emotional and mental health difficulties (SEMH)
employment experiences 15
employment opportunities ix, 13, 14–15, 80–83, **84**
empowerment 7, 86, 150
England 143
  and disabled students 76, 77, 78, 87–88
  and exclusion/inclusive education 123, 126, 128, 132, 133, 155
equality 87, 97, 99
Equality Act (2010) 2, 20, 101
  and accessibility plans 32, 36
  and disability rights approach 33, 36, 38
  and higher education 74, 75, 86, 144
Equality and Human Rights Commission (EHRC) 32, 39
equality duty 32, 100
Equality Plans 36
equality schemes 87
eudaimonia 149
eugenics 7, 8, 13
Eugenics Education Society 7
European Convention on Human Rights (ECHR) 37
European Higher Education Area 89
Evans, W. 38
Every Child Matters (ECM) initiative 58–60, 97
examinations, public 14
  and educational attainment 95, 98–99, 100, 101, 112–113
  see also GCSEs
exclusion from education 119–133, 134n1
  and academic attainment 120, 123, 125–126, 134n4
  and accountability 120, 121
  and behavioural difficulties 12, 119, 121–122
  and 'catch-up' programmes 124, 125
  and classroom composition 122, 124–126, 131, 134n4
  and curriculum 104–105, 123, 124, 125
  and England 123, 126, 128
  and learning outcomes 123, 124, 128
  and mainstream schools 121–122, 127, 129
  and Ofsted 119, 120, 121
  and primary schools 122, 124, 125, 126, 127–128
  and quality of instruction 122, 127–128, 129
  and race 111, 112, 114
  rates of 28, 119

and secondary schools 121, 122, 125–126
and segregation 9, 122, 124–126
and SEND children 121–123, 127–128
and separation 124–126, 127, 128
and skills development 123, 124
and social background 13, 119
and teaching assistants 123–124, 125, 126–128
exclusion, micro- 123–124, 125, 126
exclusion, nano 128
exclusion, pre-emptive 120
exclusion, structural 122–128
exclusion, unofficial *see* exclusion, with-in school
exclusion, with-in school 119–133, 134n4
expectation of achievement 14, 98, 111, 125
expertise, relational 66

F

family involvement
  and relationships with professionals 3, 28, 51–52, 54, 62–65, 66
  and Every Child Matters 58–59, 60–61
  see also parental involvement
family life, removal from 13–14
Family Resource Survey 76
family treatment models 146–147
feminism 83
financial burden 8, 86
Fisher, P, and Goodley, D. 65, 66
Francis, B 126
friendships, children's 13, 74
Functional Skills qualification 96
funding
  and higher education 75, 86–87
  and schools 22–23
    and disability rights approach 33, 34, 35
    and EHCPs 25–26, 35, 154, 155
    and multi-agency working 3, 61, 64
Funding Councils 87, 88
funding models 86–87

G

GCSEs 98, 120
  and educational attainment 101, 102, 103, 105, 114
  and visual impairment 101, 102, 103
  and British Sign Language (BSL) 3, 104, 105
gender 78–79, 82, 85, 89, 114
Giangreco, M.F. 129
Glasgow School of Art 88
Glasgow, University of 88
Goddard, V. 129
Goodley, D. 61
government action 154–156
  see also legislation
Government Equalities Office 2

H

Hall, S. 112–114
Handicapped Pupils and Medical Services Regulations 9
Haswell, D.O. 13
Hattie, John 122, 129–133
Heads of University Counselling Services 89–90
headteachers 4, 119
health and social care services 22, 35
hearing impairment
  and disabled students 78, *79*, *81*, 82, **84**
  and educational attainment 102–103, 104
  and segregation 10, 11
  see also sensory impairment (SI)
Hector, M. 75
helpers, passive 64
Heritage Craft Schools and Hospital, Chailey 11
HESA Graduate Outcomes Survey 79–82, 90n2
Hip Hop pedagogy 113
historical perspective of special needs and disability education 6–16
Hodkinson, A. 133
Hodkinson, A. and Burch, L. 112
Holmes Report 86
hospitals, orthopaedic 8, 11
House of Commons Education and Skills Select Committee 110–111
House of Commons Education Select Committee 130
'How the West Indian child is made educationally subnormal in the British school system' pamphlet (Coard) 4, 107
human rights 8, 110
  and community and family involvement 13, 15
  and Education Act (1981) 10, 156
  and inclusive education 6, 7, 10, 156
  and rights of appeal 12, 27, 30, 32, 33, 35–36
  see also disability rights approach

I

identity construction 62–65
identity markers 109
identity pluralism 112–114
'idiocy' 6, 11
impairments, types of 77–78
imperialism, cultural 15–16
incentives 28, 34, 100, 129–130, 155
inclusive design approach 3
inclusive education 8–12, 83, 100, 129–133, 154–155
  and accountability 129–130, 155
  Additional Learning Need 34, 39

Index

employment opportunities 13, 14–15
  and England 133, 155
  and human rights 6, 7, 10, 156
  and incentivisation 129–130, 155
  and multi-agency working 54, 57–58, 60
  and Ofsted 57, 129–130
  and parental involvement 12, 13
  and race 111, 112
  and schools 131
    and headteachers 4, 119
    and mainstream schools 9, 10, 13, 29, 57–58, 133, 154, 155
    and mixed attainment teaching 128, 131
    and special schools 10, 111, 133
    and teachers 10, 39, 131–133
  and segregation 9, 10, 13, 130–131
  and social mixing 13, 131
  and visual impairment 11, 13
  and Warnock Report 111, 133
  see also exclusion from education; integration
inclusive education dashboards 29, 130
inclusive education, structural 129–133
individual rights 32, 33
individualisation 55, 130–131
Individuals with Disabilities and Education Act (IDEA), US 99
inequalities, social 6, 13, 55, 87, 119
inequality, educational 113
information and communications technology (ICT) 96
initial teacher education (ITE) 132–133
initial teacher training (ITT) 39
Institute of Race Relations 114
Integrated Care Boards 29, 35
integration 9, 12, 29–30, 35, 150
  see also inclusive education
intellectual impairment 6–7, 8, 12
  see also learning difficulties
International Classification of Functioning Disability and Health for Children and Youth 38
intersectionality 4, 88, 89, 108–109, 111, 112, 113, 114
  see also background, social; gender; race; social class
IQ tests 11, 12

J

jigsaw approach 2, 53, 56, 154
junior training centres 9

K

Keegan, Gillian ix
key workers 59

L

labelling 38, 54–55, 107, 109, 114
Labour government 133, 134n2, 154

labour, manual 14
Lamb, Brian 2–3, 20–40
Lamb Inquiry 36
league tables 98, 99, 120
learning difficulties 38, 113
  and disabled students 78, 79, *81*, 82, **84**, 89
  and employment opportunities 82, **84**
  and multi-agency working 56, 62–63
  and segregation 6–7, 8, 10, 11, 12
learning difficulties, bands of 10
learning outcomes 123, 124, 128
legislation *see* disability rights legislation
Lewis, Ann 4
Life Chances of Disabled People report 95
local education authorities (LEAs) 12, 39, 61
  and EHCPs 24, 25, 26
  and special schools 8, 11
Local Government and Social Care Ombudsman (LGSCO) 27, 30, 35, 154
Local Government Association 154
Local Offer 23, 31, 32, 61, 155

M

managerialist approaches 87–88, 89
marginalisation 15, 123, 155
  multiple marginalisation 109–110, 112, 114
Mclaughlin, J. 62–63
McLaughlin, J. and Goodley, D. 65
mediation 22, 30
medical interventions 10–12
medical model of disability 2, 96, 108
  and disabled students 77, 83, 84–85, 86
  and multi-agency working 55, 60, 62–63
medical system of classification 9
Meijer, C. 23–27
mental health problems ix, 4–5, 119, 142–151
  and disabled students 78, 79, 82, **84**, 84, 89–90
  and social class 80, *81*
  and skills for mental health 144–145, 146–147, 149, 150–151
  and social relationships 145, 146–147
  and teachers 90, 148–149
  see also social and emotional learning (SEL); social, emotional and mental health difficulties (SEMH)
Mental Health Support Teams 147, 148, 149
Migliarini and Stinson, Chelsea 107–115
Migliarini, Valentina and Stinson, Chelsea 4
Milan Congress 10
Miller, O. 94, 102
mixed attainment teaching 128, 131
mixing, social 6, 126, 131, 150

mobility issues 78, *79*, *81*, **84**
morality 13
Morgan, Baroness 99
multi-academy trusts (MAT) 121, 134n2
multi-agency teams 57, 58, 60
multi-agency working 51–67
  and composite expertise model 53–54, 60, 62
  and decision-making 51, 55, 56, 61, 63
  definition 52
  and disabled children 56, 59, 63–64
  and Education Act (1981) 54, 55
  and EHCPs 61–62, 63, 64
  and funding 3, 61, 64
  and inclusive education 54, 57–58, 60
  and jigsaw approach 53, 56
  and learning difficulties 56, 62–63
  and medical model of disability 55, 60, 62–63
  and needs assessment 55, 57–58
  and parental involvement 3, 55, 64, 65
  and schools 57–58, 61, 64
  and service delivery 54, 60
  see also professionals; relationships between professionals; relationships between professionals and families

N

National Asylum for Idiots, Earlswood 7, 11
National Curriculum inclusive education Statement 98, 111
National Funding Formula for High Needs 25–26
National Health Service (NHS) 9
National Institute of Health and Care Excellence (NICE) 145
National SEND boards 29, 35
National Special Educational Needs and Alternative Provision Standards 29
'need' 55–56
needs, basic 150–151
neo-liberalism 64
New Labour 58
New Public Management 87
No Child Left Behind (NCLB) legislation, US 99, 100
non-statutory educational provision 22–23, 27–29, 34
Northern Ireland 77, 87

O

OECD Glossary of Statistical Terms 95
off-rolling 119–120
Office for Students 87
Ofqual 95, 99, 100, 103, 105
Ofsted 26, 29
  and academic attainment 99, 103
  Additional Learning Need 36, 39
  and exclusion from education 119, 120, 121
  and inclusive education 57, 129–130
Oliver, Michael 109
oppression, social 15, 16, 115
orthopaedic institutions 8, 11
Outcome Agreements 87, 88
ownership 56, 63

P

parental dissatisfaction xi, 60
parental involvement
  and co-production 3, 23, 26, 30–31
  and disability rights legislation 22, 23–24, 26–27, 28–29, 30
  and inclusive education 12, 13
  and multi-agency working 3, 55, 64, 65
  and statementing 12, 13
  see also family involvement
parental occupation 79, 80, *81*
Paris, D. and Alim, H.S. 113
participatory approaches 4
Partlett, M. 63
passivity 63–64
pauperism 8
Peacey, N. 38
people practice context (PPC) model 66
percentages of disabled students 75–76
personalisation 22, 23, 30
Phillipson, Bridget ix
physical activity 11
physical impairment 8, 78, *79*, *81*, 82, **84**
Plowden Report 53
poor law authorities 8
pressure groups 64
'privilege-cognisant' 52, 66
professionalisation 10, 12–13
professionals 26
  and relationships between professionals 54, 56
  and relationships with families 3, 28, 51–52, 54, 62–65, 66
  and Every Child Matters (ECM) initiative 58–59, 60–61
  see also educational psychologists; multi-agency working; teachers
Programme for International Student Assessment (PISA) 104–105
Progress 8 attainment 28, 34, 39
Progress towards Disability Equality across the Children's and Education Sector report 97
protectionism 121
psychologists 11, 12
  educational psychologists 53, 56, 57, 65
psychology 12, 13, 149
Public Accounts Committee, Westminster Parliament§ 2

Index

pupil-adult ratios 125
Pupil Referral Units (PRU) 114

Q

qualification design 100
Qualifications and Curriculum Authority (QCA) 100
qualifications, educational 95–97, 98, 99, 100–101
  and GCSEs 101, 105, 114
quality of instruction 122, 127–128, 129, 131
Quinn, P. 84–85, 86
quota schemes 14

R

race 107–115
  and academic ability 109, 110, 113
  and academic attainment 112–113, 114
  and behavioural difficulties 107, 114
  and culture 107, 113, 114
  and 'difference' 109, 112
  Disability Critical Race Theory 4, 108, 109–110, 114–115
  and exclusion from education 111, 112, 114
  and identity 109, 112–114
  and inclusive education 111, 112
  and intersectionality 4, 108–109, 111, 112, 113, 114
  and labelling 107, 109, 114
  and multiple marginalisation 109–110, 112, 114
  and schools 107, 113
  and segregation 108, 109, 110, 113
  and social model of disability 108–109, 111
relationships between professionals 54, 56
relationships between professionals and families 3, 28, 51–52, 54, 62–65, 66
  and Every Child Matters (ECM) initiative 58–59, 60–61
relationships, social 145, 146–147
Riddel, Sheila and Weedon, Elisabet 3, 74–91
Riddell, S. 79–80
rights *see* appeal, rights of; children's rights; disability rights approach; disability rights legislation; human rights; individual rights
Royal Commission 8
Ruebain, D. and Haines, S. 123
Russell, P. 55

S

safe-guarding of children 59
'Safety Valve' programme 26
Sandlebridge Boarding School 7
SATs 98

Sayers, D. 38
School Action/School Action Plus 22, 27, 143
school attendance, compulsory 7–8, 105
school meals, free 25, 91n4
School Medical Service 11
school performance 98, 99, 120
School Report Card (SRC) 98
schools 24, 31, 119–133, 154
  and employment opportunities 14, 15
  and exclusion from education 119, 120, 121–122, 125–126, 127–128, 129
  and classroom composition 124, 125, 126, 131
  and primary schools 122, 124, 125, 126, 127–128
  and secondary schools 121, 122, 125–126
  and funding 22–23
  and disability rights approach 33, 34, 35
  and EHCPs 25–26, 35, 154, 155
  and multi-agency working 3, 61, 64
  and inclusive education 131
  and headteachers 4, 119
  and mainstream schools 9, 10, 13, 29, 57–58, 133, 154, 155
  and mixed attainment teaching 128, 131
  and special schools 10, 111, 133
  and teachers 10, 39, 131–133
  and local education authorities (LEAs) 8, 11
  and multi-agency working 57–58, 61, 64
  and race 107, 113
  and segregation 6–10, 14, 15, 122
  United States 99–100, 113
schools, boarding 13
schools, comprehensive 9
schools, independent 24
Schools Information Report 23, 36–37
schools, 'magnet' 120
schools, mainstream
  and exclusion from education 121–122, 127, 129
  and inclusive education 9, 10, 13, 29, 57–58, 133, 154, 155
  and race 107, 113
  and segregation 7–8, 122
  United States 99–100, 113
schools, primary 122, 124, 125, 126, 127–128
schools, secondary 121, 122, 125–126, 131
schools, segregated 6–10, 14, 15
schools, special 6, 10, 11–12, 24, 31, 64, 107, 154
  and employment opportunities 14, 15
  and inclusive education 10, 111, 133
  and LEAs 8, 11
  and segregation 14, 15

163

Scotland
  and accountability 36, 37
  Additional Learning Need 34, 36, 37
  Additional Support Needs 37, 78, 85, 91n3
  and Co-ordinated Support Plans (CSP) 34, 91n3
  and disabled students 76, 77, 78, 87, 88, 91n3
  and social class 85, 91n4
Scottish Funding Council 88
Scottish Index of Multiple Deprivation (SIMD) 90n2, 91n4
screening programmes 102–103
segregation 6–16
  and charitable foundations 6–7, 8
  and employment opportunities 13, 14–15
  and exclusion from education 9, 122, 124–126
  and inclusive education 9, 10, 13, 130–131
  and learning difficulties 6–7, 8, 10, 11, 12
  and race 108, 109, 110, 113
  and schools 6–10, 14, 15, 122
  and sensory impairment 6–7, 8, 10, 11, 13
  and social oppression 15, 16
  and stigma and stereotyping 14, 16
self-determination theory 150
self-identification 85, 86
self-interest, schools' 120
SEN support 22, 27–28, 143
SEND Review: Right Support, right place, right time, Government consultation Green Paper 29–31
sensory impairment (SI) 3, 94–105
  and academic attainment 94–97, 101, 102–104
  and charitable foundations 6–7, 8
  and reasonable adjustments 96, 97, 101
  and segregation 6–7, 8, 10, 11, 13
  and skills development 10, 96, 101, 104
  and vocational training 11, 14
  see also hearing impairment; visual impairment
separation 124–126, 127, 128, 130–131
service delivery 54, 60, 86
service planning 36
setting 125–126, 131, 134n4
Shakespeare, T. 62
sign language 3, 10, 104, 105
Single Equality Duty 100
skills development
  and exclusion from education 123, 124
  and sensory impairment 10, 96, 101, 104
  skills for mental health 144–145, 146–147, 149, 150–151

Small Axe film series, BBC 107
social and emotional learning (SEL) 143, 144–146, 147, 148, 150, 151
social class 79–80, *81*, 82, 85, 88, 91n4
  see also background, social
social, emotional and mental health difficulties (SEMH) 142–151
  and behavioural difficulties 4–5, 142, 150
  and reasonable adjustments 144, 145
  and SEL 143, 144–146, 147, 148, 150, 151
  and skills for mental health 144–145, 146–147, 149, 150–151
  and social relationships 145, 146–147
  and strengths-based approach 5, 149–151
social media 84
social model of disability 2, 57–58, 83–85, 89, 96, 108–109, 111
socio-relational approach 146–147, 150
Special Education Needs and Disability Tribunal (later Panel) 12–13
special education programmes 113
Special Educational Needs and Disabilities (SEND) system ix, xi, 1–2, 20–40, 142–151
  see also Education, Health and Care Plans (EHCPs); exclusion from education; multi-agency working; race; sensory impairment (SI); students of higher education, disabled
Special Educational Needs and Disability Act (2001) 16, 20, 32, 57, 74, 154–155
Special Educational Needs and Disability and Alternative Provision Improvement Plan 2, 29–31, 130, 133
Special Educational Needs and Disability Code of Practice (2015) 20, 32, 37, 51, 56, 63, 110–112
  and SEMH 142, 145, 147, 149, 151
Special Educational Needs Code of Practice (2001) 142
'special educational needs' definition 9, 37–38
Special Educational Needs (SEN) system 27–29, 34, 110, 155, 156
  and Warnock Report 2, 20, 154
St Andrews, University of 88
standards 29, 30, 64, 121
Statement of SEN 12, 13, 22, 25, 26, 143
statutory educational provision 7–8, 11, 21, 22, 23–27, 143
stereotyping and stigma 14, 16, 109
Stobart, G. 96, 126
streaming 95, 125, 131
strengths-based approach 5, 149–151
Student Disability Service, Edinburgh 85, 86
students from overseas 86

students of higher education, disabled 75–83
  and assessment of disability 83–85, 89
  and autistic spectrum disorder 78, *81*, 82, **84**
  and COVID-19 3, 90
  and Disabled Students Allowance (DSA) 75, 76–77, 82, 86–87, 88
  and employment opportunities 80–83, **84**
  and England 76, 77, 78, 87–88
  and gender 78–79, 82, 89
  and intersectionality 88, 89
  and learning difficulties 78, 79, *81*, 82, **84**, 89
  and managerialist approaches 87–88, 89
  and medical model of disability 77, 83, 84–85, 86
  and mental health problems 78, 79, 82, 84, **84**, 89–90
  and social class 80, *81*
  and mobility issues 78, 79, *81*, **84**
  and Outcome Agreements 87, 88
  and physical impairment 78, 79, *81*, 82, **84**
  and Scotland 76, 77, 78, 87, 88, 91n3
  and social class 85, 91n4
  and self-identification 85, 86
  and sensory impairment 78, 79, *81*, 82, **84**
  and social class 79, 79–80, *81*, 82, 85, 88, 91n4
  and social model of disability 83–85, 89
Summerfield Report 53
support services 89
Sure Start 59
Sutherland, Caireen and McLean, Martin 3, 94–105
Sutherland, Gillian 11

T

target-setting 88, 99–100
Teacher Development Agency 39
teacher training 12, 23, 39–40, 132–133
teachers
  and inclusive education 10, 39, 131–133
  and mental health problems 90, 148–149
  and professionalisation 10, 12–13
teaching assistants 123–124, 125, 126–128, 131–132
Teather, Sarah 98
thalidomide children 11
Thomas, C. and Corker, M. 83
Times newspaper 120
Timpson Review 114
Todd, Liz and Rose, Jo 3, 51–67
Tomlinson, Sally 85
Transforming Children and Young People's Mental Health Provision, Green Paper 149

Tribunals 12–13
  First Tier Tribunal 22, 27, 30, 32, 35
  and improvement plans 29, 31
trust-led systems 121
tuition fees 75, 90n1

U

UN Convention on the Rights of Persons with Disabilities (UNCRPD) 37
UN Convention on the Rights of the Child (UNCRC) 37
United States 99–100, 113
universal provision 147–149
University Central Admissions Service (UCAS) forms 77
University of the West of Scotland 88
Utton, Nigel 4

V

visual impairment
  and academic attainment 96–97, 101, 103–104
  and disabled students 78, 79, 82, **84**
  and GCSEs 3, 101, 102, 103, 104, 105
  and inclusive education 11, 13
  see also sensory impairment (SI)
vocational qualifications 103
vocational training 11, 14

W

Waitoller, F.R. and King Thorius, K.A. 113
Wales 34, 37, 38, 77, 87, 148
Warnock Report 20–23, 28–29, 31–32, 132
  and disability rights approach 33–39, 40
  and Education Act (1981) 9, 54–56
  and inclusive education 111, 133
  and special educational needs (SEN) framework 2, 20, 154
Webster, R. and Blatchford, P. 128
Webster, Rob 4, 119–133
Weedon, E. 80
welfare state 8–10
well-being 149–150
whole-school approach 147–148

Y

Young, Iris 15
Young, Jock 15
young people, disabled 4, 36, 63–64
  see also children, disabled; family involvement; relationships between professionals and families; students of higher education, disabled

Z

'zero tolerance' approach 112, 114

www.ingramcontent.com/pod-product-compliance
Lightning Source LLC
Chambersburg PA
CBHW071707020426
42333CB00017B/2181